PLAYS OF THE

HOLOCAUST

PLAYS OF THE

HOLOCAUST

AN INTERNATIONAL ANTHOLOGY

EDITED WITH AN INTRODUCTION
BY ELINOR FUCHS

THEATRE COMMUNICATIONS GROUP
NEW YORK 1987

Plays of the Holocaust: An International Anthology is published by Theatre Communications Group, Inc., the national organization for the nonprofit professional theatre, 355 Lexington Ave., New York, NY 10017.

Designed by G&H SOHO, Ltd.

Second Printing, June 1996

Library of Congress Cataloging-in-Publication Data

Plays of the Holocaust.

  Bibliography: p.
  1. Holocaust, Jewish (1939-1945)—Drama.   2. Drama—
20th century.   I. Fuchs, Elinor.
PN6120.H73P54   1987   808.82'9358   87-9997
ISBN 0-930452-67-4
ISBN 0-930452-63-1 (pbk.)

*For Joseph Fuchs, who
first taught me about the Holocaust*

Acknowledgments

I wish to extend thanks to Robin Hirsch, my colleague at the Chelsea Theater Center in 1980, who brought the first found of these plays to my attention, and throughout has offered sympathetic interest in this project. Stanley Brechner, artistic director of the American Jewish Theatre in New York and the National Jewish Theatre in Chicago, was generous of time and suggestions, as was Prof. Alvin Goldfarb of Illinois State University. I thank Marguerite Feitlowitz for the many services she rendered this volume on the work of Liliane Atlan. I am grateful to Prof. Edward Czerwinski of the Department of Slavic Languages and Literature at the State University of New York at Stony Brook and to Prof. Daniel Gerould of the City University of New York for their assistance in obtaining material on Józef Szajna, as well as to Jessica Teich of the Mark Taper Forum, Prof. Freddie Rokem of Hebrew University in Jerusalem, and to Tamir in New York for valuable assistance in regard to *Ghetto*. My thanks as well to Pamela Billig and Eugene Brogyanyi, artistic directors of the Threshold Theater Company, its dramaturg, the late Prof. Gabriel Brogyanyi, and to Tom Cole who provided me with outlines of plays from the Hungarian and the Italian. Prof. Madeline Levine of the Department of Slavic Languages and Literatures at the University of North Carolina advised on Polish translations. I am grateful to James Leverett, Alisa Solomon, Florence Falk, Claire and Katherine Finklestein, David Cole and Dr. Susan Letzler Cole for their thoughtful readings of the Introduction. Dr. Cole's recent book, *The Absent One: Mourning Ritual, Tragedy, and the Performance of*

Ambivalence helped to shape my own thoughts on tragedy and Holocaust drama. My thanks finally to my publisher Terry Nemeth, editor John Istel and the staff at TCG, whose enthusiasm for the project and attention to a maze of detail have made the book possible.

Contents

Contents

Introduction

Of all the literature about the devastation of the Jewish people under the Third Reich, the plays are the least familiar. Even in major studies of Holocaust writing, theatre is scarcely mentioned. This volume gathers together some of the most important of these plays, chosen from scores of works searched out in Eastern and Western Europe, Britain, America and Israel. Each is from a different country, its universal theme filtered through its originating culture. All are persuasive as theatrical experience. And crucially, all are compelling as human experience.

If these works belong to what Lawrence Langer calls a "literature of atrocity," they do so with surprisingly varied theatrical approaches. A Hasidic mystery of mourning and renewal, a death journey in which children play out the "game" of life, a black farce, a theatrical performance-within-a-performance, a fantasy on the theme of modern power, a grotesque ritual performed on a funeral mound—all become means to convey the annihilating experience of the Holocaust. Here we find few recognizable "dramatic situations," and a marked absence of the devices of dramatic realism—suspense, complication, climax, denouement. Yet there are plays on the Holocaust theme that use these techniques. I will explain why none of them has been included.

In my reading for the volume, there appeared to be two types of play that grappled with the Holocaust. The first showed catastrophic historical events as the private experience of individuals or families. The second showed such events as collective catastrophe: dramatic interest was focused not on the individual but on the fate of the community. (One is reminded of the continuous use of the first person plural—the "we" rather than the "I"—in the accounts of some concentration camp survivors, such as Primo Levi's *Survival in Auschwitz* and Charlotte Delbo's *None of Us Will Return*.)

Other ways in which these two types of plays differed seemed a consequence of the scale of dramatic suffering, individual or collective If the first type of play evoked pity and sadness at the spectacle of a single life threatened, the second type, contemplating a wider and more systematic destruction, aroused more disturbing emotions—rage, revulsion, helplessness. The first type almost always took on the conventions of melodrama or family drama, dramatic patterns that in their very familiarity, including the familiar focus on the individual, seemed to offer a subtle reassurance to the spectator. The second type rejected such received structures and searched for a powerful metaphor or dramatic strategy that would lead beyond individual character and linear plot to summon the Holocaust experience in an historical, cultural or metaphysical totality. These plays do not permit us to shed tears at their characters' fates (which we have escaped), but leave us with a painful sense of desolation and even culpability. When an entire community is "exterminated," in the atrocious language of the Third Reich, the community of spectators is implicated in the crime. This second type of play, then, the play of the life and death of the community, finally emerged in my reading as the most authentic theatrical expression of the Holocaust. It is from these plays that the six appearing in this volume were chosen.

The plays were written over a period of nearly forty years. Yet between the *Eli* of Nelly Sachs, the earliest of the plays, and *Ghetto* by Joshua Sobol, the most recent, the enormity of the Holocaust appears, if anything, to have increased. Sachs could bring a fountain to life onstage and imagine however darkly a saving remnant of Jewish life, but Sobol questions whether spiritual community is not sacrificed through the very means of Jewish survival—militant nationalism. Liliane Atlan mourns a lost generation of children, but Schevill, writing nearly a decade later, envisions a new Holocaust arising from mankind's secret admiration of the last. These are different perspectives, but the artists represented here share an understanding that the next generation of writers cannot know: their lives were directly shaped, in some cases nearly broken, by

INTRODUCTION

the experience of the war and the persecution of the Jews. In no sense is the Holocaust "history" for these writers: it is the annihilation around which all ideas of history must be reorganized.

. . .

Eli: A Mystery Play of the Sufferings of Israel by the poet Nelly Sachs (1891-1970), co-winner of the Nobel Prize for Literature in 1966, was written in exile in Stockholm three years after her escape from Berlin in 1940. It has been produced in Germany, Sweden and England, and was given its American premiere at The Guthrie Theater in Minneapolis in 1981. Like all religious mystery plays, *Eli* is concerned with sacrifice and regeneration.

The scene is a Jewish village, its roadsides, its holy place, its central square. Survivors bereaved and maimed return from the camps and the burning. Somehow life begins again. But the young shoemaker Michael, one of God's thirty-six chosen Servants, will not rest until he finds the killer of Eli, an innocent child who was murdered as his parents were being led away to death. The boy had raised his shepherd's pipe to God for help, and at that moment the enemy struck him down. Michael's quest takes him into a surrealistic wilderness filled with laments from the Chimney whose stones touched "Job's body in smoke," the Tree that drank the mothers' blood, the Night that heard the children's sighs. Strange shapes emerge, huge puppet fingers of the mass murderers, teasing and tormenting. They point the way at last to Michael's goal, the killer of the child Eli.

The play is informed with Nelly Sachs's lifelong love of dance, here translated into the context of a mystic folk ritual. The very rhythms of her verse summon up the Hasidic world, full of motion and music, of her almost exact contemporary, Chagall. The lost and the found, the survivors and the sacrificed, have voices here, leading finally to a renewal of the spirit, symbolized by the collapse of the killer and the revival of the fountain at the center of the village marketplace. To the critic Robert Foot, all Nelly Sachs's work embodies confrontations with an "invisible universe," a higher reality "which is at once a land of the Dead and the region of divine mystical rebirth." Sachs's "surrealism" thus has a spiritual purpose: it lifts the spectator into an awareness of the two realms that the playwright was convinced all living beings simultaneously inhabit.

Eli is a rite of hope without sentimentality, and the one play in the book that envisions a healing of the broken Jewish community. Yet she wrote it at the "height of smoke and flame," as she described the time of frantic despair in which the work presented itself to her rapidly over three nights. The unfathomable horror of the death camps was not yet fully known. Certainly Sachs's later books of poetry, written in the light of that knowledge, constitute an almost Biblical lament for the tormented body of Israel. Still, at the deepest level *Eli* is an attempt to transcend historical suffering and to summon as a source of strength the millenial tradition of Jewish messianic hope in the face of adversity.

Liliane Atlan's *Mister Fugue or Earth Sick* won immediate acclaim when it was introduced to French audiences in 1967. It has subsequently been performed in many other countries including Poland, the United States and Israel, where it received two important literary prizes. It was the first of a number of major stage works by Atlan concerned with the Holocaust, including *The Messiahs* and the more recent *Un Opéra pour Terezin*. An important voice on the contemporary French stage today, Atlan is the recipient of major French literary prizes and honors, including the *Légion d'Honneur*.

Atlan was born in Montpellier, France, in 1932. Though her brother was taken to Auschwitz (he later escaped), she spent the war years hidden in a safe house in Lyons with her sister, away from her parents. There, to entertain themselves, the children created theatre. "She was my public and I was the theatre: the author, the actor, the stage, everything," she has recalled. After the war, the young Atlan felt that "man and his gods had died in the concentration camps." Convinced that "all paths until now had led to an impasse," she and other Jewish friends plunged into a study of the Bible, Midrash and Kabbala to search out the possibility of a non-Christian way of life and thought. These religious teachings are not systematically reflected in her plays, but "impregnate" her thought, she has said.

The French word *fugue* means flight or escapade, and Atlan's title character Mister Fugue is a runaway, a German soldier who impulsively abandons his duties to accompany a group of ghetto children, also fugitives, to their death. Atlan has written that Grol, the Mister Fugue of the play, was inspired by the great Polish-Jewish physician, educator and author Janusz Korczak, who in 1942 chose to accompany children from his orphanage in the Warsaw ghetto to Auschwitz. "He told them stories to the end," writes Atlan, and storytelling becomes the imaginative basis of her play. Atlan's character bears no exact relation to the historical Dr. Korczak, however. Indeed, she makes problematical the human possibility of heroism that Korczak represents by giving his action to a distinctly unheroic German sergeant.

Grol, "a little crazy" and with muddled instincts, befriends four Jewish children. Only moments before, he had entrapped them as they emerged from the sewers, sole survivors of a "liquidated" ghetto. Grol and the children are made prisoner in the back of a truck being driven by other German soldiers to Rotburg and the Valley of Bones, a double metaphor for the corruption and finality of the camps. In the truck, Grol tells stories and the children invent games of the imagination, principally the game of life itself. The language of the children, Atlan has said, "is a mixture of my everyday language, Hebrew, Ladino, Yiddish—in short, it is written in a language of the Jewish subconscious." Yet with its confined setting, game motif and metaphysical *"mal de terre,"* the play is at the same time in the tradition of Beckett and, before him, Racine.

The children spin tales of the courtship, marriage, success, failure, old age, illness and natural death that will be denied them in life. At the end of the journey, they appear "detached, very old." All of life has been played out, in both senses: life has been performed, that is, and exhausted.

But Atlan goes past even the atrocity of killing children to depict a nauseous universe that makes one "earth-sick." The victims of this global malaise are not only individuals. Religion, hope, aspiration, the value of achievement, a belief in order, in human goodness—the entire realm of the "ideal" is despoiled. What's left are a little love and loyalty. Atlan presents these to us ambiguously, almost as moral curiosities. Is the soldier Grol's journey with the children, which saves no one and ends in his animal-like abasement and death, a sentimental gesture in a vile and accidental universe, or does it represent a sort of fertile sediment from which a new civilization might be cultivated? Perhaps most important, in an intractably painful world ("It wasn't so gay, living," one of the children "reminisces"), there still survives a narrow pass for the imagination, both that of Atlan's characters, and our own as spectators.

The plays in this volume describe a journey into and out of the hell of Europe's death camps. Peter Barnes and József Szajna take their audiences into what Auschwitz survivor Wieslaw Kielar calls the "Anus Mundi," the place, both psychic and material, that Primo Levi simply terms "the bottom." Neither Barnes nor Szajna attempts to create a realistic representation of the concentration camps. That may not be possible or even desirable on the stage. They do bring to the horror of the camps theatre's two proper gifts: the one for concrete moral engagement, the other for sensible metaphysics, a metaphysics, that is, that we absorb through our senses and our emotions.

Best known abroad for the screen version of his stage play *The Ruling Class*, Peter Barnes is one of England's most respected playwrights. His play *Laughter*, first produced at the Royal Court Theatre in 1978, consists of two one-act plays that deal comically with evil, but its laughter gags in the throat. Part One, "Tsar," is set in the court of Ivan the Terrible. Part Two, included here, takes place in a faceless Berlin bureaucracy and in Auschwitz. "Auschwitz" is a ferocious black farce. It was written, Barnes has said, in reaction against the "pernicious explanation that the Holocaust shows the operation of abstract evil."

Barnes was born in 1931 of a Jewish mother and a father who converted to Judaism somewhat casually, as Barnes relates, in order to marry. He was evacuated as a child from wartime London, well aware that "If we had lost, we'd have been killed" like those across the water in Europe. However, he regards his Jewish identity as a "complete sidetracking" of his motives for writing "Auschwitz," one of the most devastating theatrical expressions of the Holocaust. "You have to plunge into the horror of it," he has said, "and then completely distance yourself as if you were an anthropologist of the killing-machine." In this demonic farce Barnes distances the concentration camps through the humor of the English music hall, a combination that puts the spectator in a state of extreme moral tension. Barnes intends to assault the audience. "All my plays are extreme," he has said, "but this was going across boundaries into uncharted territory."

The playwright at first seems fixed on the banal exactitude of the Third Reich bureaucracy. Its ceaselessly quoted directive and regulation numbers (all factual and meticulously researched) governing orders for concrete flues, pre-mixed cement and "rat poison" are satirized with exaggerated buffoonery. So extended is this raucous satire that we take Barnes's interest to be merely an exposure of the "towering walls of pigeonholes, skyscrapers of dossiers," where "a whole genus of office workers, preoccupied and pale, lives and dies, human typewriters," in the words of David Rousset, a French professor of history and resistance organizer who spent sixteen months in the camps.

But Barnes plays the music hall "German joke" to absurd length with another motive. He forces us to laugh not merely at but along with his obtuse characters. Little by little we become involved in their rivalries and forget the frightening title of the play. Barnes's theme here is not simply Hannah Arendt's "banality of evil," but the terrible cooperation between the banal and the diabolic. When the gas chamber is finally revealed in the play's horrific ending, our comic enjoyment has implicated us in the atrocity as surely as the play's smug, frightened Nazi bureaucrats. How swiftly Barnes is able to create a theatrical confirmation of what so many continue to find "incomprehensible"—the world's complacency in the face of the Final Solution.

In "Auschwitz," individual characters emerge more clearly than in any of the other plays: Cranach the pedant, Stroop the sycophant, Gottleb the fanatic. Only at the end of the play do we realize that Barnes has used character not to engage us, but to distract us. Our fascination with the minutiae of behavior has diverted our attention from the genocide advancing behind the characters' apparently trivial concerns. In fact the playwright's attention has remained steadfastly on the community of the suffering, revealed to us in the play's final moments.

INTRODUCTION

With *Replika* we enter the silent death realm of *"univers concentration-naire."* Józef Szajna is a painter, scenic designer, stage director, and was for many years a professor at the Academy of Fine Arts in Warsaw. Szajna was seventeen years old when Hitler invaded Poland, and spent the war years as an inmate in Auschwitz and Buchenwald. His subsequent stage work has returned again and again to this ordeal. Szajna's creation of a total scenic world that summons up the death camps began in 1962 with his design of Wyspianski's *Akropolis* for Grotowski's Laboratory Theatre. This was the beginning of a career in the tradition of the Polish avant-garde theatre created by such artist-playwrights as Wyspianski and Witkacy, and carried on after the war by Szajna's older contemporary Tadeusz Kantor, the experimental visual artist and stage director.

In 1971 Szajna was given directorship of the Classical Theatre in Warsaw, which he transformed into an art institute for scenic design with its own experimental stage, the Studio Theatre. There Szajna elaborated the scenic theme of *Akropolis* into the performance work that has become his signature work, *Replika*. From its spectral visual imagery, clangorous metallic sounds and the gutteral, half-human cries of the actors *Replika* creates a planetary world of the dead.

As a text, *Replika* is only the briefest of performance scenarios. It originated as an art installation at the Venice Biennale in 1970. By 1972, when it was invited to the Edinburgh Festival, it had evolved into a one-hour living-theatre performance with actors. Enriched with new elements it appeared at the Nancy Festival in 1973 and received its Polish premiere later that year. It was first performed in the United States in 1975. Though Szajna resigned his directorship of the Studio Theatre after the repression of the Solidarity movement, *Replika* continues to be performed in Warsaw and in the West today.

Replika is not about the death camps in a literal way. It can be understood as an apocalyptic warning about the future as well as a nightmare reminder of the past. Its stricken landscape—an arid burial mound—represents a world after the death of human culture. Out of this deadly terrain emerge human-like beings who unearth puppets and other fragments of the lost civilization. They attempt to reassemble objects, art and "order." Language has been one of the casualties of the disaster that has struck the human community. The actors form only occasional desperate words, for instance, "Mother!" "Help!" "Baby!" "Look!" "Eye!" Ironically their efforts result in the emergence of a hellish superman. Eventually the creature is destroyed, but the broken world depicted by Szajna cannot be rebuilt. What the performers create is only a replica, an inauthentic world pieced together from the shards of a vanished, once human civilization.

The final images of *Replika* include the unrolling of sheafs of thousands of photographs, lifeless replicas of those who will never return. In the last moment of the performance a child's top is set spinning at the center of the scene, an emblem of humanity's crazy optimism in the face of catastrophe, but also of global catastrophe itself as the toy careens out of control and topples. "The best now . . . is, perhaps, to be silent . . .," George Steiner has written, questioning the value of art and language in the face of the organized annihilation of the European Jewish community. Szajna's work in *Replika* may be a form of art not envisioned by Steiner, however, an anti-representation occupying a negative space, a Holocaust theatre that eerily gives voice to silence.

The two large plays that conclude the collection use the metaphor of theatre itself to dramatize the Holocaust. *Ghetto* takes its inspiration from an actual historical theatre. Its Israeli author Joshua Sobol came by chance upon a slogan that was coined in the Wilna ghetto, "One does not perform theatre in a graveyard." Realizing that there must indeed have been a theatre in the ghetto, Sobol began to collect material about it. "I discovered, to my great amazement, that the former artistic director of the theatre was living in Tel Aviv, a few blocks from my apartment." With no intention of writing a play, Sobol one day shared his research with his playwriting students. "Two hours later, the lesson had gone by . . . . I went home, sat down at the typewriter and obeyed the play."

Born in 1939, Sobol has written more than fourteen plays. Many of them were introduced at the Haifa Municipal Theater and directed by Sobol himself. For several years the co-director of this socially engaged theatre, he was appointed its artistic director in 1985. Since its premiere in Haifa in 1983, *Ghetto* has been widely performed. It received its American English-language premiere at the Mark Taper Forum in Los Angeles in 1986.

At the beginning of World War II, the Jewish population of the Lithuanian city of Wilna swelled to more than seventy thousand as Jews farther west fled the Nazi occupation. On June 24, 1941, the German army entered Wilna cheered by Lithuanians who saw the invasion as offering freedom from the Soviets. Within two weeks, the Germans began the notorious mass round-ups and exterminations of the summer of 1941. Only in September was it realized that in the preceding weeks thousands of Jews had been driven to the nearby mountain resort of Ponar and gunned down over huge pits. In early September the remaining twenty thousand Jews were forced into two ghettos. The ghetto of unskilled workers was liquidated within a month. The second, composed of twelve thousand skilled workers and their families, survived for two years. In that period more homeless Jews were periodically sent to Wilna; meanwhile incremental reductions raked the community until the ghetto was wiped out in 1943. Here, under the circumstances of ruthless hardship,

INTRODUCTION

flourished an astounding array of cultural activities. One of these was the ghetto theatre, which opened in January 1942, giving over one hundred performances in its first year.

Ghetto unfolds as a memory in the mind of the aged Srulik, former artistic director and chief puppeteer of the ghetto theatre. We follow the intertwined stories of the creation of the theatre and the destruction of the ghetto. In a setting that is both theatre and ghetto, the rear of the stage is dominated by a mountain of clothing before which the entire communal life of the Wilna ghetto is played out. The clothing, last remains of the vanished Jewish population, serves as "costume department" for the theatre troupe, and ironically symbolizes the livelihood of the struggling Jews, the tailor Weiskopf having won permission from the SS to open a ghetto factory for the repair of worn German uniforms.

In some productions all the action of the play is presented as a "performance" by the actors of the theatre, and in others a mixture of reality levels has been used. Remarkably, however, most characters of Sobol's play had their documentary counterparts in Wilna, even the fantastic German scholar Dr. Paul of the Rosenberg Foundation, whose work was dedicated to the investigation of Judaism without Jews. Similarly, the play's incidents are grounded in historical fact—its text is indebted to the diary kept by Herman Kruk, the ghetto library director, and its songs were chosen from those actually composed in the ghettos and camps. (The original Yiddish lyrics and music may be found in an appendix to the edition of *Ghetto* published by the Institute for the Translation of Hebrew Literature in Tel Aviv.)

In Sobol's treatment, the ghetto theatre becomes a major ideological battleground between intellectuals and pragmatists. In a ranging debate, characters struggle with three related questions. Does art lull the population into a false sense of well-being, or does it strengthen the population's will to survive oppression? Is Jewish cooperation with the Nazis self-destructive and immoral, or is it a necessary strategy to prolong life? And finally, if Jews organize their future survival around nationalism and force, abandoning the spiritual character of the Diaspora, will the oppressor conquer even the survivors? In raising this final question, perhaps the most unsettling raised by any play about the Holocaust, *Ghetto* seems to take place on the other side of the catastrophe, in the atmosphere of contemporary discussion within Israel today.

Sobol has said that he "heard" his play in Yiddish, but wrote it in Hebrew. In its mixture of moral debate, expressionism and burlesque, *Ghetto* owes a debt to the Yiddish theatre. (Even Sobol's wily Hasid, here a rogue palm reader, is a stock comic figure of the Yiddish theatre.) These echoes are especially evocative as Wilna had been at one time the seat of Europe's greatest Yiddish theatre.

Cathedral of Ice, the final play of the volume, examines the past but thinks about the future. Political and social themes have loomed large in the more than twenty-five volumes of poems and plays the American writer James Schevill has published over his distinguished forty-year career. A professor of English at Brown University until his retirement in 1985, Schevill began his career as a "college drop-out" studying music in Europe before the Second World War. By chance Schevill arrived in Germany to visit a friend on the night of November 9, 1938, the notorious *"Kristallnacht"* when thousands of Jewish synagogues were burned, shops and homes destroyed, and Jewish citizens swept into detention. Arriving at his Freiburg hotel late in the evening, Schevill writes:

> I saw smoke from a large fire down the street. The street was cordoned off by police and special troops. A couple was ushered into a police car. Next morning, condemned to this experience for the rest of my life, I realized I had witnessed the burning down of the synagogue and the arrest of the rabbi and his wife. A high fence had been built around the site as if to conceal a nightmare. The nightmare has never left me. It caused me to write my first poem, and somehow, to become a writer.

The "dream play" *Cathedral of Ice*, produced in 1975 by the Trinity Repertory Company in Providence, Rhode Island, emerges directly from this experience.

The title of *Cathedral of Ice* comes from a remark made by the British Ambassador to Germany on seeing Albert Speer's design, displayed at the Nürenberg Party Conference, of anti-aircraft searchlights piercing the night sky. In Schevill's often scathingly satiric play, which takes the form of a musical revue, Hitler's cathedral is a phantasmagoric "dream-machine" choked with the fantasies of power. The play uses historical characters and incidents spanning Hitler's entire career, woven into a carnival of human despotism relieved only by the figure of the Jewish peddler, who keeps turning up like a mischievous gnat. In Schevill's nightmare, the defeat of the Third Reich is a merely temporary setback. As long as men seek power by force, Hitler's future is assured. The ironically bright final song of the play is dedicated to Charlemagne, who assumes an immortal place in the "cathedral of ice," frozen "for tomorrow," when dreams of power will be mobilized again.

Schevill has situated his play in an imaginative space that perhaps could be claimed only by an American. The realm of *Cathedral of Ice* is not that of the survivor of the Holocaust, but of its inheritor. Schevill traces the "cathedral" of modern power directly to the building blocks assembled by Hitler: pornography, drugs, a fantasy Wild West, a love affair with death, the kitsch that could assimilate Wagner to Lehar.

INTRODUCTION

Schevill here anticipates the theme of *Reflections of Nazism, an Essay on Kitsch and Death*, in which French historian Saul Friedlander criticizes certain European novels and films for a morbid yet sentimental fascination with Hitler. Schevill warns that this fascination could once again plunge the world into destruction, perhaps for the last time.

• • •

In a major essay, "Writing and the Holocaust," Irving Howe considers the relationship of drama to the Holocaust:

> The Holocaust is not, essentially, a dramatic subject. . . . Of those conflicts between wills, those inner clashes of belief and wrenchings of desire, those enactments of passion, all of which make up our sense of the dramatic, there can be little in the course of a fiction focused mainly on the mass exterminations.

Howe seems to suggest that the dramatic form is inadequate, perhaps even obsolete—too weak a vessel to contain this most dreadful chapter in twentieth-century history, if not indeed in all of human history. Later in the essay Howe writes that the death camps "give little space for the tragic in any traditional sense of that term." In *Versions of Survival*, Holocaust literature scholar Lawrence Langer speculates that the "real tragedy" in the experience of concentration camp victims "is the *absence* of the truly tragic"—the denial of individual choice even in suffering.

Howe and Langer suggest that tragedy as we have understood it from Aristotle to O'Neill, the dramatic form that links human greatness with individual suffering, may finally be a victim to modern mass brutality. No more tragic hero; no more purification through suffering; no more mourning Horatio to tell the story. Alberto Moravia makes this "death of tragedy" the cruel central irony of his oratorio-like drama *Il Dio Kurt*, in which a Jewish concentration camp prisoner is forced to commit with his actual parents the crimes of Sophocles' Oedipus.

In fact, the modern stage has long forecast this loss. Nearly a century ago, Jarry's *Ubu Roi* depicted an obscene world in which tragedy, both the dramatic form and the attendant emotion, could occur only in the form of savage parody. But perhaps in the post-Holocaust era, the question of tragedy asks to be reopened, or to be reconceived. Instead of delivering the final blow to tragedy perhaps the Holocaust has shown us its new form for an epoch that can no longer summon the humanistic faith in "man" that has characterized the Western stage from its inception.

The plays presented here suggest, in their different ways, a new locus of tragedy—not in the fall of a single great and representative individual, but in the failure of the entire human enterprise. In the world after the

Holocaust, we live daily with the dark companion of extinction—by famine, plague, force, and above all by the fire of nuclear holocaust. We live in a time of tragic consciousness. For us, tragic loss is measured in groups, peoples, species. Not all the plays in this volume are tragedies as such, but all share this knowledge on a scale unimaginable before the Holocaust.

Yet the appearance of such works before an audience is at some level a refusal of this somber prospect. The theatre above all other forms of artistic practice insists on the life of the community; it cannot be be made without it. Each play presented here enacts a rite of mourning for the lost community of Jewry and by extension for the threatened human community whose doom the Holocaust may foreshadow. That rite cannot take place without the participation of the community of spectators as living witness. In the very act of representing the annihilation of the human community, then, the theatre itself offers a certain fragile potentiality for re-creation. In that spirit as well this book is offered.

ELINOR FUCHS
New York, 1987

PLAYS OF THE HOLOCAUST

Eli

A Mystery Play
of the Sufferings of Israel

Nelly Sachs
translated by Christopher Holme

Characters

WASHERWOMAN	OLD WOMAN
BAKER WOMAN	CARPENTER
SAMUEL	GARDENER
BRICKLAYERS	OLD MAN
STONEMASON'S WIFE	CREATURE
OLDER GIRL	FARMER
YOUNGER GIRL	SCHOOLTEACHER
MICHAEL	BOY
MENDEL	SHOEMAKER
MAN	SHOEMAKER'S WIFE
WOMAN	MAN
KNIFE GRINDER	WIFE
HUNCHBACK	CHILD
BLIND GIRL	DOCTOR
FIDDLER	POSTMAN
THE DAJAN	BAKER
BEGGAR	ASSORTED VOICES, WORSHIPPERS,
RABBI	MEN, WOMEN AND CHILDREN.

Time

After martyrdom.

2

The Play

—

Eli

A Mystery Play
of the Sufferings of Israel

Scene 1

The marketplace of a small Polish town in which a number of survivors of the Jewish people have come together. The houses lie around about in ruins. Nothing stands but a fountain in the middle, at which a man is working, cutting and laying pipes.

WASHERWOMAN *(Carrying a basket full of white linen. Chanting)*:
   From the laundry, the laundry I come
   from washing the garments of death,
   from washing the shirt of Eli,
   washing out the blood, washing out the sweat,
   child-sweat, washing out death.
   (To the pipelayer)
   To you, Samuel, will I bring it,
   to the Cattle Lane bring it at evening,
   where the bats flutter around in the air
   as I flutter the Bible pages
   looking for the Song of Lamentation
   where it burns and smokes and the stones fall.
   Your grandson's shirt will I bring you,
   the shirt of Eli.
BAKER WOMAN:
   How came it, Biddy, that he was struck dumb?

Nelly Sachs

WASHERWOMAN:

It was on the morning when they fetched the son,
tore him from bed, from sleep—
as they had torn open the door
to the Shrine of Shrines in the temple—
forbid, forbid—
thus they tore him from sleep.
Rachel his wife, too, they tore from sleep,
drove her before them through the Cattle Lane,
the Cattle Lane—the widow Rosa sat
at the corner, at the window
and told the story of how it happened
until they shut her mouth
with a thorn, because her husband was a gardener.
Eli in his nightshirt ran after his parents,
his pipe in his hand,
the pipe he had played in the fields
to lamb and calf—
and Samuel, the grandfather,
ran after his grandson.

And when Eli saw,
saw with the eyes of an eight-year-old
how they drove his parents
through the Cattle Lane, the Cattle Lane,
he put the pipe to his mouth and blew it.
And he did not blow it
as one who pipes to his cattle or in play,
said the widow Rosa while she was yet alive,
no, he threw back his head
like the stag or the roebuck
before it drinks at the spring.
He pointed the pipe to heaven,
he piped to God, did Eli,
said the widow Rosa while she was yet alive.

BAKER WOMAN:

Come aside, Biddy, so that he may not hear,
hear our talk, the dumb one.
Must like a sponge else suck in our words,
can bring nothing forth from his throat,
tied tight with death.

THEY *go aside.*

ELI

WASHERWOMAN:

A soldier marching with the procession
looked around and saw Eli
piping to high heaven,
struck him down dead with his rifle butt.
A young soldier he was, very young still,
said the widow Rosa.
Samuel took up the corpse,
sat down upon a milestone,
and is dumb.

BAKER WOMAN:

Was not Michael then at hand
to come to the rescue of Eli?

WASHERWOMAN:

Michael was in the house of prayer,
in the burning house of prayer,
he checked the flames,
he saved Jossele,
saved Dajan,
saved Jacob,
but Eli is dead.

BAKER WOMAN (*Meditating*):

And would perhaps have come to an end with him,
the moment
when He forsook us?

WASHERWOMAN:

And the widow Rosa added too
that Michael came a minute too late,
a tiny minute,
look, tiny as the eye of my needle
with which I had just been sewing up the torn seam
of Eli's shirt.
Why do you think he came too late,
he whom no enemy detained?
He took one step into the side street,
a single step,
there where the house of Miriam once stood,
and then he turned around—
and Eli was dead.
Then said the widow Rosa:
But Michael has the unbroken vision,
not like ours which sees only fragments—
he has the Baal Shem vision,

from one end of the world to another—
(SHE *approaches the fountain*)
Samuel, will it be ready for the Feast,
for New Year, the fountain?

SAMUEL *nods.*

BAKER WOMAN:
I'll tell you, Biddy, a secret,
I hear the footsteps!
WASHERWOMAN:
What footsteps do you hear, Basia?
BAKER WOMAN:
When they fetched Isaac, my husband,
the baker, because he baked the pretzels,
the sugar pretzels with forbidden flour,
when they fetched him from the ovens,
I gave him his overcoat,
because the cold outside was cutting—
they whinnied like horses
whinnying with joy at their oats—
"He'll be back, quicker than he can put it on—
he'll be back!"
He came back, without footsteps!
That's when the footsteps began in my ear!
The heavy footsteps,
the strong footsteps,
they said to the earth:
I'll break you open—
in between, his dragging step,
for he walked little,
breathed heavily in the cold,
at the ovens he stood,
by day and by night—
WASHERWOMAN:
Do you hear the footsteps still?
BAKER WOMAN:
They live in my ear,
they walk in the daytime
they walk in the nighttime,
whether you speak or I speak,
I hear them always.
WASHERWOMAN:
Ask Michael
if he can rid you of the footsteps.

I must ask Michael what he knows.
For he stitches sole to uppers,
he must know more than just how to wander to the grave.
Let me tell you, Basia, I'm a washerwoman,
I've made the lye, I've washed, I've rinsed,
but today at the laundry,
there where the seam was torn on Eli's shirt—
there it looked at me—

BAKER WOMAN:

If only I could,
I'd open the seam above there,
made bloody by the sun,
could Isaac's eyes but see me—
I'd say,
caught behind bars I am,
bars made of footsteps,
open the bars,
let me out of the heavy footsteps,
the strong footsteps
which break open the earth—
in between, your dragging step—

WASHERWOMAN:

The fountain's running!

BAKER WOMAN:

The fountain's running!
(SHE *cups her hands and drinks*)
Take away the footsteps,
the footsteps from my ear—
the footsteps—footsteps—
(SHE *falls to the ground*)

Scene 2

*The same marketplace, seen from a different angle. The fountain plays.
At one of the ruined houses an old* BRICKLAYER *and his apprentice,* JOSSELE,
*are working. In the background a narrow, ruined alley at the end of which
the prayer tent can be seen. Green landscape gleams through everywhere.*

BRICKLAYER:

Jossele, fill the bucket at the fountain,
run for the lime there where they're building,
building outside the gates the new town.
No gates are there anymore,
no old town anymore.

No house of prayer anymore,
only earth enough for the holy ground.
(*To himself*)
This was a house, here, this was a hearth,
there's a saucepan still, burned black.
Here's a colored ribbon,
perhaps it was a cradle bow—
perhaps it was an apron string—
who knows?
Here's a skullcap.
Who wore it?
A young man or an old one or a boy?
Did it guard the Eighteen Benedictions, the silent ones,
from idle thoughts,
from wicked thoughts,
or—who knows?

A WOMAN *in a nightdress hurries up the narrow alley, knocking with her finger on walls and stones.*

BRICKLAYER:
   Esther Weinberg, what're you knocking at?
   There's no answer locked in the stone.
JOSSELE (*With the bucket*):
   The woman has run out of the infirmary,
   now she's picking up stones and throwing them away—
BRICKLAYER:
   Wants to break out of her prison—
JOSSELE:
   But what is she doing now?
   Opening and shutting her hands like cups
   and filling them with air.
STONEMASON'S WIFE (*Singing*):
   Your right leg
   light as a bird—
   your left leg
   light as a bird—
   curls in the south wind—
   hearts can shiver like water in the hand—
   shiver like water—
   Oh . . . oh . . .
   (SHE *runs off*)
BRICKLAYER:
   She makes her child out of air—
   (HE *takes a stone*)

ELI

We make graves,
but she has broken out already—
is taking lessons already with Him—

JOSSELE *(Runs after the* WOMAN *and returns)*:
The woman is dead.
Said to a stone: "Here I come,"
struck her brow upon it and died.
This letter was lying beside her.

BRICKLAYER *(Reading)*:
"Finely veined like your temples was the stone.
Laid it to my cheek before going off to sleep,
felt its depressions,
felt its elevations,
its smooth and jagged places—
blew upon it,
and it breathes like you, Esther. . . ."
This is from Gad, her husband,
who slaved himself to death in the quarry,
bearing Israel's burden—

JOSSELE *weeps and sighs.*

BRICKLAYER:
Don't cry, Jossele.
Let us build the old house anew.
If tears hang on the stonework,
if sighs hang on the woodwork,
if the little children can't sleep,
death has a soft bed.
(HE *lays bricks, singing and whistling)*
Master of the world!
Thou, Thou, Thou, Thou!
Master of all stones!
Thou, Thou, Thou, Thou!
Where can I find Thee,
and where can I not find Thee?
Thou, Thou, Thou, Thou!

Scene 3

*The ruined alley near the marketplace, which can just be seen. The foun-
tain plays.* CHILDREN *come running.*

OLDER GIRL:
The schoolteacher said
today was the day

of Michael's wedding years ago,
the day they snatched his bride from him
before the blessing of the candles.

YOUNGER GIRL:

What shall we play?

OLDER GIRL:

Wedding and candle-blessing
And I'll be the bride—

BOY *(Seizing her)*:

And I'll snatch you away.

OLDER GIRL *(Freeing herself)*:

No, I don't want that,
I'll find myself a baby to cradle.

JOSSELE:

When I went on the ship,
the sea always traveled away with us
like the roll of yarn
when I make it pop up on the thread,
but we didn't reach the white
where it begins.
But in sleep I was there.
When I woke up, someone said:
Many are drowned,
but you are saved.
But often the water still follows me.

YOUNGER GIRL:

I sat deep below in the night,
and there was a woman there,
as kind as Sister Leah from the infirmary
and she said: Sleep, I'll watch.
And then there came a wall in my mouth
and I ate a wall.

OLDER GIRL:

Was the woman your mother?

YOUNGER GIRL:

Mother? What's that?

OLDER GIRL *(Pulling a rag out of the rubble)*:

Here is linen,
and here's a piece of wood
charred only at one end.
Now I've got a baby,
a baby with black hair,
And now I'll cradle it.

(Singing)
Once on a time there was a tale—
the tale is not a gay one,
the tale begins with singing
about a king of the Jews.

Once on a time there was a king—
a king there was, he had a queen,
the queen she had a vineyard—
Lyulinka, my child . . .

YOUNGER GIRL:

Did you learn that from Becky?

OLDER GIRL:

Yes.
(Singing)
The vineyard it had a tree,
the tree it had a bough,
the bough it had a little nest—
Lyulinka, my child . . .

JOSSELE:

Look, I've found a bone—
who makes himself a pipe of dead men's bones
will never pipe the cattle forth—

OLDER GIRL:

Does the water still follow you?

JOSSELE:

Yes, sometimes,
but more often it is the hanged Isidor who comes
and says: My friend, a roll of yarn
holds like a rope—

OLDER GIRL:

It's late,
let's go to Becky.

JOSSELE:

Give me your baby,
I'll throw it on the rubble,
there it can cry.

OLDER GIRL:

No, don't do that,
Miriam its name is,
and I'll go into the kitchen,
and ask Becky for a whisk,
that'll do for a head.

(Singing)
The nest it had a little bird,
the bird it had a little wing,
the wing it had a little feather—
Lyulinka, my child . . .
ALL *(As* THEY *go off slowly, singing from backstage)*:
The king he had to die,
the queen she had to perish,
the tree had to shatter,
the bird fly from its nest . . .

Scene 4

MICHAEL'*s cobbler's shop in the only unruined house. Through the window, moonlight and open fields. Shelves on the walls with shoes on them. Table with tools. Bench before the window.* MICHAEL, *tall, thin, with reddish hair.* HE *snatches a pair of shoes and puts them on the window bench. Then* HE *lifts up a shoe, so that it is silhouetted in black against the moonlight. It is a small woman's shoe.*

MICHAEL:
You trod so lightly,
the grasses rose behind your feet.
Here is the strap you tore,
as you hurried toward me that time—
quick is love,
the sun as it rises
is slower far.
Miriam—
*(*HE *sinks to the ground, his head between his knees)*
What constellation saw your death?
Was it the moon, the sun, or the night?
With stars, without stars?

A cloud passes across the moon. The room is almost dark. Gliding footsteps are heard. A sigh, then a rough MAN'S VOICE.

MAN'S VOICE:
Thou art fair, my love,
were I thy bridegroom
I should be jealous of death,
but thus—

Wild laughter, screams. MICHAEL *lies for a long time motionless. The moon shines again.* HE *raises himself, snatches up a pair of heavy men's shoes.*

ELI

MICHAEL:
> Isidor's shoes,
> the pawnbroker's shoes,
> heavy shoes.
> A worm is stuck to the sole,
> a trodden worm.
> The moon shines on,
> just as when it saw your death.
> (HE *sinks to the ground in the same position as before. Heavy footsteps are heard*)

FIRST VOICE:
> Don't hang it up,
> I've got it in a casket,
> of sandalwood the casket is—
> was the jewel case of the rich, then poor, Sarah—
> good customer she was—

SECOND VOICE:
> Speak, what about the casket?

FIRST VOICE:
> Buried it, behind the beech tree,
> the only beech tree among the pines—
> there's a ring inside,
> has a stone, an aquamarine,
> has a blue fire, the aquamarine—
> the whole Mediterranean is in it—
> blue, so blue, when the sun plays—
> No—in the pockets nothing rattles, empty—
> That's the night wind,
> rattling silver in the leaves—

SECOND VOICE:
> Rattle on then with the night wind, you—

MICHAEL *lies motionless.* HE *gets up again, snatches a pair of child's shoes and lifts them above his head. The morning sun begins to redden the sky.*

MICHAEL:
> Shoes,
> trodden over on the inside,
> lamb's wool sticking to them—
> Eli—
> (HE *sinks into the same position as before*)

The rending notes of a pipe are heard.

Scene 5

Room of a ruined building. SAMUEL *sits on a bed of boards. On his lap is Eli's death-shirt. A candle flickers.* MICHAEL *enters.*

MICHAEL:
Samuel,
I pray you to help me find what I am seeking,
I seek the hand,
I seek the eyes,
I seek the mouth,
I seek the piece of skin,
into which the corruption of this earth has entered,
I seek Eli's murderer.
I seek the dust
which since Cain has mingled
with every murderer's dust and waited,
meanwhile has formed birds perhaps—
and then murderers.
Perhaps it formed the mandrakes
for which Rachel gave up a night to Leah—
Perhaps it encased Sammael's exhalations of hate—
To think
that this dust may have touched the prayer book of Luria,
when it lay hidden,
till its letters spouted flames—
to think—
Oh, what dust is it that I bring you here on my shoes.
(HE *takes off his shoes*)
Samuel, let me ask your dumbness,
Was he tall?

SAMUEL *shakes his head.*

Was he shorter than I and taller than you?

SAMUEL *nods.*

His hair, was it fair?

SAMUEL *nods.*

His eyes, black, blue?

SAMUEL *shakes his head.*

Gray?

SAMUEL *nods.*

His color, red-cheeked, healthy?

SAMUEL *shakes his head.*

Pale then?

SAMUEL *nods.*

(Sobbing)
How many millions of men has the earth?
Murderers like Cain.
Crumbled mandrakes,
nightingale dust,
dust of prayer books,
from which letters spring out like flames.

SAMUEL *hands* MICHAEL *a shepherd's pipe.* MICHAEL *breathes into it.*
A weak note is heard. HE *points to the death-shirt, on which the form*
of a man's head is silhouetted.

Look, oh look,
the candle throws the shadow—
or your dumbness speaks:
Very young still,
the nose is broad,
its nostrils quiver with blood lust,
the eyes have the pupils of a wolf—
The mouth is small as a child's—

The face disappears.

Thus faces are compounded in dreams—
water poured from the invisible—
It is gone,
and burns in my eyes.
Until I find him
it will get between me and everything on this earth,

it will hang in the air—
In the bread I eat
this nightmare dust will be my food.
In the apple I eat
the murderer's face will lurk—
Samuel,
your speech has already reached
where all dust is at an end.
Beyond the Word this thing was compounded.
(HE *backs to the door, where* HE *puts on his shoes*)

Scene 6

Open side of the marketplace, giving on to the fields. The splashing of the fountain is heard. On a sandy path in plowland, PEDDLER MENDEL *stands and cries his wares, surrounded by onlookers.*

MENDEL:
　　Bargain offer! Amazing opportunity!
　　It is my privilege to show you:
　　Apron material, washable, colorfast, with flower designs,
　　with butterfly designs.
　　Stockings of wool, stockings of silk, straight from Paris.
　　Elastic, look, you can stretch it
　　from here to kingdom come, and back it springs—
　　direct from America.
　　From England I have lavender for headaches
　　and peppermint for a bad digestion—
　　But this linen now from Russia—
　　not now for the dead, no longer,
　　not for the feet pointing toward the door—
　　no, for the lovely bride, for baby too—
WOMAN (*To her husband*):
　　Look here,
　　what a holiday dress that'd make for me,
　　just now with the New Year coming in.
MAN:
　　We live in the poorhouse,
　　you have neither table nor chair,
　　what do you want with such stuff?
WOMAN:
　　Why, look now,
　　the little Sterntal woman

has a better husband than I,
he's bought her the fine scarf already.

MAN:

Where you now stand, it ran with blood—
We are saved . . .

WOMAN:

. . . and ought to have joy in our safety.

MAN (*To* MENDEL):

You're spoiling the women all over again.
This love of finery
will bring even mourning crepe out in pleats and flounces.

MENDEL:

I have no wife,
but if I had one, I'd vie with Solomon.
He who praises the virtuous wife
praises her attire as well—

MAN:

Very well, measure me a length of the stuff.

KNIFE GRINDER:

Scissors to grind,
Knives to grind,
Sickles for the new crop—

ANOTHER WOMAN:

I wish he'd be off
and do his grinding away from here—
The noise of knives grinding
is more than a body can stand—

KNIFE GRINDER:

Next time you eat
you'll need a knife—
Next time you harvest
you'll need a knife—
When next you dress
two knives you'll need.
(HE *grinds on*)

ANOTHER WOMAN:

A lot it matters to you—
or don't you feel it? That your grinding
carves up the world in pieces.

KNIFE GRINDER:

I hate nobody,
want to give no offense—
I grind because it's my trade—

ANOTHER WOMAN:
> So it's his trade,
> as it's mine to weep—
> and another's to die.

TWO TEENAGE GIRLS *enter.*

ONE GIRL *(Speaking to* MENDEL*)*:
> Peddler, I want to buy a hank of woolen yarn.
> *(To her companion)*
> Let me lay the hank around your wrists.
> You hold them still while I wind
> and it's like saying goodbye.
> Me they held fast by the wrists
> and took my mother away—
> and the goodbye went from her to me—
> from me to her,
> till it was at an end—

THEY *walk on. A* FIDDLER *has come and starts to play.* THEY *all begin to dance.*

HUNCHBACK:
> What longing in the bones—
> the old Adam ferments in the notes,
> the new man has his first rib already.

A BLIND GIRL *enters with hands stretched before her, holding twigs and sticks.* SHE *is barefoot and dressed in rags.*

BLIND GIRL *(Coming to a halt in front of the* FIDDLER*)*:
> There's a twitching under my foot.
> The pavement of our longing must be here at an end.
> There go all my journeys.
> *(*SHE *throws down the sticks)*
> Always, when my feet got a new wound
> a journey was at an end
> like a clock that strikes.
> I wanted to see my love once more
> but then they took away my eyes—
> from that time on, I counted midnight.
> Now I am but a tear removed from my love,
> and the last wound has opened in my foot—

ELI

(SHE *sinks to the ground and is taken away*)

HUNCHBACK:

She's brought with her only the skeleton of her journeys—
The flesh is all consumed with longing—
She wanted to see her love once more—
but the Devil
shies from the mirror of love in a human look
and shattered it—

TWO CHILDREN (*Collect the twigs and sing*):

We've got sticks,
we've got journeys,
we've got bones,
ei, ei, ei—

MENDEL:

This one stick
I could use to tie up my bundle
the others you can keep.

The FIDDLER *plays on, and* EVERYBODY *dances.*

HUNCHBACK:

Don't dance so heavily
knocking at the walls of sleep—it could flood you,
too many young hearts inside them—
there'll be love dust—
Who knows how that grain will taste—
who knows?

YOUNG WOMAN (*With a child on her arm, to the* HUNCHBACK):

Don't stare at my child like that!
God preserve it from the evil eye—

HUNCHBACK:

Forbid that I should scorch it with my look.
I only wonder
how you were able to bear it
in these times—

YOUNG WOMAN:

In a hole in the earth I bore it,
in a hole I suckled it—
Death took its father,
me he did not take,
saw the milk in my breasts
and did not take me.

HUNCHBACK (*Repeating her words*):
  And did not take you—
YOUNG WOMAN:
  Forgive me if I offended you.
  But God preserve me,
  I thought at first
  you were a living piece
  of Israel's
  misfortune.
HUNCHBACK (*Pointing to his hump*):
  You saw the satchel
  in which the scapegoat carries its people's misfortune.
YOUNG WOMAN:
  To me it seems
  a hundred or more years have passed
  since I sat in my hole—
  I can't bear the light anymore—
  I only blink—
  To me these seem not human beings,
  mounds of earth I see dancing—
  night can preserve no names.
  Whatever barks, whatever sings
  I've long forgotten—
HUNCHBACK (*Pointing to the long shadows thrown by* MENDEL):
  It's a late hour already in Israel.

All the DANCERS *throw long shadows. Their bodies are as if blotted out by the glare of the evening sun. Only the* YOUNG WOMAN *with her child stands out clearly in the light.*

Scene 7

The marketplace as at the beginning. In the background the narrow alley ends at the prayer tent. A crowd of WORSHIPPERS *is gathering for the Festival service.*

FIRST WORSHIPPER:
  Here is the place
  where baker Isaac of the shuffling gait
  was struck down because of a sugar pretzel.
  His shop sign was an iron pretzel,
  on it the children's eyes
  had fastened with longing,

ELI

and eaten their fill of it—
One child fell dead,
had eaten enough.
Thought Isaac,
I'll bake a sugar pretzel,
then another and once again,
so that they'll not eat themselves to death
with their eyes on the iron pretzel.
One pretzel he baked, no more.
The iron pretzel glowed
as in the baker's oven fire,
until a man of war took it away,
melted it down for the next death.

A MAN *with a looking glass in his hand passes by, looking into it.*

MAN:
There, where you carried your children—
I believe we were seven in number—
there your body collapsed onto the grave gaping below,
your withered breasts hung over it in mourning.
O my mother,
your murderer held a mirror before you
so that you might have a comic death—
Mother, you looked at yourself
until your jaw sagged onto your breast—
but the great Angel spread his wings over you!
Through the barbed wire of the times
he came hasting to you
with torn wings—
for iron and steel have grown rampant, Mother,
building primeval forests in the air—
murderers' brains have grown rampant—
vines of premeditated anguish sprouting from them.
Mirror, mirror,
echo from the forest of the dead—
victims and hangmen,
victims and hangmen
played with their breath upon you the dying game.
Mother,
one day there'll be a constellation called Mirror.

(HE *passes on*)

SECOND WORSHIPPER (*To* THIRD WORSHIPPER):
>Is he still saying kaddish into the mirror?

THIRD WORSHIPPER:
>Yes. Holy Baal Shem,
>last sheaf-carrier of Israel's strength,
>weaker your people has become and weaker,
>a swimmer
>whom only death brings to land.

THE DAJAN:
>But I tell you:
>Many a one of you has had the potent faith,
>behind the curtain of night
>has forced down
>the great tranquilizers life and death.
>*(Pointing to a house wrecked by gunfire)*
>Not with such weapons alone was the battle fought,
>I tell you:
>Battlefields there are—battlefields
>which the inventors of daylight murder
>have never dreamed of.
>Many a prayer
>has hung with flaming wings before the cannon's mouth,
>many a prayer
>has burned up the night like a sheet of paper!
>Sun, moon, and stars have been arrayed by Israel's prayer
>along the potent strings of faith—
>diamonds and carbuncles
>about the dying throat of her people
>O! O!—

HUNCHBACK:
>They say,
>because of my jerking shoulders
>they hate me—

KNIFE GRINDER:
>They say,
>because of my perpetual smile
>they hate me—

MENDEL:
>They say,
>because of this heap of stone
>which was once my house
>they hate me—

BEGGAR *(With a feather in his hat)*:
> When I turn the hat over
> it's a grave for money,
> or I put it on,
> and it's something
> which has to do with flying.
> What are riches in a Jew
> but an ice pit around a frozen tear!—

THE DAJAN:
> I see,
> see the beginning of your jerking shoulders, Simon—
> when with Abraham you dug the well of the "Seven
> > Oaths"
> in Beersheba—
> I see,
> I see the beginning of your smile, Aman—
> on Horeb planted in the seventy elders,
> to sprout again
> sprout in the wandering dust of the lip.
> Stones are stones—
> Earth of Paradise in them, but in greed destroyed.
> But they do not know the beginning,
> not the eternal beginning—
> and that's why they hate us—

ALL THE BYSTANDERS:
> That's why they hate us—

THE DAJAN *(Shouting)*:
> Eli, because of you,
> to know your beginning—
> *(HE collapses)*

Scene 8

The same. The WORSHIPPERS *have disappeared into the prayer tent. Murmurs are heard, then the voice of the* RABBI *pronouncing the Shophar lines.*

RABBI'S VOICE:
> *Tekiá—*

A long note is heard, of a single pitch.

Shevarim—

Three notes in succession.

Teruá—

A trilled note. The shadow of the seven-branched candlestick is silhouetted on the tent wall. The tent is opened. The WORSHIPPERS *march out.*

FIRST WORSHIPPER:
　The air is new—
　gone is the smell of burning,
　gone is the smell of blood,
　gone is the smell of smoke—
　the air is new!
SECOND WORSHIPPER:
　In my ear there's a noise
　as if someone were pulling
　the barb from the wound—
　the barb that is sticking in the middle of the earth—
　Someone takes the two halves of the earth apart
　like an apple,
　the two halves of today and yesterday—
　takes out the maggot
　and joins the casing together again.

　THE WORSHIPPERS *march across the marketplace.*

SEVERAL WORSHIPPERS:
　Happy New Year!
　May the moment when He forsook us
　be at an end!
OTHER WORSHIPPERS *(Joining them)*:
　And Israel emptied forth its soul for death—
　The horn has sounded to call us home.
　He did not forget us.
　On the palms of both hands engraved
　has He His people!

　EVERYONE *goes off. The marketplace is empty. An* OLD WOMAN *comes and sits on the edge of the fountain.*

OLD WOMAN:
　Isn't he coming yet, the Rabbi?
　Still not here yet, the Rabbi—
　(SHE *gets up and goes to meet him, weeping)*

ELI

There comes the Rabbi!
A cake I baked
in the oven out there in the fields—
the other women said:
That's a fine cake you've baked,
your holiday cake. I said,
It's for the Rabbi, the cake.
I took three measures of flour,
as Sarah did when she baked for the angels,
the angels
when they came to Abraham at evening—

RABBI:
There's nothing in the scripture
about their coming at evening—

OLD WOMAN:
Always the angels come at evening.
And the water at the spring
has a mouth that speaks.

RABBI:
Why are you crying, Grandma?

OLD WOMAN:
Have I not a right to cry?
The rats have eaten the cake,
the cake for the Rabbi.

RABBI:
New flour will be given you
and we'll eat the cake together—

OLD WOMAN:
Can't bake anymore,
can't eat anymore,
can only weep.
(Weeping more violently)

RABBI:
Do you live in the house with the old people, Grandma?

OLD WOMAN:
I live in the third cellar
on the marketplace.

RABBI:
Why don't you live with the old people?

OLD WOMAN:
Because I must live
there where I live.

Yehudi was born there,
Natel was born there,
Taubel was born there—
their cry is still in the place,
and Taubel's dance is in the place—
Michael gave me a pair of shoes
because the grave-earth had entered into the old ones,
Yehudi's earth,
Taubel's earth,
Natel's earth.
They're shoes from Rabbi Sassow,
they're Tzaddick shoes,
holy shoes, holy dancing shoes.

(SHE *laces them up tighter*)

Taubel's dancing is in them.
Look!

(SHE *begins to dance*)

Scene 9

Marketplace at the fountain. The GIRLS *fill the jugs and hand them to the dusty* BRICKLAYERS *as* THEY *pass, building the new town.*

BRICKLAYER (*To a* GIRL):
Thanks for the drink,
I am going now to build the new town.
GIRL:
Cement this in too.
It's got the Holy Words in it,
given to me by my love,
and I wore them on this chain about my neck.
BRICKLAYER:
How can one part with such a gift?
GIRL:
Short my life will be,
but the walls,
they must hold.
SECOND BRICKLAYER (*To another* GIRL):
Let us wed in spring,
for it is written:
Marry in winter
while the chrysalis lives on its dreams,
and your dream will shatter

before spring comes.
But when it flies,
then God himself will open brooks and buds—
THIRD BRICKLAYER (*Drinking thirstily*):
Always Israel was thirsty.
What people can ever have drunk at so many springs?
But now, thirst upon thirst,
all deserts together have worked at this our thirst.

A CARPENTER *with a door passes across the stage. The* BEGGAR *with the feather in his hat enters.*

BEGGAR:
That is a door.
A door is a knife
and parts the world in two halves.
If I stand in front and knock on it
because I'm a beggar,
then perhaps it'll be opened to me
and the smell of roast meat
and the smell of soaked clothes stream out.
It is the smell of human homes.
He who has a fine beggar's nose
can smell tears too
or built-in well-being.
But the housewife says:
"No, it's too early in the day,"
and "No" says the closing door.
At the next door I come too late,
all I get is a glimpse
of a bed thrown open,
and the door shuts,
sad as an evening blessing.
Carpenter, hang no doors,
they are the knives
which cut the world apart.
CARPENTER:
Man, collect your feather wits,
doors are for the cold and for burglars.
And since cold too is a burglar,
things are right as they are.
BEGGAR (*Going up to the door and knocking*):
Here is Israel, door of the world,
Door of the world, open!

CARPENTER:
> It is well made,
> it does not move,
> but behind it,
> the swallows migrate.

BEGGAR (*Throwing himself on the sand before the door*):
> There's your threshhold!

TROOP OF YOUNG BRICKLAYERS:
> We build, we build
> the new town, the new town,
> the new town!
> We bake, we bake
> the bricks of the new town!

THE DAJAN:
> And Abraham raised his hovel
> again and again
> and set it in direction toward Him.

FIRST BRICKLAYER:
> Moses baked bricks,
> David baked bricks,
> now we bake bricks,
> we the survivors!
> His thornbush in the desert
> are we, we, we!

SECOND BRICKLAYER:
> We bake!
> And this here is our candle!
> (HE *stamps the earth with his foot*)

THIRD BRICKLAYER:
> We have new miracles!
> Our desert too had quails and manna,
> for a time I lived on snow,
> ate clouds and sky—

CARPENTER:
> What do you say to the secret of a potato peeling
> washed up at my feet by the flood of hate?
> That was my Ark.
> If I now say "God,"
> you know where the strength comes from.

GARDENER (*With an apple tree*):
> For a new Adam,
> for a new Eve.

ELI

ALL *(Singing)*:
> We bake, we bake,
> to build the new house—

THE DAJAN:
> I fear you don't trench deep enough,
> those foundations will only bear the easygoing.
> *(Drinking at the fountain)*
> The new Pentateuch, I tell you, the new Pentateuch
> is written in mildew, the mildew of fear
> on the walls of the death cellars.

FIRST BRICKLAYER:
> Anguish of worms on the fishhook,
> anguish of fish over the worm,
> anguish of beetles under my foot—
> enough of the gravedigger's spade!
> *(To* THE DAJAN*)*
> Save your hay of memories for next winter—
> here is fresh grass.
> *(*HE *wreathes a* GIRL *with grasses)*
> Dust worshippers we are.
> As long as the dust bears such fruit,
> so long will we grub in its furrows
> and make paradises of dust
> with the apples
> which like grim forebodings smell of departure—

GARDENER *(With apple tree)*:
> This comes from the alien earth.
> The patriarchal dust is missing,
> has nourished the holy citron—
> Rachel of the well-deep eyes nourished it—
> David, the shepherd of lambs.
> My fingers crook themselves,
> to sink its roots in alien earth—

FIRST BRICKLAYER:
> Perhaps the air will turn into a new plant habitat,
> in virtue of new inventions—
> citron in the air,
> home in the air.

ALL *(Singing)*:
> We bake, we bake—

THE DAJAN *(To himself)*:
> I saw one who gnawed his own flesh
> filling himself out to one side like the moon

and thinning down toward the other world—
I saw a child smile
before it was thrown onto the flames—
Where is that now?
My God, where is that now?

Scene 10

Country road. Uprooted or burned trees on either side. Fields churned up by warfare. Rank reeds flowering over them. KNIFE GRINDER *and* PEDDLER MENDEL *walking together, the latter with his stock on a handcart.*

KNIFE GRINDER (*Pointing back along the road*):
They're all on edge a bit there, Brother Mendel.
MENDEL:
He who sits in the dark
lights himself a dream—
He who loses his bride
embraces the air—
He whose garment was touched by death
so that he cried out
has thoughts eating at him like worms—
A good thing I had hidden my stock
under the stonework.
Business wasn't bad today—
KNIFE GRINDER:
What did that man mean
when he picked out the one whose shoulder jerks
and you others?
MENDEL:
How should I know?
Once I saw a dowser,
his wand jumped up
whenever a spring was found.
So the Dajan seeks everywhere
the spring of hate
which was given Israel to drink.
But even though I knew better than I do,
you from another tribe,
how could I explain it to you?
KNIFE GRINDER:
Brother, why do you speak such words!
When we lay in the hayloft,

in the Pole Yarislav's hayloft,
then we were both one!
Eyes only, to espy the enemy,
ears only, to listen for creaking steps—
hair on the head
to rise to heaven in damp terror—
there came to us *one* sleep,
one hunger, *one* awakening,
came the yellow-eyed owl
who collects twigs
when she smells death—
looked into the loft window,
cried out like a hangman's daughter,
if he had had one:
Tuwoo!

MENDEL:

You made a gurgling sound in your dream
like a drowning man—

KNIFE GRINDER:

You spoke much about a light
that had set fire to your stock—

MENDEL:

Do you hear the crickets, Brother?

KNIFE GRINDER:

No.

MENDEL:

Pity.
It is the brighest sound in this world,
not every ear can catch it.
But did you see one?

KNIFE GRINDER:

No.

MENDEL:

Worse the pity.
They sit where the invisible begins.
They're beggars already at the gates of Paradise,
said Grandmother to us children.
But once a cricket was sitting
on a roll of rose-pink satin ribbon—

KNIFE GRINDER (*To a stray dog which runs past*):

Here, here, comrade.
With your four paws
you can accompany my two.

If Mendel has his cricket,
I'll have my dog.
When I grind, he'll bark—
There'll be two for the wind to stroke,
two to hunger and stand outside,
with the earth under our paws.
When sun, moon, and stars enter his pupils—
and a whole world too.
O you warm, walking grain of earth
with two mirrors—

An OLD BEGGAR MAN *comes to meet them.*

MENDEL:
Who are you, Grandpa?
OLD MAN:
I am not nor am I Grandpa!
MENDEL:
You are not, yet you speak!
Where do you come from?
OLD MAN *(Pointing to the grinding wheel)*:
Are you a knife grinder?
KNIFE GRINDER:
Yes.
OLD MAN:
So you know the truth.
KNIFE GRINDER:
Why do you answer as in a question game?
OLD MAN:
For the reason that there's fire in the stone,
and therefore life,
and in the knife death—
Therefore day by day you grind life with death.
That's where I come from.
KNIFE GRINDER:
Alive out of death?
OLD MAN:
From there where the murderers sowed my people in the
    earth.
O may its seed be full of stars!
KNIFE GRINDER:
By you?
OLD MAN:
I was only half sown,
lying already in the grave,

knew already how the warmth leaves the flesh—
how motion leaves the bones—
heard already the language of the bones when corruption
    sets in—
language of the blood when it congeals—
language of the dust
striving anew after love—

KNIFE GRINDER:
    But how were you saved?

MENDEL:
    Had you a ring,
    a fine pearl to sell,
    paid for your life with a secret glint?

OLD MAN:
    You wretched sacks,
    stuffed with questions and quarreling.
    What do you know of it,
    when the bodies become empty
    whispering like seashells,
    oh, when they rise on the white-flecked waves
    of eternity?

KNIFE GRINDER:
    But tell us, how were you saved?

OLD MAN:
    We had fled,
    Amschel, brown Yehudi, and I.
    Three nations were taken captive
    three languages taken captive,
    hands taken captive
    to be made to dig their own graves,
    to grasp their own death.
    Bodies were slaughtered
    and the remains poured out on the ground.
    How many thousands of millions of miles of anguish from
        Him!

MENDEL *and* KNIFE GRINDER:
    But you, you?

OLD MAN:
    The soldier
    who filled in the earth over us
    and buried us—
    blessings be on him—
    he saw by the lantern light,
    for it was night,

that they had not slaughtered me enough
and that my eyes were opening—
and he fetched me out
and hid me—
KNIFE GRINDER:
Very hard to believe.
MENDEL:
There's no telling,
speak on.
OLD MAN:
The soldier that morning—
so he told me later—
had had a letter from his mother.
Blessings be on her!
For that reason he was not intoxicated like the rest
and saw the blinking of my eyes.
The mother wrote:
"Really I meant to put this letter with the socks,
the home-knitted ones.
But my longing gave me no peace—"
blessings be on it!
"And I am writing today
without waiting till they are finished.
But your suit, the blue one,
has been brushed and hung out to air
because of the moth powder.
So it won't smell of it
when you come."
But it didn't happen
that she was able to post the letter at once,
for she fell ill during the night.
And a neighbor came—
blessings be on her!—
asked how she was—
but really all she wanted was an onion—
a small one to cook with her potatoes,
for her own were finished.
Ah, that she ate potatoes
and not turnips—
Blessed be all onions!—
and she was given an onion
and took the letter to the post
and the soldier got it on that morning

and did not get intoxicated like the others—
and saw the blinking of my eyes—

KNIFE GRINDER:

How many onionskins came together there to save you!
And what more will sprout
from your onion luck?

OLD MAN:

I'm going to the Rabbi in the grave town.
My body will hold out no longer,
sand has touched the sand—
yet now it is the *one* death I die,
the other, which resides in a hangman's hand muscles
like a skeleton key in the burglar's fist,
that I don't need anymore,
I have the right key!

KNIFE GRINDER *and* MENDEL *resume their walking.*

MENDEL:

I am pleased, I am pleased!

KNIFE GRINDER:

What pleases you, Brother?

MENDEL:

I am pleased
that I gave Michael a pair of laces
for his walking shoes.
If he reaches Paradise
he'll have my laces on his feet.
The death-shirt of Eli too was of my linen—

KNIFE GRINDER:

Why was it good,
that you gave the shoemaker the laces,
and why should he die,
young as he is?

MENDEL *(As if telling him a secret)*:

I don't know,
but good it is in any case.
He may be one of the Thirty-six
on whose deeds the world rests—
one who follows the course of the waters
and hears the turning of the earth—
one for whom the vein behind the ear
which for us throbs only in the hour of death

throbs every day,
one who wears Israel's walking shoes to the end—
KNIFE GRINDER (*To the dog*):
  Here, then, come,
  you look as if you were hungry.
  The tongue hangs from your throat,
  so you are thirsty too—
  We'll go into the village,
  if a twig of a stork's nest is still left of it,
  to a farmer,
  if a fingernail of a farmer's still to be found,
  look for a sickle,
  sharpen it
  and cut with it the weeds in the field—
  Perhaps we'll find a pool of water too,
  in which death has not yet washed his bloody hands—
  and then we'll drink—
  (HE *nods goodbye and walks across the field with the dog*)

MENDEL:
  Now it's as before.
  Saved, but alone.

Scene 11

Night. A wood. An invisible light source illuminates a fallen CHIMNEY
and some trees with twisted branches. MICHAEL *in his wandering stops
and listens.*

VOICE FROM THE CHIMNEY:
  We stones were the last things to touch Israel's sorrow.
  Jeremiah's body in smoke,
  Job's body in smoke,
  the Lamentations in smoke,
  whimpering of little children in smoke,
  mothers' cradle songs in smoke,
  Israel's way of freedom in smoke—
VOICE OF A STAR:
  I was the chimney sweep—
  my light turned black—
TREE:
  I am a tree.
  I can no longer stand straight.
  It hung on me and swung
  as though all the world's winds hung and swung on me.

ELI

SECOND TREE:

Blood pressed onto my roots—
All the birds which nested in my crown
had bloody nests.
Every evening I bleed afresh—
My roots climb from their grave—

FOOTPRINTS IN THE SAND:

We filled the last minutes with death.
Grew ripe like apples from the heavy tread of men—
the mothers who touched us were in a hurry,
but the children were as light as spring rains—

VOICE OF THE NIGHT:

Here are their last sighs,
I kept them for you,
feel them!
Their abode is in the never-aging breezes—
in the breathing of those to come,
inconceivable in the sadness of night—

While MICHAEL *listens, there is seen, scarcely distinguishable from the tree roots, a* CREATURE *sitting on the ground, sewing at a white prayer shawl. Near him a death's head in the grass.*

CREATURE:

Michael!

MICHAEL (*Approaching*):

Hirsch the tailor
in his lifetime looked like that
You have perishable company with you—

CREATURE:

Hirsch am I, the tailor, and my neighbor there
was someone's wife, perhaps my own—
I don't know—for although, there . . .
(HE *points to the* CHIMNEY)
. . . I was employed as Death,
once over the frontier it is hard to find anything again. One
minute past midnight
everything looks the same—
But however that may be,
if I'd listened to my blessed wife
I'd be sitting with the living in America,
among whom I have a brother—
not here among my like.
Look, she said

when it all began—
You're a stag, Hirsch, a stag,
so you must scent it coming
or hasn't the Jewish people
a nose for what's in store?—
The knives are stirring in the drawer,
the scissors of the great tailor are grating,
and the fire in the stove is forming grisly faces
as in the Witch of Endor's cave—
But above all, I feel glances,
glances squinting like the cat's—
Michael, Michael—
you they have not touched,
you they have spared,
and you stood up to them everywhere,
so to speak to windward,
As my one-time customer, the gamekeeper, would have
    said,
like a game animal
which has lost its scent—
but me they brought to bay
because of my protruding cheekbones
and also because of my legs.
Death, you have two sickle blades,
they said,
it's quicker that way.
Unless you send your people up in smoke,
unless you burn your own flesh and blood
we'll unscrew your pelvis
and remove your two sickle blades.
And then you'll have better food
than all of us together.
Smoke weighs more heavily in the stomach than bread—
(HE *lays the prayer shawl aside. Points to the death's head*)
It is too dark, that one there
doesn't shine anymore—
And I burned them
and I ate smoke,
and I stoked Him into the fire.
And I ran into the wood
and there stood raspberry canes,
and I ate raspberries
after I had stoked Him into the fire,

and I could not die,
because I am Death
but look there—
(Shouting)
look there—

CHIMNEY:

I am the Camp Commandant.
March, march
go the thoughts out of my head!

*Smoke begins to rise and transform itself into transparent shapes. Moon
and stars shed a black light. The tree roots are corpses with twisted limbs.
The* CREATURE *gets up and throws the prayer shawl high into the smoke.*

A GIANT FORM *(Wraps itself in the shawl and rises singing into the sky)*:

Hear, O Israel.
He our God.
He the One—

The CHIMNEY *crumbles.*

CREATURE *(Is struck, dying)*:

Hear, O Israel
He our God,
He the One—

FOOTPRINTS IN THE SAND:

Come gathering, gathering, Michael,
a time is there again,
a time which had run out—
gather it up—
gather it up—

MICHAEL *(Stoops, walking in the footprints)*:

He who goes gathering death moments
needs not a basket, but a heart to fill—

Scene 12

Frontier of the neighboring country. Heath and moorland.

MICHAEL:

All signposts point downward.
Foxgloves grow here—
no, not gloves but fingers

grow here like weeds,
not like those flowers
with which Miriam filled her little shoe
when she broke the strap:
"The gloved fingers will stroke you," she said,
"as you sew it up."
The fingers which grow here
are fingers of men's hands.

VOICES OF THE FINGERS:

We are the fingers of the killers.
Each one wears a premeditated death
like a false moonstone.
Look, Michael, like this—

A FINGER *(Reaching for* MICHAEL's *throat)*:

My finger's specialty was strangling,
the compression of the windpipe
with a slight turn to the right.

There is a gurgling noise. MICHAEL *has sunk to the ground.*

VOICE OF THE SECOND KILLER:

Your knees, Michael,
your wrists—
do you hear, of glass—
everything is fragile on earth.
A good man's not afraid of dust,
and here's a wineglassful of blood—

MICHAEL:

Great death, great death, come—

VOICE OF THE SECOND KILLER:

That's out of fashion.
Here are the small dainty deaths—
your neck—
just there where the hair gets downy—

VOICE OF THE THIRD KILLER:

In the name of Science—
this injection—
Whoever volunteers turns light-colored
like rotten wood—

LONG BONY FINGER:

Don't be afraid.
I want neither to bid good night to your windpipe

nor to be rough to your joints.
I'm only the professorial finger
of the new wisdom.
I want a little conversation with your gray matter—

MICHAEL:
Away—

VOICE OF THE PROFESSORIAL FINGER:
Job is grown weak,
tired organ-grinder of a once-fresh tune.
The seas have been drawn out into horsepower on one
hand
and into tap water on the other.
Their ebb and flow are in the hands of a moon-man.
Michael the shoemaker
sews sole and uppers together
with his waste-product thread—
Shoemaker saint!
Were the fountain pens asleep among you
which should have bought your people free?

VOICE OF THE WILDLY GESTICULATING FINGER:
I am the conductor's finger.
I conducted the music for their good night.

March music is heard.

Old the world had to become
before the hate
which bloodily sought
to solve the Jew puzzle
hit on the notion
of banishing it from the world with music—

The music becomes weaker. THE FINGERS, *held by a giant finger on strings,
dance their respective activities.* THE PROFESSORIAL FINGER *taps* MICHAEL
on the head. The Earth falls like a black apple.

MICHAEL *(Shouting)*:
Is that star lost?

ECHO:
Lost!

MICHAEL'S VOICE:
Hear me . . .

Scene 13

An open field. MICHAEL, *lying on the ground, gets up. A* FARMER *with a cow on a halter approaches.*

MICHAEL:
The fingers last pointed in this direction,
murderers betray the murderer in the end.
How peaceful in daylight this spot looks.
The crickets sing,
a jay calls its mate.
The cow has the primeval face
of a creature just stroked by its Creator's hand.
As everywhere, the farmer is tasting out the secret of the
    wheat grain.
(*To the* FARMER)
A good evening to you,
would there be a shoemaker's in this neighborhood?

FARMER:
You come from over there, across the frontier?
You've death on your brow—

MICHAEL:
How can you tell?

FARMER:
When a man has something shining between the eyes,
big as a snowflake—

MICHAEL:
May be
that the death of my people shines in me.

FARMER:
A Pole are you or even—a Jew?

MICHAEL:
On this earth I am both.

FARMER:
That is much!
There beyond the big meadow
is the way to the village.
Next door to the inn garden
is the shoemaker's shop.

A CHILD *has joined them.* MICHAEL *pulls out his shepherd's pipe and plays.*

CHILD:
If I'd a pipe like that
I'd be piping day and night,
I'd be piping in my sleep—

MICHAEL:
It's from a dead child—
FARMER *(Repeating)*:
From a dead child—
MICHAEL:
From a boy
who was murdered—
FARMER:
Who was murdered—
MICHAEL:
As his parents were being driven to their death
he ran after in his shirt—
FARMER:
After in his shirt—
MICHAEL:
On this pipe he piped to God for help—
FARMER:
Piped to God for help—
MICHAEL:
Then a soldier struck him dead—
FARMER:
Then a soldier struck him dead—

MICHAEL *plays his pipe.* CHILDREN, *calves, sheep and foals come frisking to it. The* MOTHERS *lift up their babies. Some* MEN, *sickle in hand, lower their heads.*

Scene 14

The house of the village SCHOOLTEACHER. *In the garden the* SCHOOLTEACHER *and his* SON *are looking up into the great linden tree.* BOYS *are practicing stone-throwing at a scarecrow, made of old bits of war gear and metal parts that stand in the plowed field.*

BOY *(After throwing)*:
That sounded as if someone had cried out.
CHILD:
Yes, it was Isidor the peddler's voice
as we drove him out of the village.
Oy, he said, oy,
and there he lay in the ditch.
BOY:
And reached out for his cap,
look, like this, with his hand turned inward,

just as he used to do when weighing things—
and Hans called out:
"Has the evening sun caught your cap?"
and gave him another to remember us by—

SCHOOLTEACHER:

There hangs the bee swarm.
Hark to the music it makes.
There'll be honey,
never has the linden tree flowered so well,
what luck
that it was spared by men's wars.

BOY:

How nice it smells here, Father, O!
And then the honey on our bread, O!

MOTHER (*From the house*):

I'll just pick the lettuce
and chop the chervil for the soup,
dinner will soon be ready.
Why don't you get out your butterfly net, Hans?
Look at all those moths on the thyme—

BOY (*Picking up a stone*):

Just a minute!

SCHOOLTEACHER:

Leave the scarecrow alone,
too much corpse smell in the field,
the crows get more and more—

BOY (*Pointing at* MICHAEL):

No, there I'll throw it.

SCHOOLTEACHER:

Don't do that!

BOY:

Why yesterday and not today?

SCHOOLTEACHER:

Although I teach arithmetic,
that's a mathematical puzzle I can't solve—

MICHAEL *walks past.*

BOY (*To himself*):

Yesterday I'd have sent the stone after him,
it'd have fallen near the manure pit, I expect,
after first tripping two feet.

Today it stays in my hand,
but I'll throw it into the pond,
to give something a fright at least—

Scene 15

The SHOEMAKER'*s shop in a frontier village.*

SHOEMAKER:
No, not like that, no truly!
Only—perhaps you are for us
like shoes of former times, of long ago.
They fitted nobody,
good leather, but unsuited—
not for our climate,
not for the deserts perhaps,
for the Holy Land perhaps,
for those markets perhaps
where the Isidors hawk their wares differently from us—
but of course as things went with you then—
no, that we didn't want—
not like that—

MICHAEL:
Since Abraham wandered forth from Ur
we have spent our efforts to build our house toward Him
as others build facing the sun—
True, many turned themselves in the opposite direction—
Old shepherds let the star clocks strike unheeded
and slept like Isidor the pawnbroker with crooked fingers—
But there was a boy—
Master, the sole cries out in my hand,
it reeks of death—

SHOEMAKER:
May be so,
for a dying steer stretched out its paws
and then—

A MAN *enters, holding a small* CHILD *by the hand.*

MAN:
Are my shoes ready?
SHOEMAKER:
My assistant's just working on them—

MICHAEL:
> This sole can't be patched,
> it's torn up the middle.

MAN:
> Make me a new sole then—

CHILD:
> Father, this is the man
> who had the pipe.
> There it is on the flowerpot.
> O let me play it!

MAN:
> You don't play strangers' pipes.

CHILD (*Crying*):
> The pipe—

MAN:
> She's crying
> because she wants her mother.
> She always wants something:
> One day it's the blackbird
> which used to come for scraps
> and disappeared,
> another it's the old sheepdog
> which ran across the rails
> and was run over—

MICHAEL:
> Everything begins with wanting.
> Even this here—
> (HE *lets earth from the flowerpot trickle through his hands*)
> And these here—
> (HE *points to the hides from which the shoes are cut*)

CHILD:
> The pipe—

MAN:
> I'll buy you a pipe.
> When you've got it,
> all the children will follow you
> and give you their toys—

CHILD:
> No, *this* pipe,
> then the cows'll come and the little calves.

The MAN *takes the* CHILD *by the hand, and* THEY *start to go out.*

SHOEMAKER'S WIFE (*At the door as* THEY *leave*):
    I want something too.
    Farmer, when'll you have a roast to spare?
    With me it's the mouth
    that does the wanting.
    What kind of want is that?

Scene 16

A farmhouse bedroom. The CHILD *sleeps.*

MAN:
    Teeth everywhere,
    do you hear how it rattles?
    Hollow tooth where oats should be.
    Black horse climbing,
    shaking its mane,
    and showing its teeth.
    The calves drink with their teeth
    and fleck the udders with blood—
    the rye-stalks bitten off—teeth without rats—
    Do you hear it, Wife,
    here in the room,
    there, there!
    (SHE *points to the wall*)
    Teeth where bricks should be—
    Wife, the bricklayer must to the gallows—
WIFE:
    Be quiet now,
    the child's asleep,
    the fever's very high!
MAN:
    Now it's rattling,
    the whole house rattles—
    (*His teeth chatter*)

CHILD (*In a dream*):
    All the trees go walking
    all the trees go walking
    lift up their root-feet and walk
    when I pipe—
MAN (*Singing*):
    All the shades go walking,
    come, dear hearse-cloth,

cover up the white moon-tooth for me.
Wasn't it a milk-tooth
which dropped from his mouth with the pipe—
Wife, wife,
the milk has teeth,
teeth—

A knock on the window.

MAN *(Opening the window)*:
Who's there?
BAKER:
Baker Hans.
Here's a sugar pretzel for little Annie.
The iron pretzel,
my good shop sign from the Jew baker in Poland,
has turned red.
They're whispering already.
The dead children don't touch the pretzel crumbs
I scatter for them into the night,
and drag the malt away.
Lately they sat like a swarm of wasps
on the shop counter.
The squint-eyed child stamped its feet on the wood,
as if to warm itself,
then it climbed bolt upright to the ceiling
and hung there like flypaper.
In the morning it fell off.
The flies had eaten it up.
MAN *(Rattling the windowpane, which is lit up by the moon)*:
Look, that's how you did with the squint-eyed one—
Here's the pretzel,
there's the pretzel,
till it had ceased to squint.
Now it's squinting your day away,
as mine is chewed by the milk-tooth.
BAKER:
They say
you once killed a holy child?
MAN:
Stuff and nonsense!
All children are holy.
POSTMAN *(Coming on)*:
Why do you quarrel for first place in child murder?

BAKER:

Sorter of cry-baby parcels!
Did no sender
write "Fragile" on them?

POSTMAN:

My orders were
to heed the addressee,
not the sender.

DOCTOR *(Coming out of the bedroom)*:

Your child—

WIFE *(Coming on)*:

The child is dead!

Scene 17

A country road. On either side, thick pine forest. MICHAEL *walking. Behind a pine tree, the* MAN *is standing.*

MICHAEL:

A look has pierced my back,
I am held fast.

THEY *look at one another.*

MAN:

If he hadn't thrown his head back
I shouldn't have struck him down,
the milk-tooth wouldn't have fallen out with the pipe.
But—that was contrary to Order—
to throw the head back—
that had to be corrected.
And where did he pipe to?
A secret signal?
A signal through the air—
beyond all control—
Help, shoemaker,
the milk-tooth is growing out of the earth—
beginning to gnaw at me—
right through my shoe—
my feet are crumbling—
becoming earth—
(Shrieking)
Where's the Order in all this, the World Order—

I am alive,
I am not dead—
not hung—
not burned—
not thrown live into the earth—
(*At the top of his voice*)
It's a mistake, a mistake,
I'm crumbling, crumbling—
I'm a stump—
sitting on the sand
that a moment ago was my flesh—

The air has opened out into circles. In the first circle appears the EMBRYO
in its mother's womb, with the primal light on its brow.

VOICE:
   Child with the light of God,
   read in the hands of the murderer—
MAN:
   My hands, my hands—
   don't leave me, O my hands—
   (*His hands crumble off*)

The horizon opens out as the greatest of the circles. A BLEEDING MOUTH
appears like a setting sun.

VOICE:
   Open,
   dumb mouth of Samuel!
VOICE OF SAMUEL:
   Eli!

The mother's womb dissolves in smoke. The primal light fastens on to
MICHAEL's *brow.*

MICHAEL:
   Crumbling one!
   His eyes become holes—
   the light seeks out other mirrors.
   I see through the holes—
   glasses for the sun's eclipse—
   into your skull
   which frames that world

which you, as commanded, have packed inside it,
as in a soldier's knapsack—
There it lies—twitching,
an insect star with wings torn off—
In it stirs a hand
that stole a lightning bolt—
A raven consumes a human leg—
lightning consumes the raven—
I see nothing more—

VOICE:

Footprints of Israel,
gather yourselves together!
Last earthly moments of Israel,
gather yourselves together!
Last moments of suffering,
gather yourselves together!

MICHAEL:

Under my feet it jumps up.
From my hands it plunges down.
My heart pours something out—

VOICE:

Your shoes are worn to pieces—come!

MICHAEL *is gathered up and vanishes.*

END OF PLAY

Nelly Sachs

POSTSCRIPT TO *ELI*

Michael, a young shoemaker, is the leading character in this mystery play. According to Hasidic mysticism, he is one of the thirty-six Servants of God who, unaware of it themselves, carry the invisible universe. The Lord puts the arrow He has used back in its quiver so that it may remain in darkness, according to the prophet Isaiah. Thus Michael feels, darkly, the inner call to seek the murderer of Eli, the child who raised the shepherd's pipe to heaven to play to God as his parents were being taken away to their death (the same pipe with which he called the cattle together, "like the stag or roebuck before it drinks at the spring"). A young soldier, believing this to be a secret signal, struck the boy dead—a symbol of non-belief.

Michael goes his quiet way through this legend made of truth. He sees the face of the murderer in the shadow thrown by a light on Eli's death-shirt, and in transcendental fashion, once more during his travels experiences the bloody events of our forsaken age. The murderer, when Michael finally sees him face to face, crumbles to dust before the divine light shining from Michael's countenance (a picture of remorse).

In this world of night, where a secret equilibrium seems to triumph, the victim is always innocence. The child Eli and the child of the murderer both die, victims of evil.

This mystery play was the outcome of a terrible experience at the height of the smoke and flame of Hitler's reign, and was written in a few nights after my flight to Sweden.

The shepherd's pipe raised in desperation by a child to God is the attempted outbreak of the human in the face of horror.

The soldier says, "If he hadn't thrown his head back, I shouldn't have struck him down . . ."

It was a sign beyond any control—possibly a secret signal: No more trust in good on Earth.

Through mime and the rhythm of the words, the performer must make the Hasidic mystical fervor visible—an encounter with divine radiance which accompanies each of our everyday words. The play is designed to raise the unutterable to a transcendental level, so as to make it bearable, and in this night of nights, to give a hint of the holy darkness in which both quiver and arrow are hidden.

Mister Fugue
or Earth Sick

Liliane Atlan

translated by Marguerite Feitlowitz

"Ever since the day the temple was destroyed, the
gift of prophecy was taken away from the prophets
and given to children and madmen."
    —The Talmud, Baba Batra, p. XII, a.

Time

After the total destruction of a ghetto.

Places

The mouth of a sewer, barbed wire, ruins.
A truck in the fog.
Rotburg, or The Valley of Bones.

Characters

The soldiers, dressed in green:
CHRISTOPHER
FROBBE
GROBBE
THE COMMANDANT

The children, who are no longer real children:
YOSSELE (pronounced Yō-sel-uh)
RAISSA (pronounced Ry-ees-sa)
IONA (pronounced Yōna)
ABRACHA (pronounced with a soft "sh"—Abrahsha—a diminutive of
    Abraham)
TAMAR'S DOLL (through her, the children, especially Iona, are able to keep
    Tamar, who has been dead a long time, present)

GROL, or MISTER FUGUE

The children, covered with mud and wearing rags, are savage, disabused, cruel; at the beginning, if it weren't for their wild eyes, they would be close to animals.

Grol's gestures are slow, sometimes he gives the impression that he is paralyzed. He is sweet and simple. He is very disturbing.

THE CART　In the ghetto, a cart came round every day to take away the dead, whom those surviving the day covered with newspapers.

THE TREE　There was only one tree in the ghetto.

A few notes for readings and productions . . .

The children do not describe, *they see*, they live what they see.

They do not search, *they find*, instantly.
　　For example, when Yossele says, "Today, it's a holiday," Raissa *finds* instantly, "It's the holiday of the dog-Rabbi."

The closer time presses, the faster they find.

The Play

Mister Fugue
or Earth Sick

The Mouth of a Sewer

The ruins of a ghetto. Barbed wire. Flames. THE COMMANDANT,
CHRISTOPHER, GROL, GROBBE *and* FROBBE *contemplate the fire. A beat.*

THE COMMANDANT: For eight days, this ghetto's burned. The rats that
lived here are dead. Those fleeing toward the forest, we captured
and sent to Rotburg. Those who stayed in the sewer, we hosed, for
fifty-six hours you've guarded every exit, all of them drowned. The
affair is done. We can leave.

THEY *separate.* CHRISTOPHER *detains* GROL.

CHRISTOPHER: Loosen this cover. Not too much. So it looks natural.

GROL, *dazed, obeys.*

Lie down. Play dead. If any of those rats are left, you're going to
see what they'll do to you.

GROL *plays dead, his eyes open.* HE *doesn't move, is preoccupied, distressed.*
CHRISTOPHER *slips into his pocket bread and cigarettes, then moves off.*
Sound of a truck pulling away.
The cover is lifted. The cadaverous, emaciated faces of YOSSELE *and*
RAISSA *become visible.* THEY *climb out without a word.* THEY *creep about;*

57

both, but especially RAISSA, *are like nightbirds. Then* IONA *(holding to his chest a death-doll with a skeletal gaze, enormous head and skinny limbs, a doll that resembles them) and* ABRACHA *emerge from the sewer.* THEY'*re wild-eyed and in rags.* YOSSELE *and* RAISSA *have seen the bread, snatch it without a word. Silently,* ABRACHA *and* IONA *rob* GROL, *take his boots, see the bread and jump* YOSSELE *and* RAISSA. THEY *devour it on the ground, all the while on the lookout.*

YOSSELE *(In a broken voice)*: Shit, there's fire everywhere.
RAISSA *(Even more broken-voiced)*: We go back down?
ABRACHA *(The most emaciated of all, in a thin, reedy voice)*: You crazy, or what?
YOSSELE: We're gonna tear down the wires. Quick.

THEY *do, except for* IONA, *who hangs back, muttering.*

RAISSA: There hands somewhere in all this blood?
YOSSELE: Damn well better be.
ABRACHA: Iona, where do you think you are?
RAISSA *(Spitting)*: He's praying.
ABRACHA: To a shit god.
YOSSELE: Pray tearing down these wires, at least that would help.

IONA *helps them, holding the doll and never ceasing to pray.* THEY *don't see* CHRISTOPHER *watching them from behind.* GROL *sits and watches them; neither can* HE *see* CHRISTOPHER.

ABRACHA: Pray and I'll break your face, you hear me?

Furiously, THEY *tear down the barbed wire, wounding themselves.* IONA *is crying like a child who has been chased for a long time.* HE *keeps trying to stop, but cannot.*

GROL: Stop, for God's sakes, it won't get you anywhere.

IONA *mutters even more as* HE *tries to escape,* ABRACHA *cringes,* YOSSELE *and* RAISSA *are like hyenas, ready to pounce.*

GROL (HE *suddenly gets up)*: Come, children, I'll drive you to the forest.

THE CHILDREN *don't move.*

I'm a soldier, it's true. . . . I set fire to this ghetto, it's true. . . . I played dead in order to catch you, that's true, too, but for God's sake, come quickly!

The CHILDREN *huddle together, keeping their distance from* GROL. CHRISTOPHER *appears, laughing.*

MISTER FUGUE

CHRISTOPHER: Just as I thought. Like bugs, they always come out. (*A beat.* HE *whistles*) Frobbe!

WE see the mouth of the truck. The CHILDREN, *huddled close, move back, still keeping their distance from* GROL. THE COMMANDANT *returns.*

THE COMMANDANT: So there were some left.

CHRISTOPHER: Four, Commandant, the last of them.

THE COMMANDANT: You've got a flair for this, Christopher. Have them join the others in the Rotburg valley.

The truck moves forward, driven by FROBBE *and* GROBBE. *It is a huge, wire cage, full of straw, the kind of half-van, half-bus used to transport animals. Though it's a machine, there is something both human and bestial about its mouth. There's an elevated, windowed cab, from the inside of which one can observe the interior of the truck proper.*

THE COMMANDANT: And so, children, you're going to join your parents. Hop in. There's meat in this truck, you're going to eat.

THEY *don't obey.*

Get in. (*Beat*) Get in. (HE *hits them with his stick*) Ladies first, be gallant, good sirs. (HE *hits them again with his stick*) Get in. Get in.

GROL: *a flash.* HE *wants to climb in behind the* CHILDREN, *without saying a word.*

THE COMMANDANT: Don't bother, Grol, such a light load!

CHRISTOPHER: If Sergeant Grol had had his way, Commandant, these rats would have gotten away.

THE COMMANDANT: You've never been to the Rotburg valley, Grol? To the Valley of Bones? (GROL *doesn't answer*) I should have you shot on the spot? (GROL *doesn't answer*) Then take your place next to the driver, Sergeant Grol. You'll be less chilly there. (GROL *still doesn't answer*) Special treatment, you know what that is? (*Beat*) Sergeant Grol, do you persist?

GROL: I'm no longer Sergeant Grol.

HE *pushes* THE COMMANDANT *aside and gets into the truck.*

THE COMMANDANT (*To* CHRISTOPHER): Consider him as one of the inferior race.

THE COMMANDANT *moves away.*

CHRISTOPHER: How long, Frobbe, for this last trip?
FROBBE: Should be about an hour, Lieutenant, but with this fog . . .
CHRISTOPHER (*Shaking off his fatigue*): Let's go.

The Truck in the Fog

The truck starts. The noises of the fire soften, are replaced by those of the motor.

GROBBE: It's the first time, Lieutenant, we're making a trip for just four.
CHRISTOPHER: Five.
GROBBE: It's not many, Lieutenant, four or five.
CHRISTOPHER: But they're the most important. The last ones.
GROBBE: The fog's getting worse, Lieutenant, we're not finished yet.
CHRISTOPHER: We got 'em, we'll finish.

In the back of the truck, the CHILDREN *huddle together in a block, facing* GROL.

ABRACHA: So, it's sure, they're going to kill us?
GROL: Yes. (*Beat*) Me too.
YOSSELE: We'd rather be alone.
GROL: I know.
YOSSELE: So why don't you leave?
GROL: People say I'm a little crazy, I don't know.
YOSSELE: Leave, go up front.

GROL *doesn't move. Beat.*

IONA (*As though possessed by the doll*): May Tamar sit down?
RAISSA: Yes, she may. Here, you may.
ABRACHA (*To* TAMAR): And you may even make noise. Here, play with this.

HE *gives her one of* GROL's *boots.*

IONA (*Trembling*): She doesn't want to play.
RAISSA: She's caught her death again.
IONA (*Frightened*): No. I don't want that. Not that.
RAISSA (*Tough, to* TAMAR): Don't bother to make a fuss, there's no more sewers, no more hiding, and it isn't cold.

IONA/TAMAR *starts to cry.*

YOSSELE (*To* TAMAR): Don't be dumb, I can't go running after doctors here.
RAISSA: She still caught her death.

YOSSELE: What did she say?

IONA: I don't know. She just vomited blood.

ABRACHA: It's nothing. It's cause she's scared of the flames.

IONA: That's not it, she hasn't seen them. I didn't want her to see that.

GROL (*To* IONA): Don't tremble like that, I beg you, you're making me sick.

YOSSELE: Shit. He's sick.

Barking laughter from the KIDS. *Beat.*

IONA (*To* TAMAR, *like a lullabye*): Don't tremble, don't tremble, it's not really cold. Here, the cart won't take you away.

Anguished, the CHILDREN *lean over* TAMAR. RAISSA *hums something, a lullabye without words. Slowly,* GROL *gets up, covers the doll with his overcoat, then returns to his place. Beat. Then suddenly:*

RAISSA (*Giving him back his overcoat*): We don't want it.

IONA: We do, too.

YOSSELE (*Taking back the coat*): We didn't get her out of there so she'd . . .

RAISSA: Bah! All she does is groan.

GROL: I know lots of stories.

YOSSELE: She doesn't believe stories anymore.

GROL (*To the doll*): Once upon a time, there was a truck. Its name was Earth. It rolled toward the trenches. It's been a long time since the drivers stopped trying to stop it.

IONA/TAMAR *keeps crying, as hard as before.*

YOSSELE: She doesn't like that one.

GROL: Once upon a time, there were some children. They hid in the sewers. They had turned the hoses on them. They would climb out and the soldiers would capture, then kill them.

YOSSELE/TAMAR: That's not a story.

GROL (*Still to the doll*): It's something you can believe.

Beat.

RAISSA/TAMAR: Something else.

GROL (*To* RAISSA): Once upon a time, there was a soldier. He would have wanted to lead them to the forest, but the children hadn't followed, he could have lied to them, but he didn't, the proof, he got in the back of the truck, they'll kill him in the Rotburg valley.

YOSSELE: That doesn't interest us.

Beat.

Liliane Atlan

GROL *(To the doll)*: They've often thrown lots of people into lots of trucks, some in back, others in front. Some were killed, others killed them.

YOSSELE: And then?

GROL *(To the doll)*: I was among those who killed. I was so afraid of being killed myself.

RAISSA: Shit. We're going to end up comforting him.

Barking laughter from the CHILDREN.

GROL *(To himself)*: The soldier climbed into the truck, to his place. They didn't try to escape, you can't get away from the earth. But there are the stories, they told them to each other.

YOSSELE *(Sad, without aggression)*: The real stories, you don't know.

GROL *(Putting on his boots)*: Before the war, I didn't work, I didn't like anything, like the others, they told me I was stupid, from time to time I'd go away, so the children in my village called me Mister Fugue, I liked that name because it's true, I didn't much like all that earth, so I'd go away.

YOSSELE: Where?

GROL: To the city. I'd stare at the streets, I loved their lights. But the people made me sad! When I had money, I'd give it away to see them laugh. But they didn't laugh, ever, war broke out. I set fire to houses, I wounded people, I was happy, there were no longer any doors. And then we waited, fifty-six hours, I counted them, near the sewer for you to come out and we set this trap for you. So I saw you when you were still down there, as you are now *(Looking at* TAMAR*)* especially her, she hurt like no one ever has, she'll hurt forever, it's as though we'd been family in I don't know which world, I recognized you, everything hurt and in my head I started everything all over again— from the earth's beginning, without soldiers, without people in pain.

Beat.

YOSSELE: You must be a little nuts, Mister Fugue, we'll take your shirt.

GROL smiles sweetly and awkwardly, morbidly, painfully good. HE *tends to* YOSSELE *with awkward gestures. From now on,* THEY*'ll call him* FUGUE, *or* MISTER FUGUE.

YOSSELE: Start with her, that's Raissa, my fiancée. We're not old, but since we're going to die, Iona will marry us. That's him, he knows all the prayers. He said the one for the dead while we took their clothes. That way, we weren't doing them any harm.

MISTER FUGUE *(Tending to* RAISSA*)*: For me, Iona didn't say prayers.
YOSSELE: Who knew you were crazy. That's Tamar. She spent two years
    in a closet, won't sit or stand without asking permission. They hid
    her at a neighbor's house, that's why. And then the neighbors died.
    That's Abracha, he went searching for Tamar and her doll, and we
    took them with us. Abracha can worm his way into anyplace. He
    ran guns, papers, everything. That's how we kept from dying. Tamar,
    she couldn't. They covered her with old newspapers, they came with
    the cart, but Iona snatched her doll, and Tamar was on the shuttle
    again with us. And then, there was no one anymore to take what
    we were running, we left this sewer because we were too hungry.
MISTER FUGUE: That's right, there's meat . . . Christopher, the meat. We
    promised it to them.

Anguished, religious silence from the CHILDREN.

CHRISTOPHER: Grobbe, feed the dogs.

    GROBBE *throws them a little meat through the bars. The* CHILDREN *madly
    tear into it, devouring it, except for* IONA.

IONA: Blessed Art Thou, Lord of the Worlds, thank you for this meat.
    (HE *eats, the doll in his arms)*
ABRACHA *(Mouth full)*: Shit on prayers.
MISTER FUGUE: Right, and shit on the whole world. But not so fast, don't
    eat so fast.

    THEY*'ve finished their meat and are waiting for more.* CHRISTOPHER
    pretends to throw them more, keeps it, then suddenly makes his throw. The
    CHILDREN *do as* THEY *did before. Beat.*

YOSSELE *(Anguished)*: Why aren't you eating?
MISTER FUGUE: I'm not hungry.
ABRACHA: It's no good. The meat's no good. (HE *is taken with a fit of
    trembling)*
YOSSELE *(Mouth full)*: Sometimes, it's all night he shakes like that, then
    it's over.

Beat.

RAISSA *(Drying her mouth with her fingers)*: How long until this valley?
MISTER FUGUE: The whole Earth.
RAISSA: He's crazy, this old geezer.

YOSSELE: Completely.

ABRACHA (*Still trembling*): If he had just a small ration of beard, he'd look like my grandfather, also a nut who prayed, was praying but they shoved him to the left and when they fired at him . . . and when they fired . . .

MISTER FUGUE: And when they fired at him?

ABRACHA: He died, what do you think?

Barking laughter from the CHILDREN.

CHRISTOPHER: And here's dessert, some chocolate, ready?

IONA: My God, chocolate!

RAISSA (*Almost smiling*): Of course, chocolate!

CHRISTOPHER, *without a word, throws the chocolate out of the truck. The* CHILDREN *press their faces to the wire grating.* CHRISTOPHER *laughs.*

MISTER FUGUE: Stop this truck, stop it.

CHRISTOPHER *laughs harder.*

Stop it, or I'll . . . (HE *lunges at* CHRISTOPHER, *throwing himself against the bars*)

YOSSELE: Don't yell, Mister Fugue, with them, it doesn't do any good . . . we just ate.

IONA: But not the chocolate. (HE *forgets about* TAMAR)

ABRACHA: Blessed Art Thou, Lord of the Worlds, that you did not want us to eat chocolate . . . . The prayer machine broken, Iona?

IONA: You're the one who broke it.

ABRACHA: It broke when my grandfather went to the left and instead of praying . . . or before, I don't know anymore. Or when they split my sister's kidneys with a hatchet, it gushed over everything, he's red all over, our merciful God, and I piss on him.

MISTER FUGUE: Abracha, you worry us. It was men who did all that, not God. Hey, I'm going to tell you the story of the crazy captain. He steered his boat into the cliffs, which wrecked it, then he said, "God damn those cliffs."

ABRACHA: I don't know what they are, cliffs.

YOSSELE: Me neither. We've never seen any.

MISTER FUGUE: Cliffs, well, they're hard to explain. They're hard things, the sea crashed into them. The sea never dies, neither do the cliffs. They get worn down a little, that's all. And in the morning, and at night, sea birds gather there. They have large feathers, warm and white, they come from far away, from a land that fell long ago, they have hoarse, broken voices, they tell love stories forgotten for millenia, they themselves don't understand them, then they take off, again alone.

YOSSELE: What good does that do?

MISTER FUGUE: None. It's marvelous, that's all.

RAISSA *(Hurt)*: You are really very stupid, Mister Fugue, you believe in things that are marvelous.

MISTER FUGUE: Of course!

RAISSA: In this truck?

MISTER FUGUE: Where else?

ABRACHA: Love, they do it on the stairs, in front of everyone, before they die. I know, I stood guard.

YOSSELE: Or on the cobblestones, in the streets, as long as there are streets. We've done it too, but it's not funny.

RAISSA: Tell them, tell your fairy tales.

ABRACHA: My brother, he wasn't married long, I often stood guard. But when they came, he didn't hesitate, he gave over his wife.

Barking laughter from all the KIDS *except* IONA; HE'S *occupied again with* TAMAR.

RAISSA: So, what about those love stories of your big white birds?

THEY *laugh, even more savagely. Beat.*

MISTER FUGUE: The great white birds come from another world where trucks don't exist, where children don't stand guard. They descend to earth at high tide, they cry with their strange, broken voices words of love from another world. They look at one another, and they recognize each other. Then they take to the air again, and disappear, for millenia.

RAISSA: It's stupid, your story.

YOSSELE: Tell us about the sea instead. Boats.

MISTER FUGUE: The sea, she is a great lady, she, too, is slightly stupid. She seems to be sleeping, then strength takes hold of her, making her whirl, throwing her over black holes, boats pass, happy, tranquil, but strength leaves her, so now the sea, sick, eats the gathering blackness. She forgets everything, closes in on herself . . .

YOSSELE: That's not the sea.

MISTER FUGUE: Maybe, I never saw her.

YOSSELE: Me neither. But I know the sea, that's how you escape, and one day you see chimneys smoking, far away, that's the promised land guarded by soldiers, and guarded so well you can never get in. That's what the sea is, she smells of gunpowder and cannons, 'cause of the soldiers who have fired on her.

IONA: Even on God.

YOSSELE: Now God, he went crazy, he knocked around in the sea like a fish, in the air like a bird, nothing but barbed wire, he doesn't dare anymore to sit or stand, he steals passes, but he doesn't leave, he doesn't dare anymore to do anything. He's sick, our good God.

ABRACHA: There were some like that in the ghetto, and to finish with it, they slept in the snow, near the soldiers who were firing at them.

RAISSA: You remember the dancer—who—recited—psalms?

Barking laughter.

RAISSA *(Miming)*: The soldiers were hitting him and him, he was dancing, like this, he was old and thin, so thin you heard his bones creak. He closed his eyes, leaned his head like at shul when you pray, you know, like this, and he rocked, he jumped, and the soldiers were hitting him like madmen, they were red, they'd been drinking.

ABRACHA *and* YOSSELE *mime the soldiers.*

The more he hopped, the more they hit him. He recited psalms, the ones for the Day of Atonement, *Ani Kéli mále bouchá,* I am a vase full of shit, and he drooled, I swear it, he drooled.

ABRACHA: And after that, he barked. Like this. (HE *barks*) They killed him anyway.

Laughter.

RAISSA: Your big white birds, they're not so funny.

ABRACHA: Even when he was barking, he didn't stop reciting psalms.

YOSSELE: ". . . from the Red Sea to the charnel house
my tribe carried the star . . .
full of shit . . ."

Laughter.

ABRACHA: My grandfather, when they fired at him, he did it in his pants.

Laughter.

RAISSA: You don't know life, so you, you talk about birds, but birds, I'm gonna tell you, birds . . .

MISTER FUGUE

Crazed laughter.

YOSSELE: They came right into the street to eat our dead.
RAISSA: That's why we covered them with newspapers.

Laughter, in crescendo. Beat.

(*Not laughing anymore*) Birds, that's how they were, Mister Fugue.
MISTER FUGUE: I didn't know. I was only a soldier.
RAISSA: So tell us about that.
MISTER FUGUE: I'm ashamed.
YOSSELE: He's ashamed!
RAISSA: Ah shit.

Beat.

IONA/TAMAR: What's shame?
MISTER FUGUE: It's a black doll that eats your heart.

The truck stops suddenly.

YOSSELE: Shit.
ABRACHA: Rotburg.

THEY *press their faces to the wire grating.*

CHRISTOPHER (*Who was dozing*): What is it, Frobbe?
FROBBE: I can't see, Lieutenant . . .
YOSSELE: Can't see anything.
FROBBE: It looks like a wounded animal, I'll go see.
IONA: Does it hurt to die?
MISTER FUGUE: Of course not.
RAISSA: You're lying.
MISTER FUGUE: Just a little, Raissa.
FROBBE: It's a deer, Lieutenant. Run over.
GROBBE: Probably by the last convoy.
CHRISTOPHER: The bastards.
YOSSELE: He's right, it doesn't hurt. What hurts is not having been
grownups.

THEY *keep standing, one against the other.*

CHRISTOPHER: Let's go now.

FROBBE: There, Lieutenant.

GROBBE: Christ, it's cold.

CHRISTOPHER (*Passing the canteen after taking a drink*): Drink some of this, it'll warm you up.

The truck starts up again. Its noise. This will not fade as the CHILDREN *dream again, will not disappear until* THEY *are totally absorbed in their game.*

ABRACHA: We're going again.

YOSSELE: The next time it stops, it'll be for good.

MISTER FUGUE: A truck, it doesn't go fast when there's fog.

YOSSELE: You sure we couldn't break down these bars?

MISTER FUGUE: They're watching us, they'd shoot us.

YOSSELE: And later, it'll be different?

MISTER FUGUE: No. Not necessarily. War or no war, at the end they put us in the earth and it's the earth you can't escape, whether you die in bed or in a valley! What counts is to have done something before that, whether or not it does any good. Let's do something. Here.

RAISSA: That's as stupid as your big white birds.

YOSSELE: I wanted to live, for real.

MISTER FUGUE: For real, what's that, for real? Here is all we'll ever want, here.

ABRACHA: The old people, in the trucks or the trains, I know they bawled or went crazy.

MISTER FUGUE: So let's cry, let's go crazy.

RAISSA: That's stupid too.

MISTER FUGUE: So let's do nothing.

Beat. IONA *has moved closer to him, with* TAMAR.

RAISSA: Tell us about shame, the black-doll-that-eats-your-heart.

MISTER FUGUE: You don't want to play living?

RAISSA: No.

MISTER FUGUE: Shame, I have become shame, I can't tell you about it.

RAISSA: So tell us about going away!

MISTER FUGUE: Watch closely. First, I'm at the table, or rather, no, I can't come to the table. I'm afraid. Of doors. I can't come in, or go out, or dress, or undress. All I do is tremble.

ABRACHA: There're soldiers in your house?

MISTER FUGUE: No.

ABRACHA: Trucks, out front?

MISTER FUGUE: Of course not.

ABRACHA: Nothing? For real?

MISTER FUGUE: I get dizzy, that's all, terribly dizzy.

ABRACHA: 'Cause of the soldiers, just the same?

MISTER FUGUE: No, 'cause of nothing. People make fun of me. Go ahead, make fun of me.

YOSSELE: You're too stupid, we can't.

ABRACHA: We'll have to take him to the doctor.

RAISSA: What good will that do? They don't know anything. What he needs is a good spanking, no doubt about it.

SHE *spanks him. But* HE's *absent, beatific, doesn't feel it.*

YOSSELE: He's out of this world.

RAISSA: Out of this world? What, again? Look at that! He's all out of joint.

IONA: It's Tamar's doll! *(For* TAMAR*)* May I?

ABRACHA: Yes, Tamar, you may.

IONA/TAMAR *pulls* MISTER FUGUE's *hair and laughs.*

IONA/TAMAR: I want to put him in the closet.

YOSSELE: Here.

THEY *push him into the straw,* HE *looks more beatific.*

IONA/TAMAR *(To the Mister Fugue doll)*: Don't make noise, ever. *(Becoming the doll, terrorized)* Oh, no ma'am, never.

RAISSA: What if we climbed on him? (SHE *does so, dancing and barking)* Ani Keli malé boucha, Ani Keli malé boucha . . .

IONA/TAMAR: You're hurting him.

RAISSA *(Dancing and barking)*: All she had to do was not call me, all she had to do was not breathe.

ABRACHA *(Pushing her away)*: Get down from there, don't dance like a rabbi.

IONA *brushes* MISTER FUGUE's *clothes, laughing,* YOSSELE *watches him.*

YOSSELE: It hurts me to see him.

RAISSA: 'Cause he's no longer a man, he's a chubby beast, eats greens and everything, wait I'll get my pitchfork, shit, he broke through the wall, the beast's inside, there's his tail.

YOSSELE: Don't hit him, he's happy.

RAISSA: Hey, I know when to watch my manners! Look, he's come out the wall, like a real man again, but full of the holes I, I put in him! (SHE *laughs)* This way, he'll never again join his birds.

YOSSELE: You're mean, Raissa, he wasn't doing any harm, he was rolling in the grass.

ABRACHA *(Aggressive, to* RAISSA*)*: Me too, when I was a kid . . .

MISTER FUGUE *gradually becomes panicked.*

RAISSA: You, you were a kid? I don't believe it, you couldn't have been.

ABRACHA: I couldn't have been, why not?

YOSSELE: Beacause your grandfather locked you in a dark room and read you stupid books.

ABRACHA: They were Holy Books. And the room, it couldn't have been dark, or I couldn't have read.

YOSSELE: That's what I'm saying, you were doing the Talmud while you were still in diapers.

ABRACHA: I couldn't have, I wasn't talking yet.

MISTER FUGUE *screams, throws himself against the bars, and shakes them with a terrible strength.*

YOSSELE: Act up, they'll shoot you.

MISTER FUGUE *pushes him away, and shakes the bars harder and harder.* CHRISTOPHER *shoots him in the leg.*

YOSSELE: You see!

MISTER FUGUE *(Stuttering)*: It's happened, before, sometimes I'd come back wounded, I never knew why.

RAISSA: And why did you scream like a jackal?

MISTER FUGUE: Strength left me, and it hurt.

RAISSA: Well, now you hurt for a reason.

IONA *(Hugging* TAMAR*)*: Your black doll's in pain.

ABRACHA: Throw us something so we can take care of him. . . . Hey, you up there. . . . He doesn't answer.

RAISSA: So what else is new.

MISTER FUGUE: It doesn't matter.

RAISSA: You must come from another world, Mister Fugue, a world where birds chatter, feed on music, and then at night come to earth to die. But they're dumb, your stories, in the end, they're just dumb.

MISTER FUGUE: Very dumb.

RAISSA: Another thing, your eyes are eating away at your face, that's not normal.

YOSSELE: Have you ever seen owls before, Mister Fugue?

MISTER FUGUE: Yes, maybe, I don't know.

YOSSELE: Me, yes, in books, when I went to school.

RAISSA: That wasn't any good, school.

YOSSELE: But you were always top of the class.

RAISSA: Only so you wouldn't be.

YOSSELE: Yeah, well I was anyway and more often than you.

ABRACHA: That's not possible, you said she always was.

YOSSELE: You, you'll try to reason with the worms in the earth. I don't know anymore what I was trying to say.

MISTER FUGUE: Owls.

YOSSELE: Oh . . . yeah, they had eyes like yours and Raissa's. Big, stupid eyes that looked into the night, and it wasn't cheery, night, so they screamed.

ABRACHA: In the book?

YOSSELE: Yes, in the book, you're a lousy Talmudist, no imagination . . . this is school, here.

IONA: Let there be school, and there was school.

ABRACHA *becomes the teacher, the* OTHERS *seat themselves as at school.*

RAISSA *(To* MISTER FUGUE*)*: You, you're the dunce, go to the back.

ABRACHA: Ruth and David will never come again, Iona, stand watch.

IONA *(Pushing* TAMAR *to the side)*: You, you're in nursery school.

RAISSA *(Becoming* TAMAR'S MOTHER, *febrile, imploring, hunted)*: It's not a safe place, I don't want to put her there, Mrs. Kross, take my little one. *(Becoming* MRS. KROSS, *a shrew)* Oh yes, in times like these, it's dangerous, Mrs. *(Scornfully)* Rosenblum! *(Again,* TAMAR'S MOTHER*)* Here are my rings, my diamonds, the key to my jewelry box, to my apartment, take care of her and it's all yours. *(*MRS. KROSS*)*—With all this money why don't you escape? It's true you don't look very well. But your husband, isn't there a chance he'll come back? *(*MRS. ROSENBLUM*)*—You know very well I got his ashes a long time ago. *(*MRS. KROSS*)*—Okay, then, I'll put her in my closet, with her doll *(Gently)* and don't worry, she'll be taken care of. *(Giving* TAMAR *a brutal shove)* No one must hear you. Don't talk, and don't breathe. Never call me. I'll come when I come. You're old enough to understand, you're here on my charity.

IONA *waves: end of the alert.*

ABRACHA: Take your geography books. Nothing resists erosion. It makes hard rocks protrude, and weak ones disappear.

YOSSELE: Mister, what do you mean protrude?

ABRACHA: I don't know. Take your geography books, spit on them, there's nothing in there but stupidity and filth. Take your poetry books. You Okay, Iona?

IONA: The old folks say we make noise.

RAISSA: Oh them! Tonight, in hiding, they forced Lydia to strangle her kid, the greens found them anyway.

Barking laughter.

ABRACHA: Quiet, Raissa. Your book.

RAISSA: Didn't bother them to tear it to pieces for me.

YOSSELE: Just do like me, I learned the whole book by heart.

ABRACHA: Recite, Yossele Morgenstern.

YOSSELE: "I have seen the strange sea abandon the sea
Your shadow deported to the ends of our universe . . ."

ABRACHA: Enough! Always the same old story. Come on, let's sing.

THEY *sing in raucous voices,* "Rhevlei maschiar, rhevlei maschiar . . ."

IONA: Ssh! There're people in the courtyard, green plants.

Beat. Silence.

They're gone.

ABRACHA: Alone?

IONA: No. With the nursery schoolers.

ABRACHA: Let's sing anyway.

THEY *sing same song.*

MISTER FUGUE: *Rhevlei maschiar*—what does that mean?

RAISSA: What an ass! "The ropes of the Messiah . . . when he comes . . ."
I don't know the rest.

ABRACHA: That's all there is, probably.

MISTER FUGUE: Why ropes?

ABRACHA: The old people said there are some and that they reach around the worlds. When things go badly down here, you give a tug, and there's a response from up there. If you don't pull, nothing answers and nothing comes. If you don't call him, then God, he can't guess that you need him. He's an old schmuck. Recreation.

THEY *play.*

IONA: I'm the soldier.

YOSSELE: No, me.

IONA: You always are.

YOSSELE: That's how it goes. I'm the leader. You'll be the truck. Ready?
ABRACHA, IONA *and* RAISSA: Ready.

ABRACHA *and* RAISSA *walk up and down in front of* YOSSELE, *the soldier who makes the "selection."*

YOSSELE: To the right, left, left, right, left, step on it or I'll crack you one. You, old man, to the left, left.
MISTER FUGUE: This isn't a real game.
ABRACHA: It's the only one we know.
YOSSELE: To the left, left, faster, faster, you little bug, left, to the left . . .
IONA *(Still playing)*: They're coming. For real.
YOSSELE: To the left, left, left, and for real this time, let's go, kids, all of you.

THEY *all get into the "Iona-Truck."*

ABRACHA: I'm getting in, too.
YOSSELE: Not necessary, professor. You've got a pass.
ABRACHA: I'm getting in.
YOSSELE: So he got in. Like you, a little while ago.
ABRACHA: They all died. The professor too.
IONA: It seems he'd driven the soldiers crazy, he made all the kids laugh.
RAISSA: That can't be right, you can't laugh in a truck.
MISTER FUGUE: And you, where were you during the round-ups?
YOSSELE: Us! In the sewers, we were lucky . . .
RAISSA *(Proud, a burst of enthusiasm)*: That's why we ran guns. For the Revolt.
ABRACHA *(Same tone as* RAISSA*)*: Inside the doll!
YOSSELE *(Same energy)*: And since she and Tamar looked alike, every time they caught us, we fooled them!
IONA *(Without giving them time to add anything)*: And the ghetto burned, we made it to the forest.
ABRACHA: They killed all the green plants.
YOSSELE: And then we ate, for centuries.
IONA: Chocolate, nothing but chocolate.
YOSSELE: You. But I, I had pineapple.
IONA *(HE makes* TAMAR *come out of her closet)*: We ate everything.
YOSSELE: And then the ghetto burned, we couldn't get to the forest.
ABRACHA: We couldn't even find the sewers, there weren't streets anymore.
RAISSA: We stayed in the gound, lying low, completely covered, but everything was burning.
ABRACHA: We went to the sewers anyway. They were completely blocked.
RAISSA: And we had to get in the truck.

Liliane Atlan

THEY *laugh, lay the doll across* MISTER FUGUE*'s knees. It is obvious that* HE *is suffering. Beat.*

YOSSELE: It's blocked. I can't find anything. It's black.

MISTER FUGUE: Yes, of course. All of a sudden, you're two years older, five years in your house, you sleep, you eat, but at the heart of it, nothing's happening, it happens to us every day, it's black for everyone.

YOSSELE: Well, I was blocked six years. The time it took to get over the sewers, and all that, have clothes a little less filthy, and well! I'm twenty.

RAISSA: At twenty, you're still at the stupid age.

YOSSELE: You, my dear, are only fifteen.

RAISSA: Eighteen!

YOSSELE: That's even more dumb. You think only of dancing, but you're flat as a board. I moved to a different city and forgot you.

RAISSA: Me too. I go out with boys that are handsome and live in palaces. My servants wash my feet, and I, I eat. Continuously.

YOSSELE: Me too.

IONA: I sleep in a real bed, a featherbed.

ABRACHA: Well me, I don't do anything, I remember, that's all I do, I remember.

YOSSELE: I stroll through town and I steal a chicken. I eat it. I steal another, and I eat that. I steal a third. I keep it, then I swallow it.

RAISSA: A varied schedule.

ABRACHA: He had imagination!

YOSSELE: Then I meet a strange girl with owl eyes, flat as a board, rouged up like a whore. I think she'd be prettier with a mouthful of shit. I go on my way.

ABRACHA: So.

YOSSELE: I go to a bar and get drunk. Drown my sorrows.

ABRACHA: Banal.

YOSSELE: I go to shul. I see a small rabbi with thin legs. I go to him. He doesn't respond. He's stuffing a tiny god covered with blood, a little god killed at the shoulder. I go out. I go back. They're stuffing the little rabbi. It was Iona. I start to cry.

IONA: Crazy!

ABRACHA: Completely crazy.

YOSSELE: So I cry, and then I go . . .

RAISSA: Eat.

YOSSELE: Right. I meet a guy who's all excited, tubercular, with a bomb in his hand. I go up to him. So, you moth-eaten revolutionary, what do you want to do with that?—I want to throw it . . . at the trucks.—

My poor Abracha, the trucks *(Showing him)* are there! —That's why I'm not throwing it, he says. But I can't live. —Me neither. I eat.

RAISSA *laughs.*

What do you hear about Raissa? Did you ever see her again? — Never. —Well, I heard she turned out badly. She wanders around, at night, barking. —Not bad, I go. We're quiet. Then he says to me: I'm going to change the world. Tell them everything. Everything they did to us. —My poor friend, I say to him, come, let's nosh on some pineapple. So we nosh.

RAISSA: You're not smart, Yossele.

YOSSELE: It's that the old people I knew disgusted me, I wouldn't want to do like them. And since I was never old for real, I don't know what I'd have done.

RAISSA: Well, I know. Look there's a big city with trains and lots of lights. Lots of noise. Iona, you're the train. Mister Fugue you'll be the garbage can. Abracha, you're the sea, make sea sounds.

ABRACHA: In a city?

RAISSA: Idiot! If it's a port? Yossele, you don't exist, you're ugly. Tamar, you're the cat, go meow. Got it? Good. I need a rope. Well all right, Yossele, be the rope. Okay, so the cat and me, we're digging through the garbage, picking out things we can eat. I'm the owl, the bat the hyena and god in heaven, it's all the same, I'm digging through the garbage. A banana skin. I pull it out, prowl around with it and come back, I dig through the garbage.

YOSSELE: If you hurt Mister Fugue, I'll scratch out your eyes.

RAISSA: Go 'head, let's see if you can.

THEY *fight.*

You're not smart, Yossele. Just a frayed rope. I'll put a match to it. That way, human beings, you won't be able to call me by tugging on it. And if you do tug on it, you'll burn.

ABRACHA: My grandfather always said that God came to earth preceded by fever and followed by plague.

RAISSA: You have nothing to say, you're the sea.

YOSSELE: What if you played becoming a little girl, a pretty little girl, Raissa, good and gentle.

RAISSA: I spit on pretty little girls. I prowl around, I dig through garbage cans. I hear trains passing, I'd like to catch them. I hop one. The train wants no part of me. No use crying, this train's going to

Rotburg. The whole earth is Rotburg. I leave. I can't. The rope is broken. They're after me. I'm afraid. It was the kids. It's funny, on this earth there are lots of trucks, it's not very cheerful, this earth. . . . A café! Iona, you're the café, make café noises. Garçon! Café au lait!

IONA: There isn't any.

RAISSA: Café au lait for the good little god who can no longer escape from the earth.

IONA: I can't, there isn't any more.

RAISSA: For the good little god deported to earth, to the bad earth, the earth-cage for big white birds with broken voices.

Wild laughter.

IONA: All I've got is water.

RAISSA: Thank you garçon. For you I shall open the heavens. They're on fire, garçon, look at them. Climb in, climb in I'm telling you, to the left, to the left, faster, to heaven, garçon!

IONA: I don't want to.

RAISSA: You don't want to? You don't want to?

SHE *hits him.*

MISTER FUGUE (*As though crazy*): Enough. God's not coming to earth, the earth is lost, she's a big house, a big house in the fog, full of holes, doors that whistle, they're mouths, they close on us . . .

RAISSA: I don't like your house. I prowl around it. I set it on fire. It crackles. Like this. A dry little noise. Finished. Nothing left.

MISTER FUGUE (*Looking at her*): You fell into the trap first, then you then me, they replace us. The house doesn't die, from the cellar to the attic, in the halls, they tell and retell the stories, they love each other, they laugh and wait their turn. ·

RAISSA: They don't love each other and they don't laugh. For the old folks, it was good to laugh. To butter each other up.

IONA: My parents weren't like that.

ABRACHA: They recited psalms!

IONA: Yes, practically all the time.

ABRACHA: They were the first to die, your parents.

YOSSELE: My old folks, they were stupid. "Don't steal. . . ." Don't steal, you don't stay alive. It's funny, when I see them, I see them only from the back.

The truck stops.

CHRISTOPHER (*To* FROBBE): Now what is it?

FROBBE: I can't see the road anymore, Lieutenant.

CHRISTOPHER: Grobbe, walk on ahead, you'll mark the way.

GROBBE *gets out. The truck starts off very slowly.*

YOSSELE: They can't find the road anymore.

ABRACHA: Too bad. We wouldn't be so cold anymore.

RAISSA: You're all pale, Mister Fugue, were you scared it was time to get out?

MISTER FUGUE: It hit me . . . the way it used to, when I would fly away . . .

RAISSA: What does it do to you, to think they're going to shoot you?

MISTER FUGUE *(Far away)*: It frightens me.

RAISSA: And the house that doesn't die, where you laugh and wait your turn, none of it's true, is it?

MISTER FUGUE: No, not yet.

RAISSA: It'll never be true.

YOSSELE: You shouldn't play anymore. It's not funny.

MISTER FUGUE *trembles.*

RAISSA: The real truth is that now you think it was dumb to get into this truck.

YOSSELE: You're stupid, Raissa.

RAISSA: So why have you got the shakes?

MISTER FUGUE: I've lost my stupidity.

RAISSA: Doesn't look it.

MISTER FUGUE: I have killed. I lost consciousness I hurt so bad, I hit, I hit, I don't even know what.

RAISSA: All you had to do was look. Maybe it's nothing but flies.

MISTER FUGUE: I hear screaming. Children.

RAISSA: So it's children you killed.

MISTER FUGUE: Maybe.

RAISSA: They'd be dead anyway. In bed or in a valley!

Wild laughter. Beat.

YOSSELE: You're weird, Fugue, you're sentimental.

RAISSA: Can't you see he's a wise man? That he knows things? *(Beat. To* FUGUE*)* Have you often traveled in this truck? *(Beat)* So, you talk? *(Beat)* White birds, broken voices, where do you get your jokes?

MISTER FUGUE: I see them.

RAISSA: And the flames? There where we're going? Go 'head, Sergeant Grol, do it here, pitch your fairgounds.

Liliane Atlan

MISTER FUGUE: You're blacker than night, Raissa, it was you made me lose my stupidity, yes, 'cause of you. Before I saw you I could feel you'd be this way, I saw you in those sewers, I was suffocating, I was hungry, I'd become you, I wanted us to leave, Christopher and me, you could have made it to the forest, we wouldn't have told stories, I'd like to live a little more but backwards, so we'd be in the forest. (HE *weeps*)

YOSSELE: Don't you see we are?
ABRACHA: Listen to the birds . . . trees!
YOSSELE: Hide, Mister Fugue, they'll see us.
IONA: Ssh, Tamar! I hear someone.
MISTER FUGUE: It's only an animal. Come.

The CHILDREN *follow him. Beat.*

IONA: If we rested?
YOSSELE: Not already. There, there'll be wheat, taller than we are, we'll get there and be safe.
ABRACHA: Sing us something, Raissa, I'm beat.
RAISSA: I don't want to.
YOSSELE: Raissa, we're in the forest, sing us something.

Beat.

RAISSA (*Sings in her broken voice, sometimes very sweetly, then again hoarsely*):
    Don't ask why
    Ill-loved and mortal mother
    We the golem with dreams gone dry
    Our hands are made to be broken.
IONA: Not so loud!
RAISSA: Whose fault if you sleep
    On an earth that despises you.
ALL: We the golem with dreams gone dry
    Our hands were made to be broken.
MISTER FUGUE: Where does it come from, this song?
RAISSA: It's not a song.
ABRACHA: At shul one day, instead of saying the prayer, they said that. Then we repeated it.
MISTER FUGUE: But golem? What are they?
RAISSA: Misfits, people don't want any part of them.

Beat.

IONA: Tamar's hungry.

YOSSELE: It's not time. It's time to sleep, now, or tomorrow we'll have no strength. I'll stand watch.

IONA: No, it's me.

YOSSELE: Later, you'll relieve me.

THEY *try to sleep.* ABRACHA *is trembling.*

IONA: Don't tremble. Don't tremble, you make Tamar tremble.

YOSSELE *(To* TAMAR*)*: It creaks, but like in the closet, it's nothing, just the forest.

Beat.

IONA: You don't hear the dogs anymore.

ABRACHA: So much the better.

RAISSA: All I have to do is close my eyes and I hear them. . . . They must have turned them loose again.

YOSSELE: Not possible. We're in the forest.

RAISSA: They must have seen us leave. They've turned the dogs loose.

YOSSELE *(Giving her his hand)*: Don't be foolish, Raissa, they haven't. *(Beat)* We'll go all the way to the sea, get a boat, and after we've crossed the border, people will come all the way to the beach, they'll see us and say: there are the children who came through the flames. They'll admire us, they'll give us everything, anything we want, and we will always have food, always.

RAISSA: It's not true, they've turned the dogs loose.

YOSSELE: You made me sad, Raissa.

RAISSA: I can't do otherwise.

YOSSELE: We'll go to school again, and afterwards, I'll marry you, because . . .

RAISSA: Your soul's not pretty, then.

YOSSELE: She won't dare walk through the door, that's why.

Beat.

ABRACHA: Don't sleep, don't sleep, you gotta think back, remember, to change everything.

YOSSELE: Laugh.

RAISSA: Can't.

YOSSELE: Have to.

IONA: Everything's spinning.

YOSSELE: It's 'cause you're hungry. We gotta go now. Later, we'll eat.

ABRACHA: Wake up, Tamar, we're going.

YOSSELE: Time to fly, Mister Fugue.

MISTER FUGUE *(Doesn't move)*: On the beach, they'll shoot me 'cause I was the enemy.

YOSSELE: We'll tell them you're okay.

MISTER FUGUE: They'll shoot me.

RAISSA: It's true. They don't like people with eyes as big as holes.

ABRACHA: My grandfather had eyes like that too, and the old man who taught me the law. Then everyone, all of a sudden. It's seeing, does that.

IONA: They can't shoot you for that.

YOSSELE: Come on, Mister Fugue!

MISTER FUGUE: I can't. Really.

YOSSELE: Listen. What you did before, it doesn't concern us. *(Looking* RAISSA *up and down)* And even.

YOSSELE: We need you, Mister Fugue. . . . If we don't go. . . . Maybe they have turned the dogs loose . . .

> MISTER FUGUE *makes a terrible effort to walk,* YOSSELE *and* ABRACHA *hold him up. Beat.* CHRISTOPHER *watches them.*

IONA: A house!

Beat.

Nothing but corpses in there, let's go.

YOSSELE: They're not corpses, they're people having a quiet dinner, they're going to recognize us, they're going to give us everything, you'll never again be afraid . . . they're not laughing, you're right, they're corpses.

ABRACHA: What if we told them everything?

RAISSA: You crazy? They'd turn us in.

IONA: Fugue's gone!

RAISSA: I knew it, he was lying to us.

IONA: He went maybe to turn us in?

YOSSELE: Doesn't matter. Gotta keep walking while it's dark.

> *Beat.* THEY *walk.*

MISTER FUGUE: I stole three chickens! Cooked!

IONA: Blessed art Thou, Lord of the Worlds, Blessed art Thou!

ABRACHA: You starting again?

CHRISTOPHER *(To* GROBBE *who has just climbed back into the truck)*: Grobbe?

GROBBE: Lieutenant?

CHRISTOPHER: Look.

RAISSA: We gotta stop, it's getting light.

MISTER FUGUE: We're going to eat.

IONA: Blessed art Thou, Lord of the Worlds, who makes wheat grow in the earth, and roast chicken grow in the forest.

THEY *eat voraciously, but a bit less than before.*

MISTER FUGUE: Eat nicely, not like that. From a plate. Slowly.

RAISSA: Pass my napkin, my dear, no, I don't feel very well today, I'm getting a cold. . . . Life is hard, my dear, a cold and no money. . . . Still I heard you'd bought a villa? A hovel, my dear, a hovel. —I do like your chandeliers and your Persian rugs. —Oh, but we're camping, Madame, I still don't have my tapestries.

THEY *laugh and eat.*

ABRACHA *(Stops laughing, ecstatic)*: Pass me the salt, please, Mister Fugue.

MISTER FUGUE: Here, Abracha, do you want the wing or the thigh?

ABRACHA: Both.

RAISSA: Me too.

IONA: Each may have a bit of both.

MISTER FUGUE: And, Tamar, what does she have to say?

ALL *(At once)*: It's good, it's good, it's delicious.

YOSSELE: Don't eat standing up, Iona.

IONA: I'm not hungry anymore.

THEY'*re happy.*

CHRISTOPHER: Frobbe?

FROBBE: Lieutenant?

CHRISTOPHER: Is it still far to Rotburg?

FROBBE: At this rate, yes, Lieutenant, very far.

CHRISTOPHER: Then stop.

FROBBE: We're almost at the village, Lieutenant.

IONA: Thank you, Lord of the Worlds, for this meal in the forest.

RAISSA: And thank you 'cause we're going to die?

IONA: Thank you 'cause we're in the forest.

YOSSELE: Quick, let's go, while it's night.

ABRACHA: The forest is so beautiful, you see, Tamar, it's not all black, there's lots of sky.

RAISSA: Blackberries.

YOSSELE: We don't have time.

IONA: There'll be some on the beach.

ABRACHA: Blackberries, on a beach!

MISTER FUGUE: I can't walk anymore . . . my leg . . .

YOSSELE: Don't be a baby.

RAISSA *(Sings)*: Don't ask why
  Ill-loved and mortal mother
  We the golem with dreams gone dry
  Our hands are made to be broken.

ABRACHA, IONA *and* YOSSELE: We the golem with dreams gone dry
  Our hands are made to be broken.

RAISSA: Who's to blame if you sleep
  On an earth that detests you.

ALL: We the golem with dreams gone dry
  Our hands are made to be broken.

CHRISTOPHER: Grobbe, they're singing!

GROBBE: Sad songs, Lieutenant!

CHRISTOPHER: Frobbe, stop, if they can have fun, so can we.

The truck stops. This time, we don't hear the brakes. CHRISTOPHER *opens the back.* GROBBE *and* FROBBE, *armed, stand guard.*

MISTER FUGUE: This isn't Rotburg.

CHRISTOPHER: Get out!

HE hits FUGUE with his stick; FUGUE doesn't move.

RAISSA: Not worth it to get beat up. Come on.

THEY get out, FUGUE last.

CHRISTOPHER: So, having a little party? Don't stop, let's all have fun. *(To* MISTER FUGUE*)* You, dance. *(Hits him with his stick)* Come on, dance, it'll loosen your legs, Sergeant Grol.

YOSSELE: Don't dance, Mister Fugue.

CHRISTOPHER *(HE fixes on IONA who has taken TAMAR in his arms)*: You, dance, or . . . *(FUGUE dances)* You, sing. *(Hits RAISSA with his stick)* Well, little bat, you gonna sing?

HE hits her again. SHE *doesn't flinch.* HE *hits FUGUE's wounded leg.*

RAISSA *(Sings in a broken voice)*: Nothing lasts save erosion
  This is the code
  You will smile

Even if living hurts you
To smile you will smile . . .
ABRACHA, IONA *and* YOSSELE: To smile you will smile . . .
RAISSA: Even if living hurts you
To smile you will smile . . .

FUGUE *dances in spite of his wounded leg.* CHRISTOPHER *keeps hitting him with his stick.*

CHRISTOPHER: That song is completely stupid. A different one. (HE *hits them)* Come on, come on.
RAISSA: Nothing lasts save erosion
This is the code
You will smile . . .

CHRISTOPHER *hits her.*

You will smile.
ALL *(The rhythm is more and more gay, but more lacerating, their voices false, harsh)*:
And the grass
The birds the stones
Will remember you . . .

CHRISTOPHER *hits* RAISSA.

will remember . . . will remember . . . will remember . . .
MISTER FUGUE: Stop, Raissa.
RAISSA: No, I don't give a damn. Me, I'm singing. It's a song we made up In the ghetto. We'd sing it all night long. Still and all, we didn't smile. (SHE *sings)* Nothing lasts save erosion . . .
This is the code . . .
You will smile . . .

CHRISTOPHER *hits* FUGUE *in the face;* RAISSA *stops singing.*

CHRISTOPHER: And so, you smiling? No? You'd rather sing? So sing.

HE *hits* MISTER FUGUE.

RAISSA: I don't want to anymore.
CHRISTOPHER *(Suddenly coming to his senses)*: Get in, now. And keep quiet. Otherwise, it starts over again. Got it?

HE *hits them until* THEY'*re all back in the truck.*

I don't want to hear any more laughing.

The truck starts off again. Lots of noise, the gears grind. Beat.

YOSSELE *(Very low)*: We've spotted a commando. But it doesn't matter. We play dead, then, we'll take off again.
MISTER FUGUE *(Exhausted)*: It's still far, the beach, let's go right now.
IONA: I'm standing guard.
YOSSELE: Yes, but from heaven's side.

THEY *start walking again, but more slowly than before.* THEY *are exhausted, fearful, discouraged.* THEY *stop. Noise from the truck.*

CHRISTOPHER: That bitch, I'll get her.
GROBBE *(Oily, stupid laugh)*: She won't go much farther, Lieutenant.
CHRISTOPHER: You don't understand. They're resisting us, from the inside.
IONA *(Still very low)*: I don't see it, I don't see the beach.
MISTER FUGUE: Walk anyway.
RAISSA: It's not worth it anymore, they must have turned the dogs loose, they'll be on the beach, there will be so many dogs, we won't see the sand.
YOSSELE: I'm the boss, we keep walking.

THEY *walk. Noise from the truck.*

GROBBE: Lieutenant? Why did Grol do that?
CHRISTOPHER: And why was he a soldier? Do you know what a donkey sees when he walks down the road? *(Beat)* He's part of the race that's slow, stubborn, unalterable, we'll get at them only from the inside. I'll have them. Especially her.
FROBBE: Looks like the fog's lifting, Lieutenant . . .
CHRISTOPHER *(To himself, continuing his train of thought)*: I'll skin her alive.

Beat. The truck goes faster.

RAISSA: That's it. The dogs.

An attack of nerves, which spreads, fear of the dogs possesses them.

MISTER FUGUE *(To* ABRACHA*)*: Don't bark. Listen to me. They captured you, beat you, then threw you on the ground. You can't even tell anyone your troubles anymore, all you can do is howl. People can't stand it anymore, they'll never quit chasing you. But us, look, we speak your language.

ABRACHA *smiles.*

Raissa, the dog recognizes us.

RAISSA: There's more than one.

MISTER FUGUE *(To all of them)*: Listen, they've said, "Men, *(Meaning the dogs* HE *is addressing)* dogs, *(Meaning the* CHILDREN*)* tear them apart." They've spoken to you as men, and to us as though we were dogs. You and us, they've humiliated us. So come, we'll go to the beach, we'll gallop whole nights through, on the sand, our feet in the water, we'll feel the fresh air, horses pass, we follow them, they whinny, we bark and we sing, we're content, we're not crazy. Well maybe, but too bad, so much the better. It's that we see holes where others see doors, and doors where others see holes. *(Exalted)*

ABRACHA: The dogs love us. We keep going.

YOSSELE: My God! The sea!

ABRACHA: She's black! And mean! She's coming toward us!

MISTER FUGUE *(To the sea)*: Listen. They walked through the flames and came out with their lives. They come from a land where people know the real stories. Let them leave for a land where children don't have to stand guard.

IONA *"hears" the sea.*

MISTER FUGUE: You see, she'll help us.

RAISSA: No boat, we can't leave.

YOSSELE: So beautiful, the sea is so beautiful!

RAISSA: Don't cry, Yossele.

YOSSELE: She's too beautiful, it hurts.

MISTER FUGUE: There, there are cliffs, look how they're split, between them flows the sea . . .

ALL *except* RAISSA, *give a hoarse cry, sudden departure suggesting a flock of birds taking flight.*

ABRACHA: Gulls, Yossele!

YOSSELE: Their voices are broken, because the sea, she's beautiful, and it hurts them too.

MISTER FUGUE: Everything smells of the sky.

RAISSA: Idiot, why are you always talking about the sky? It's the sea, only the sea.

ABRACHA: Still, the sea is frightening.

IONA: Tamar doesn't see her.

ABRACHA: It's not her fault! She's never seen anything!

RAISSA: Not even her doll. It was dark in her closet.

ABRACHA: One time, I brought her to the tree. But there was a round-up.

YOSSELE: And then, when she'd caught her death, we put her back in hiding. She was waiting for us to come home.

ABRACHA: We told her everything we'd seen, but running guns she didn't understand.

YOSSELE: She was only four years old.

IONA *tries to stop trembling the way* TAMAR *stopped crying.* HE *is mumbling, without realizing it.* HE *clings to God as* TAMAR *to her doll.*

MISTER FUGUE (*To* TAMAR): Climb up on my shoulders. Don't cry, or I'll scold you. Look, the sea. It's a house the color of sky, a grand house, fragrant with grand voyages, and with the flavor of salt.

IONA: Above it, are there clouds?

MISTER FUGUE: Foam.

YOSSELE: The hurricane, my God, the hurricane, what marvels! Hurricanes!

RAISSA: We won't leave if it lasts, the hurricane.

YOSSELE: Too bad, I like it.

ABRACHA: All the same, we'll have seen some beautiful things, the forest, the dogs, the sea . . .

RAISSA: We still had to put up with him, him and his birds, the color of the sky.

YOSSELE: You didn't sing for him, before?

RAISSA: I was just singing. To annoy the greens. Not for Mister Fugue, he's too stupid, all he sees is sky, sky . . . and dogs that don't bite if you talk to them, you've seen that for real, have you?

YOSSELE: Yes, I've seen it. All I gotta do is look at you.

RAISSA: Look at your own mug a little, for the sake of comparison.

YOSSELE: I'm not going to marry you.

RAISSA: 'Course not, I'm not the hurricane!

YOSSELE: Oh no, you're made of coal, coal that won't burn, fool's coal.

RAISSA: So you're a wimp. You let them put this over on you. And you don't see the barbed wire anymore. But me, I see it.

YOSSELE: Hard to tell, sometimes.

RAISSA: Me, I see the fog that's lifting and us arriving at Rotburg. That's what I see.

YOSSELE: Me too, Raissa. I see it all. The barbed wire, the forest, the hurricane. I see more of it than you.

MISTER FUGUE

RAISSA: You're like him, you're crazy.

YOSSELE: You're the crazy one, you've got to see it all at once.

HE *hits her.*

You make the sea go away.

ABRACHA *(Separating them)*: The two of you, when you're married, you'll
hire me as your valet to pick up the pieces.

RAISSA: You won't have to bend too far, where we're going.

YOSSELE: Bitch.

Noise of the truck. THEY*'re jolted.*

MISTER FUGUE *(As though suddenly inspired, clownesque)*: Eleven o'clock,
already. But they're late. Young people today have no *savoir-vivre.*
Mr. Freneticus, where are the banns? The sugar almonds? The couple? I have a town council meeting this afternoon.

Grimaces. THEY *laugh.*

ABRACHA: The couple is fighting, Mr. Mayor. The're drawing crowds
in the white, green and multicolored streets. Thirty wounded. It's
'cause the wife bit them.

MISTER FUGUE: Bit them, my God! That's cute, Freneticus, that's really
cute! . . . Bit them!

ABRACHA: She scratches too, even the dogs are afraid of her.

MISTER FUGUE: How cute! cute! But where is my monocle, Freneticus,
but where?

ABRACHA: Here, Mr. Mayor, on the windowsill.

MISTER FUGUE: What's it doing there, my good man?

ABRACHA: It was going away, Mr. Mayor.

MISTER FUGUE: It's not serious then (HE *looks for the couple on his hands and
knees, in the straw)* Little, little, little couple, where are they hiding?

IONA: They can't come, 'cause of the round-up.

MISTER FUGUE: But where have you been, my good man! The war's been
over twenty years, my good man, there are no more round-ups, we
love each other, Mr. Vertigo, are mad for one another, what can I
say, truly mad. . . . That phone again! Hello, it's I, the Mayor and
Municipality, what do you want this time? What? What are you saying? That the wife is howling? That the husband is desperate? But
that's banal, my good man, send them over. For dinner, my wife
made pheasant, Freneticus, à la vanille!

ABRACHA: A la vanille! What a feast!

MISTER FUGUE: I'll bring you the leftovers. If I have time to go eat.

YOSSELE: Here we are.

MISTER FUGUE: Finally! Finally! But where are the witnesses?

YOSSELE: We brought the dogs, there was no one else.

MISTER FUGUE: Miss . . . your name, please?

YOSSELE: Raissa Dollfuss, and me, Yossele Morgenstern.

MISTER FUGUE: Miss Raissa Dollfuss, do you take, before dogs and God, Yossele Morgenstern as your husband?

RAISSA: Since there's no one else.

YOSSELE: Hey.

ABRACHA: That won't work. If there's no more war, how come there're only dogs left? That won't work.

YOSSELE: Out, reasoner!

ABRACHA: I don't believe it. It's not possible.

MISTER FUGUE: Mr. Freneticus, one doesn't reason when one marries, or one wouldn't marry. Sign the marriage license.

ABRACHA: I don't believe it.

MISTER FUGUE: Okay, no marriage.

YOSSELE: You see, it wasn't fated, the two of us.

RAISSA: What does that mean, fated?

YOSSELE: I don't know, my father used to say it.

RAISSA: You're an ass, you repeat what you don't understand?

YOSSELE: All you had to do was see the sea and the hurricane and not talk about the rest.

RAISSA: It's my fault, maybe, if the fog lifts?

YOSSELE: It is your fault and isn't your fault, you've ruined everything for us.

RAISSA: All right, all you have to do is tell us about death. At least we believe in that, tell us about death.

Noises from the truck.

MISTER FUGUE: Death, she's an old woman, she has a pinched nose, yellow lips, her skin is brown, creviced, as though she'd already become earth.

RAISSA: Tamar, she was all white, all hunched over, she was scared, and in pain, even afterward.

IONA: She wants us to go.

MISTER FUGUE: Our boat is ready, get in, get in, there's the bridge, that's where we'll sleep, facing the stars, they gambol behind our sails, a sun is going to rise, nothing will be the same *(To* YOSSELE *and* RAISSA*)* you will be able to marry.

YOSSELE: I'm not coming.

MISTER FUGUE: But Yossele, we're going to the Promised Land.

YOSSELE: Too bad.

MISTER FUGUE: You'll see, it's no longer being guarded, we'll be able to land.

YOSSELE: I can't leave her.

MISTER FUGUE: We're going to carry her, whether she wants it or no.

YOSSELE: Better not. She carries calamity.

RAISSA: Hey.

The truck pitches.

YOSSELE: The proof, their boat's going to sink.

The truck pitches.

RAISSA: It's all right. It's all right!

SHE *"gets in." The truck pitches more and more.*

MISTER FUGUE *(Happily, illuminated)*: It's the hurricane, the true hurricane, the one that makes things move, like at the world's beginning, light breaks, bubbles, holes form, planets fly, their masts crack, collapse, their passengers are lost in the wind, in the fire that carries them off.

ABRACHA: I'm seasick.

MISTER FUGUE: You can be earth-sick too, but the earth was shipwrecked, there's nothing left of her, all the fogs are lifting, from door to door the boat dances, flies, toward the true Earth!

Pitching.

ABRACHA *(Scared for real)*: It's pitching too much here, say sailor, you know the sea? Really know her?

YOSSELE: I'm a sailor, aren't I? *(HE laughs)*

RAISSA: In the boat, the reasoner doesn't reason anymore!

CHRISTOPHER *(Hearing their laughter, harshly)*: Grobbe! You hear?

GROBBE: Yes, Lieutenant, but we're almost there. See, there, that white cliff. On the other side is the Valley of Bones.

Laughter.

CHRISTOPHER: Frobbe, stop.

FROBBE: Impossible, Lieutenant, the road's too slick.

The CHILDREN *pitch, laugh.*

CHRISTOPHER: I order you to stop.

FROBBE: I really can't.

RAISSA: There's trees on this sea, strange trees, an odor of rot . . .

YOSSELE: I don't know if I love you, but I'm going to marry you, right away.

RAISSA: I prefer Abracha.

YOSSELE: Hey!

MISTER FUGUE: So you do love her!

RAISSA: Abracha doesn't like the sea, he's all pale, bald, with big sad eyes, and a girl's voice, and no, I don't love him, he's a wimp, too.

YOSSELE: And at night, when you're afraid? And in the basement, when you were practically dying, who carried you on his shoulders, who held your hand when you had nightmares? And who gave you his jacket when you were cold, who gave you his potatoes, a wimp, maybe?

RAISSA: And who was it kicked you so you wouldn't fall asleep in the snow, after your parents, they'd left? And who sang to you when you cried at seeing them only from the back? And who put your jacket over you when you thought I was asleep? It wasn't me, maybe?

YOSSELE: Mister Fugue was right, you're blacker than night, but there are nights that are full of moonlight.

RAISSA: I don't understand what you're saying.

YOSSELE: It doesn't matter. Mr. Rabbi, say the prayers for us.

ABRACHA: You can't do without?

YOSSELE: No. Not for this.

ABRACHA: You're like the old people you didn't like before. For marrying and dying they ran for the rabbi, the rest of the time they didn't give a damn. But for the Day of Atonement, every last fool was in shul, just in case God, he should exist. Fakes, all of them.

YOSSELE: Maybe, but with me it's different.

ABRACHA: And how is that?

YOSSELE: I can't say. I'm not a reasoner.

ABRACHA: Well me, I know. It's 'cause you're scared, like the others.

YOSSELE: That's not true. It's 'cause I've seen the sea.

ABRACHA: That's true, is it?

YOSSELE: Yes, though just quickly.

IONA: Clean youselves up first, I don't marry slobs.

RAISSA: My servants will attend me. *(*SHE *calls)* Tamar! No, hairdresser, hairdresser . . .

ABRACHA: Here. You're getting married?

RAISSA: Something high.

MISTER FUGUE

ABRACHA: With your face so thin and pinched, something low would be better.

RAISSA: I don't give a damn. Perfume me. Essence of pineapple.

ABRACHA: If you please?

RAISSA: My fiancé loves pineapples and hurricanes.

ABRACHA: More than you?

RAISSA: I'm afraid so.

ABRACHA: What a shame! (HE *untangles her hair with his hands*)

IONA: The soap, please. Whether I need it or not, I wash once a year, when I do a marriage.

MISTER FUGUE: What have you done with my melon hat?

RAISSA: Quick. My dress. Not that one. The one made of diamonds. And my heels made from bits of the moon. My fiancé loves the moonlight.

ABRACHA: He a poet, then?

RAISSA: That's what you think! He's a gutter-rat. He's had typhus, you know, but he got over it. It's since the typhus, he's dreamed of hurricanes, pineapples and the full moon. And then, he fell in with a bad crowd. A guy whose pockets are full of white birds.

ABRACHA: My word!

MISTER FUGUE (HE *has covered himself with straw, is grotesque*): My evening clothes are ready. (*Bowing and scraping, grimacing*)

The CHILDREN *laugh heartily.*

CHRISTOPHER: Frobbe, I'm giving you three minutes to stop.

FROBBE: I'll try Lieutenant. (HE *does try to stop*)

YOSSELE (*Anguished*): Isn't anyone going to help me?

MISTER FUGUE: There, there, does the gentleman wish to be coiffed high or low?

YOSSELE: Backwards, idiot.

MISTER FUGUE: Nervous on account of the wedding, perhaps?

YOSSELE: I dunno. Do it fast.

While FUGUE *does* YOSSELE's *toilet,* IONA *does* TAMAR's.

MISTER FUGUE: Your fiancée is waiting eagerly, no doubt?

YOSSELE: She doesn't love me.

MISTER FUGUE: That's impossible, sir, you're not that bad.

YOSSELE: I see her only from the back.

MISTER FUGUE: It's love, does that.

YOSSELE: It's not love, this weight that makes me old, I can't get it out of my heart.

MISTER FUGUE: Earth-sickness, perhaps?

YOSSELE: Oh no, I don't know what it is, the war, yes, the war.

MISTER FUGUE: No, sir, I don't think so. For you see, me, I've known peace. We've all had heaviness in our hearts. It's that made it painful to stand, to love each other, to leave each other, sir, it's living that hurts.

YOSSELE: Me, I don't believe that.

MISTER FUGUE: Because you're young.

The truck stops. CHRISTOPHER *and* GROBBE *get out.*

IONA: Ready?

ABRACHA: Let's go.

YOSSELE: The prayer.

IONA: I've forgot.

ABRACHA: Then make it up, you idiot, the one time we're letting you.

CHRISTOPHER: Frobbe, the shovel.

FROBBE: Here, Lieutenant.

CHRISTOPHER: Dig just a little, to mark the spot.

IONA: Blessed art Thou, Lord of the Worlds, who made Yossele Morgenstern and Raissa Dollfuss meet in a sewer.

HE *chants, davens quickly in all directions.*

THE OTHERS *(Same game):* In a sewer . . .

CHRISTOPHER *opens the door of the truck.*

IONA: Blessed art Thou, Lord of the Worlds, who did not give them time to grow rotten from being too old.

CHRISTOPHER: Mr. Rabbi, that's not how you celebrate a marriage, get out.

IONA: Blessed art Thou, Lord of the Worlds, who placed them in the hurricane to marry them like white birds.

THE OTHERS: To marry them like white birds.

CHRISTOPHER: I said: get out.

IONA *(Obeying, showing him* TAMAR*):* Don't let her catch cold again.

CHRISTOPHER: Take this shovel and dig your hole.

IONA *obeys.*

RAISSA *(Hoarse):* In the hurricane like white birds . . . alleluia.

THE OTHERS *(Against the grill):* Alleluia . . .

IONA *(Digging, in a weak voice):* Blessed art Thou, Lord of the Worlds, who made our boat pitch, with all those millions of stars . . . behind

our sails . . . under the newspapers . . . don't take it so hard, Lord
of the Worlds, things aren't good here, but they go on. . . . Let the
fête go on, so I can hear it, too . . .
THE OTHERS: All those millions of stars, that gambol behind our sails . . .

IONA: Our house gambols, like before, the sea and the mountains, when
you'd come to us with fever and plagues.
CHRISTOPHER: Dig, Rabbi. Faster.

HE *strikes him.*

IONA: They were dying, the mountains, they were spitting blood, they
fell like old people and still, Lord of the Worlds, they danced, and
us too, we're dancing, for Yossele and Raissa, you see, are getting
married.
RAISSA: In the commandos' faces, alleluia.
THE OTHERS: Alleluia.
IONA: And I pronounce Yossele and Raissa man and wife. Dance,
dance . . .

Wild ronde. THEY *sing* "Rhevlei Maschiar." IONA *sings with them,
and digs.*

CHRISTOPHER *(Screaming)*: Silence!
ALL *(Louder)*: "Rhevlei maschiar, rhevlei maschiar . . ."

CHRISTOPHER *makes* IONA *walk down into the hole. The dance stops.
A long silence.*

CHRISTOPHER: Go 'head, one more prayer, your prettiest, field mouse.

HE *strikes him.* IONA *moans. Hoarse cries from the* CHILDREN.

MISTER FUGUE *(Brusque, desperate, holding* TAMAR*)*: Blessed art Thou, Lord
of the Worlds, who brought Yossele and Raissa together like two
hoarse and solitary birds . . .
IONA *(Seeing* TAMAR*)*: Not the cart, I don't want that, I don't want, I've
already got earthfuls of mouth, I . . .
CHRISTOPHER: He's barking, the Rabbi's barking. The rest of you, laugh.
So laugh, since I'm allowing it. You're the ones who'll be throwing
handfuls of dirt. Get out. *(HE hits FUGUE with his stick)* You don't want
to get out? I get it, now you're sorry?

FUGUE *panics at the door of the truck.*

The rest of you, get started.

THEY *don't obey.*

ABRACHA *(Throwing dirt on* IONA *as* THEY *would have for* TAMAR): This is the chicken, the chocolate, the wedding cake, blackberries, the boat, the sea, pineapples, the black doll.
IONA: I don't want anymore, Tamar, I don't want anymore.
CHRISTOPHER: Your turn, Sergeant Grol.
RAISSA: Don't you see he's sick? Come down, Mister Fugue, there're no holes, there's us and that's all. Yossele, come help me. What wimps these men are. Lean lightly, you crazy old man.

SHE *helps* FUGUE *down.*

We're going to give him the earth, don't cower like that anymore.
CHRISTOPHER: Let's be done with it. Throw.

RAISSA *takes some dirt in her hands, approaches* IONA, *but instead starts digging him out.* CHRISTOPHER *shoots* IONA, *who falls dead. Beat.*

CHRISTOPHER: Bitch. I wanted him alive. On his feet and buried alive. But you'll see what I've got waiting for you. You and your nonsense. You've seen what that's worth. His howling wasn't bad. We'll do better next time. Get back in.

The truck starts off again. The gears grind. CHRISTOPHER *plays the harmonica. In the truck, the* CHILDREN *grow old, as though paralyzed, especially* FUGUE, *who from now on, holds* TAMAR *on his lap. Beat, for as long as we can stand it.*

YOSSELE: He wouldn't have felt the earth, you did right, Raissa.
RAISSA *(Crying):* Don't cry, don't cry.
ABRACHA: I shouldn't have stopped him from praying like that. They're not true, those prayers, but all the same I shouldn't have stopped him. Gotta laugh, Mister Fugue, he said so, Iona.

HE *trembles. Gradually,* FUGUE *calms down.* HE *seems to be living elsewhere.*

YOSSELE: Hey, Mister Fugue, don't go away. *(Beat)* It wasn't nonsense.

MISTER FUGUE

RAISSA: You're so old, my poor Mister Fugue, all of a sudden! You're white, wrinkled *(Forcing herself)* even so, Grandpa, if it isn't shameful I've got to wash and feed you. As if I didn't already have too much work with my kids.

Though HE *doesn't speak anymore,* MISTER FUGUE *remains the* CHILDREN's *center, their center of light.*

RAISSA: Did you find work, Yossele?
YOSSELE: I was a sweeper in a hospital but since I sang all the time they threw me out.
ABRACHA: What were you singing, Yossele?
YOSSELE: Dumb things. That the earth is a boat in the fog, that it sunk, that we pitched and tossed in the hurricane, that we could disembark. They didn't like that.
RAISSA: They like thinking of the price of potatoes.
YOSSELE: It's being less than a person to not think of what is black.
RAISSA: What's Grandpa trying to say? That he's right, my Yossele?
YOSSELE: Of course I'm right. But I'm out of a job.
RAISSA: So what. We know already what hunger is.

Time passes. Little by little, MISTER FUGUE *loses his sadness.*

YOSSELE: I have something to do but I'm not sure what.
RAISSA *(To* ABRACHA*)*: And you? You don't come round very often.
ABRACHA: It's that I haven't been well.
YOSSELE: It's that you're like the others. You don't think about it anymore.
ABRACHA *(Crying out)*: About what?
YOSSELE: You see! You don't want us to talk about it anymore.
ABRACHA: Talk, all you do is talk. A real man of the cloth.
YOSSELE: That's not true.
ABRACHA: You do nothing. Except your holidays.
YOSSELE: That's not true either. But I can't talk to you about it yet. It's too big.
ABRACHA: For me, too, Yossele, it's so big.

Time passes. THEY *dream.* CHRISTOPHER's *harmonica.*

YOSSELE: Make them shut up, those kids, I can't think.
RAISSA: It's Iona who's playing music, he doesn't play very well.
ABRACHA: I started my opera. A hoarse song with broken voices, and then gears grinding when it starts up again, but I haven't finished it, I don't finish anything. Nothing but bits.

Liliane Atlan

YOSSELE: Sing them to us anyway since it's a holiday.

RAISSA: Iona's holiday, the little dog-Rabbi, who recited psalms, and who made the mountains gambol, it's a long time since then, miles and miles.

ABRACHA: I can't sing . . . I'm cold inside my chest and it burns my lips. *(HE trembles)*

RAISSA: It's funny how sicknesses, they continue in peacetime.

YOSSELE: I've brought pineapple for our holiday.

RAISSA: Again! And with what did you pay for them?

YOSSELE: I didn't pay for them, I took them.

ABRACHA: Back to your old habits.

Normal laughter.

RAISSA *(To ABRACHA)*: It doesn't keep him from getting old. *(To YOSSELE)* Why are you all hunched over? And never laughing?

YOSSELE: It's that I haven't changed the world, Raissa.

RAISSA: But that doesn't matter, doesn't matter at all.

YOSSELE: We eat, we sleep, we eat, that's all we do, that's not enough.

RAISSA: We don't love each other, at times?

YOSSELE: It's still not enough.

RAISSA: You don't know anything. When you're here, there are no longer any holes in the floor. I don't see them anymore.

YOSSELE: Me yes, I feel them all the time.

RAISSA: It's that you don't love me.

YOSSELE: Yes I do, but I see Grandpa, and what he's become, how he goes away, like that, without moving.

RAISSA *(Very gently)*: Grandpa, is it true you go away?

Beat.

YOSSELE: And when you're sweet like that, that hurts me too.

ABRACHA: Yossele, you should do like me, make music, or something, anything. *(Sententiously)* It makes the pain slide past.

YOSSELE: You don't remember anything, do you?

RAISSA: It's true, when we talk about the truck, you scream.

ABRACHA: It's that I'm not like you, I can't keep harping on dead things and valleys of bones. The two of you, you're always whining.

YOSSELE: And you, you go to the theatre, you have fun, you practically never come for the holidays.

ABRACHA: It's that I don't believe in it anymore, I don't believe in anything, and then your holidays commemorate nothing but the dead, nothing but trucks.

YOSSELE: Because that's how it is. We must remember.

ABRACHA: Well me, I can't, it made me sick, I couldn't get up anymore, I couldn't eat, I didn't want to go crazy.

YOSSELE: You were wrong, Abracha.

RAISSA: Quiet. It's the holiday.

> THEY *chant all together but in different keys, on different rhythms. Then* THEY *laugh, very softly, and eat. The harmonica stops.*

RAISSA: It's the holiday of the little dog-Rabbi who made the mountains gambol.

YOSSELE: And us, we eat.

ABRACHA: Of course, we eat. . . . Why was he called the dog-Rabbi?

RAISSA: No one knows anymore. Too many miles between then and now.

YOSSELE: In books they say he hurt too much, he'd scream and the dogs would answer every time, he screamed like a dog. But he made the mountains gambol.

ABRACHA: When it's a holiday, you don't talk about dogs. You eat and joke around.

YOSSELE: Then it's not a holiday. A holiday, it's seeing everything at once.

ABRACHA: You won't be able to live, Yossele, if you see everything at once. Look at Grandpa, it turned him into a mollusc.

YOSSELE: He lives maybe better than we do.

RAISSA: He doesn't look it.

> ABRACHA *coughs and trembles.*

YOSSELE: You either, you don't look well.

RAISSA: You take care of yourself, sometimes? Go to a doctor, maybe?

ABRACHA: They said I have a hole in my lung, or in something else, I don't know anymore.

YOSSELE: I saw my father, last night, my mother, too.

RAISSA *(Gently)*: Tell us, Yossele.

Beat.

YOSSELE: They'd been in the earth, and for a long time, they were suffocating, but still they couldn't die.

ABRACHA: It's like that for everyone, it isn't serious.

YOSSELE: My father looked at me, his lips moved, but he couldn't say anything, and still I knew what he wanted to say to me.

RAISSA: He was saying what, your father?

YOSSELE: He was saying that I stole everything, ammunition, bread, air, all the air, it's 'cause of that he can't breathe anymore.

RAISSA: You misunderstood. He couldn't have said that to you.

YOSSELE: He was. That's what he was saying. And for that he turned his back on me. Because I stole everything.

RAISSA: And your mother, was she talking?

YOSSELE: She had too many wrinkles, all over her body, there was dirt inside them.

RAISSA: Me, I believe that if your father, he hasn't been able to die completely, it's 'cause he's worrying about you.

YOSSELE: Then all I have to do is die.

RAISSA: You're stupid, Yossele.

ABRACHA: You can see I'm right, you can't live if you see everything.

Rotburg, or the Valley of Bones

In the distance, flames.

FROBBE: Rotburg, Lieutenant.

CHRISTOPHER: Finally!

GROBBE: The fires from the last load aren't out yet.

THEY *climb down.* GROBBE *and* FROBBE *get out the shovels.*

CHRISTOPHER: Get busy with the graves. I'll take care of *them.* (*To himself*) Hope, until the last moment, let them nibble on hope. Them too, I'll burn, but from the inside.

HE *stays in the cab and from time to time will play the harmonica. In the truck,* YOSSELE, *even older and more stooped, prays.*

ABRACHA (*Visiting*): Still praying, your Yossele?

RAISSA (*Old*): Of course.

ABRACHA: He doesn't see everything anymore, then?

RAISSA: I don't know. He barely speaks anymore.

ABRACHA: You ready, for the Opera?

RAISSA: Almost. I even went to the hairdresser.

ABRACHA: Gotta say it doesn't help.

RAISSA: Hey!

ABRACHA: Much.

RAISSA: And your music, they're still not playing it yet?

ABRACHA: I don't like to talk about it.

RAISSA: Because you failed!

ABRACHA: Because at the heart of it, it doesn't console me.

Beat.

RAISSA: Me, I think his prayers are about nothing but holes.
ABRACHA: And Grandpa? Is he senile?
RAISSA: I don't know. When I'm sad, I look at him, and my sadness, it goes away. Funny, no?
ABRACHA: Funny, yes.

Beat.

RAISSA: He smiles as though he were glad to leave the earth. . . . He's going away, softly.
ABRACHA: Maybe that's what it is, getting old.
RAISSA: Me, the old people I've known, they've drooled, they were crazy. I remember, there was one who went out in the snow, all skinny, all yellow, you could see his bones dance, and well, you won't believe it, but he was jumping rope.
ABRACHA: Those weren't real old people.

CHRISTOPHER *plays the harmonica.*

RAISSA: Give me my hat. The one for holidays. Yossele, it's time.

YOSSELE *mutters.*

ABRACHA: He hasn't held up, poor guy, he saw too much at once.
RAISSA: I knew he was a wimp.
ABRACHA: That's what you said about me, too.
RAISSA: It was true, too, you never did manage to marry. (SHE *laughs*)
ABRACHA: I loved you, Raissa.
RAISSA: Not true.
ABRACHA *(Child's sing-song)*: Is too.
RAISSA: Then why didn't you say so?
ABRACHA: I wasn't the leader.
RAISSA: You waited for us to be old and gray, dummy.

SHE *takes his hand.*

ABRACHA: Don't betray your husband.
RAISSA: And why not?
ABRACHA: Because that's bad.
RAISSA: You're a fine one to talk, you're another one rotten with religion.

ABRACHA: Hey!

RAISSA: Hey what? I say what's true, you're a wimp.

ABRACHA: And you, you're a bad woman.

RAISSA: The real article, you idiot, the real article. I'm the only one who's held up. Me, I saw the black and didn't build walls of fakery or music to hide it, and I still haven't fallen, and I can damn well betray you all at once if I want to, because that's how it is, I allow it.

ABRACHA: You disgust me.

RAISSA: You didn't love me, at times?

ABRACHA: You still disgust me. (HE *coughs*)

RAISSA: More than anything, you're sick, my poor old man, put on your scarf. Oh children, don't shout. For once I'm going out. I'm not going to spend my life doing your wash. I am going to the Opera, and I will knock them dead!

YOSSELE: Idiot.

RAISSA: You weren't praying?

YOSSELE: To forget you.

ABRACHA: Fifteen years of marriage, that's bad for love.

YOSSELE: Twenty years, very bad. You did right to stay a bachelor.

CHRISTOPHER *stops playing, climbs down from the truck.*

ABRACHA *(Anxious)*: Raissa, Yossele, the Opera!

YOSSELE: I'm not going, I hurt too much.

RAISSA: No, wait, I was kidding.

YOSSELE: It's my cancer hurts me.

RAISSA: You think about it too much.

YOSSELE: It hurts too much.

RAISSA: 'Cause you're afraid.

YOSSELE: It's not that, Raissa. I don't feel like anything anymore. Not even the Opera.

RAISSA: Then I won't go either.

YOSSELE: But I want you to. He'd be unhappy to be happy all alone. That hurts, too. Go quickly, Raissa, I'm watching the children.

RAISSA: Watch over him, Grandpa.

FUGUE *absent, smiles. Harmonica.* RAISSA *and* ABRACHA, *at the Opera.*

RAISSA: How beautiful! How beautiful!

ABRACHA: So what if I didn't finish my own!

THEY *"listen."* GROBBE *and* FROBBE *return. Beat. Suddenly,* CHRISTOPHER *opens the door to the truck.*

CHRISTOPHER: Last stop. *(Beat)* All out.

MISTER FUGUE

THEY *obey, slowly, as though numbed.* GROBBE, FROBBE *and* CHRISTOPHER *hit them with their sticks.*

YOSSELE: Don't hit. It wasn't so gay, living. *(To the* OTHERS*)* I'll be better off at the hospital.

HE *climbs down, very old, very dignified.*

CHRISTOPHER: I'm giving you one chance. Frobbe, the rope. Those who can jump it will live. *(To* YOSSELE*)* Start.

GROBBE *and* FROBBE *hold the rope.*

YOSSELE: Don't lie like that, doctor, I'm not going to last much longer.
CHRISTOPHER: You jump, I let you leave, the forest isn't far, you walk, free.
YOSSELE *(Still to his imaginary doctor)*: Don't give me all these drugs, I don't want to go to sleep, I want to see everything, right up to the end, like at a fête.
CHRISTOPHER: You're young, you'll make it to the sea, you'll be saved.
RAISSA *(Visiting the hospital)*: The nurses say it isn't visiting hour, but me, I don't let myself be pushed around. . . . You . . . you feel better, Yossele?
YOSSELE: I'm going away, Raissa.
RAISSA: That's not true. You just have to eat.
YOSSELE: Go get Abracha. I'm going to throw my party.
RAISSA: What party?
YOSSELE: I don't know. Go quickly, I can't breathe anymore.
CHRISTOPHER: It's good, being alive, here, take it, fix the height yourself.

ABRACHA *and* RAISSA, *visiting the hospital.*

YOSSELE: Don't tell me I'm getting better.
ABRACHA: Oh no, Yossele, we know very well that you . . .
RAISSA: We'll go with you, part of the way.
YOSSELE *(Like a poem)*: Speak softly, I hurt everywhere, tonight.

Beat.

ABRACHA: I brought you my opera. I finished it, for you.

YOSSELE, *increasingly feeble, says something incomprehensible.*

RAISSA: Yossele . . . Yossele . . .

Beat.

YOSSELE *(In great pain)*: You remember . . . Raissa? . . . When I said . . . your soul . . . that you were my soul. . . . That it was black . . . it's not. . . . And don't cry, I've had enough of all this . . . *(Beat. To* ABRACHA*)* Sing it to me, your opera. Quickly.

Beat.

ABRACHA: I can't, Yossele.

YOSSELE *(Dying, intones)*: Nothing lasts save erosion . . . *(*HE *"dies")*

CHRISTOPHER: You wanted it, you'll die, for real. Like your father, like your brothers. You've filled this valley with your bones, no prophet will awaken them.

THEY *carry him off and throw him down, in front of the grave.*

ABRACHA *and* RAISSA *(*THEY *sing like a Kaddish)*:
Nothing lasts save erosion
This is the code
You will smile
You will smile
Even if living hurts you
To smile, you will smile
Even if living hurts you
To smile, you will smile
And the grass the birds the stones
Will remember you
And the grass the birds the stones
Will remember you.

After the song, RAISSA, *mute, petrified. Beat.*

ABRACHA: There's nothing to say. Howl, that's all. *(Beat)* Cry. But cry. *(Beat)* Did you go to the cemetery, Raissa? Did you say the prayers?

RAISSA *(Haggard, like an amputee)*: Yes.

ABRACHA: Already more than a year ago. You've got to live, still and all.

RAISSA: Yes.

ABRACHA: It's such a long time. Five years, already! Raissa, gotta live.

RAISSA: Of course.

ABRACHA: Gotta take care of your little children.

RAISSA: It's the morning . . . when I look for him . . . I still believe he's there, I can't live, in the mornings.

CHRISTOPHER: Grol, if you play the dog, I let these two live.

FUGUE *seems not to understand.*

MISTER FUGUE

CHRISTOPHER: Go 'head, bark, they'll live.

Beat. FUGUE, *absent, miserable, senile, plays the dog.*

(Without touching or striking him) Louder. I'm telling you, they'll live.

FUGUE *gets down on all fours, licks, barks.*

(Throwing the doll) Better than that. Go fetch! Hut! But . . . Hut! They'll live, I swear to you, if you put your face in this rag. There . . . nicely. . . . They laughed, right, they laughed! But we're licking it, aren't we, we've got the game now!

RAISSA *(Taking back* TAMAR*):* It's very evil to do that. Get up Mister Fugue. Look, I'm not afraid. Tamar's not afraid of anything anymore. (SHE *brings* TAMAR *back to* FROBBE. *Then turns)* Nor in pain.

CHRISTOPHER *lunges, snatches the doll from* FROBBE'S *hands, throws it under the truck.*

CHRISTOPHER *(Lunatic):* Start up the fires.

The SOLDIERS *move off.* FUGUE, *still a dog, howls, as though* HE *senses death, then softly whines.*

ABRACHA *(Very old, without energy):* It's since the little one had her accident. The driver of the truck, he didn't even dare to come see us.

Beat.

Tumors, trucks, sewers, already it wasn't exactly gay, but that . . . that . . .

RAISSA *(A renewal of violence):* That, that's not just. That's dirt. I don't understand why God does dirt to children.

ABRACHA: There is no God. Only accidents.

Beat.

RAISSA: That should have been dealt to me. I'm not good for anything anymore.

ABRACHA: Me neither, nothing interests me anymore. Not even my opera. I won't finish it.

Beat. Their gestures recall MISTER FUGUE *in the truck.*

RAISSA: We're used up.

Beat. Detached and serene, like MISTER FUGUE *in the truck.*

ABRACHA: It means nothing to me, that I've done nothing.
RAISSA: It's good, going away.

Beat. In the distance, shoot up flames from the fires.

CHRISTOPHER: Hellfire. They're making hellfire.

GROBBE *and* FROBBE *return for* MISTER FUGUE, ABRACHA *and* RAISSA, *who come toward them.*

RAISSA *(Helping* MISTER FUGUE *stand)*: Come, Mister Fugue, we're going now.

THEY *leave by themselves, detached, very old.*

RAISSA: I still would not have wanted to see all this dirt.
ABRACHA *(Sad smile)*: Oh, you know, in a bed or in a valley!

END OF PLAY

Auschwitz

Peter Barnes

Characters

VIKTOR CRANACH
HEINZ STROOP
ELSE JOST
HANS GOTTLEB
GEORG WOCHNER

GOTTLEB'S MOTHER
ABE BIMKO
HYMIE BIEBERSTEIN
TWO SANITATION MEN

Time

Christmas Eve, 1942.

Place

An office in Berlin.

106

The Play

Auschwitz

"Deutschland Über Alles" blares out briefly then fades. Lights come up on an office in WVHA Department Amt C (Building) Oranienburg, Berlin, 1942. An eight-foot high filing unit stretches across half the back wall. Its shelves are stuffed with gray files. Smaller filing units are placed to the right and left. There is a photograph of Adolf Hitler festooned with holly above the door and a Nazi flag in a stand. Nearby is a small cupboard. The executioner's block remains to the left.

VIKTOR CRANACH *sits at his desk dictating a memo to* FRÄULEIN ELSE JOST *while an elderly clerk,* HEINZ STROOP, *replaces a file on the shelves, and returns to his desk, which is next to* FRÄULEIN JOST'S.

CRANACH: WVHA Amt C1 (Building) to WVHA Amt D1/1. Your reference ADS/MNO our reference EZ/14/102/01. Copies WVHA Amt D IV/2, Amt D IV/4: RSHA OMIII: Reich Ministry PRV 24/6D. Component CP3(m) described in regulation E(5) serving as Class I or Class II appliances and so constructed as to comply with relevant requirements of regulations L2(4) and (6), L8 (4) and (7). Component CP3(m) shall comply with DS 4591/1942 for the purpose of regulation E(5) when not falling in with the definition of Class I and II. There shall be added after reference CP 116 Part 2: 1941 the words "as read with CP 116 Addendum 2: 1942.·. . . ." Six copies, Fräulein Jost. Dispatch immediately. "Will comply with requirements of regulations L2(4) and (6) L8(4) and (7)!" I don't mince words. I've always believed in calling a CF/83 a CF/83. How dare Amt D1/1 send me an unauthorized, unsigned KG70? Gottleb's trying to cut our throats behind our backs. He's out to destroy this department. (HE *chuckles*) "Component CP3(m) shall comply with DS 4591/1942 for the purposes of Regulation E(5)!" A *hit!* . . . A word with you, Fräulein. As civil servants we must be ready at any time to answer for our administrative actions. Actions based solely on past actions, precedents. It's therefore essential we keep accurate records. That's why everything has to be written down. It's the basis of our existence. Words on paper: Memo to Amt D III; memo to Sturnbannführer Burger, Amt D V etc., etc. Without them we can't function. They tell us what's been done, what we can do, what we have to do and what we are. The civilization of the Third Reich'll be constructed from the surviving administrative records at Oranienburg, 1942 A.D. Unless of course they've the misfortune to dig up a memorandum of yours, Fräulein. (HE *picks up a memo from his desk*) Will you please retype this. I know the first step's hard, but once you've tried it you'll enjoy using commas. Paper size A4 not A3 and the margins should be nine elite character spaces, seven pica on the left and six elite, five pica on the right.

ELSE: Naturally, Herr Cranach, if you look for mistakes you'll find them. (SHE *takes memo*) My OS 472 states I can do shorthand, typing and filing—but not all simultaneously. We're overworked and underfed. I can't keep Mother and me fit on a daily ration of a hundred and twelve grams of meat, eight grams of butter, forty of sugar and shop signs saying: "Wreathes and crosses—no potatoes."

CRANACH: Please, Fräulein! Remember, where there's a will there's a Gestapo.

ELSE: Coming to work this morning, I stopped to pull in my belt. Some idiot asked me what I was doing. I said, "Having breakfast."

CRANACH: I hear they're experimenting with new dishes. Fried termites from the Upper Volga and grilled agouti with green peppers.

ELSE: They can't be worse than those dehydrated soups. They actually clean the saucepans while they're cooking.

CRANACH: It doesn't worry me too much. I've got worms and anything's good enough for them. I can recommend Dr. Schmidt's liver pills to alleviate any deficiency in your diet, Fräulein. They'll stop your hair from falling out too. . . . Have you searched this morning yet?

ELSE *shakes her head and while* CRANACH *continues talking,* THEY *all carefully search the office—*ELSE *and* STROOP *the filing shelves,* CRANACH *round his desk.*

Everyone realizes, Fräulein, our department has special problems. It's why Obergruppenführer Dr. Kammler had us upgraded and seconded from the Reich Ministry. We're now dealing with an estimated 74,000 administrative units in the three complexes in Upper Silesia alone, instead of 15,000 of just a year ago, and that's only the beginning. At the moment we still lack staff, equipment, space. You know I've been waiting two months for my own office, *ahh.* (*HE finds something stuck under his desk and pulls it out: it is a bugging device, attached to an electric cord.* HE *barks into it*) And interdepartmental jealousies don't help!

HE *pulls the cord savagely and there is a faint cry of pain far off; without pausing,* HE *takes a pair of clippers from his desk, neatly cuts the cord and puts the bugging device into his drawer.*

As the first non-volunteers to work in WVHA, naturally Gottleb and Brigadeführer Glucks and the other hard-liners want us out. The knock in the night, the unexpected Foreign Service Allowance, the quick transfer to the Occupied Eastern Territories!

THEY *shudder.*

We're under great pressure, but we'll triumph, just as our armies did last month at Stalingrad and El Alamein.
STROOP: Rissoles. Soya-bean rissoles with onion sauce à la Riefenstahl. I have 'em every day for lunch in the staff canteen, bon appétit. Very filling, Fräulein.
ELSE: I must try them.
STROOP: Early in the week.

STROOP *sighs loudly.* CRANACH *groans and* ELSE *sadly shakes her head.* STROOP *sighs,* CRANACH *groans and* ELSE *shakes her head again.*

CRANACH: That's enough. We musn't talk politics. It's too dangerous. Fräulein, bring me the material on the CP 3(m) tender.

THEY *resume work.* STROOP *picks up two files with memos attached and takes them to* CRANACH, *while* ELSE *goes to the files.*

STROOP: What you just said, sir, about helping others, reminded me of Oberdienstleiter Brack.

HE *places the files in front of* CRANACH *who glances at them.*

You remember Brack, sir. OMTC transferred to Resort K2 RMEUL. Big man, fat eyes, but made up for it with a bad cough. Almost as eloquent as you, sir, on the ideals of the service. Each man giving of his best, blending with the best other men give. His mind was such, I think, he could've been a world famous surgeon.

CRANACH: I remember him. Tragic case. He always wanted to help suffering humanity but never had the necessary detachment. It must've been his experiences in the Great War; kept turning over corpses in his mind. I'm sure that's why when Bouhler set up the Foundation for Institutional Care at T4, he applied for the post of Oberdienstleiter and became a member of the Party. *(HE signs the two memos attached to the top of the files)* All those cretins, mongoloids, parapalytics, sclorotics and diarrectics—who doesn't want to root out pain? It's not true Goethe died peacefully, he screamed for three days and nights in fear of death. But there was no pain or fear at T4 under Brack, only five cc's of hydrocyanic acid. Incurables were finally cured. It was all repugnant to me on moral grounds, but I must say Brack always stressed the mercy in mercy killing.

ELSE *comes back with three files.*

ELSE: Cardinal Galen denounced it from the pulpit. Only God can play God, make a tree, choose who lives, who dies. My mother would've been a beneficiary of Herr Brack's social surgery. It's true she's eighty-three and has developed whining into an art unsurpassed in Western Europe. But it's a sin to deprive the sinner of a last chance to reconcile herself to God.

CRANACH: Public opinion was completely opposed to the euthanasia program, even when Brack pointed out its benefits were only available to German-born nationals. The Führer—make-him-happy-he-deserves-it—had to drop the whole project. You see, despite what our enemies say, he can only govern with the consent of the German people.

HE *hands the files back to* STROOP.

STROOP: It broke Herr Brack. He was prematurely retired on half-pay and a non-recurrent service gratuity. It could happen to any of us! You pull yourself up hand over hand but someone's always there with a knife, waiting to cut the rope. No one understands the arbitrary terror we all live under nowadays in the Third Reich—redundancy, compulsory retirement with loss of pension rights! *(HE returns to his desk)* Today Herr Brack just sits in his room, unable to hear the word Madagascar without screaming.

ELSE: *Requiescat in pace.* Amen. (SHE *has finished checking the files and puts them on* CRANACH*'s desk)* The tenders for appliances CP3 (m). Krupps AG of Essen, Tesch and Stabenow of Hamburg and Degesch of Dessau.

CRANACH *opens the files, while* ELSE *crosses to the small cupboard to prepare coffee.*

CRANACH: Herr Stroop, I'd like your opinion. Obergruppenführer Dr. Kammler'll want the department's recommended choice. Krupps's DS 6/310 tender's a high twenty thousand marks. They claim lack of trained personnel on the site justifies pre-mix concreting and the installation of chuting and pumping. I'm not prepared to encourage wild experiments in new building techniques at government's expense. I favor Tesch and Stabenow.

STROOP: I agree, sir. They've proved most satisfactory. Amt D already've a contract with them for two tons of Kyklon B rat poison a month. Two tons. There can't be that many rats in the whole of Germany.

CRANACH: Kyklon B isn't being used to kill rats but to discredit this department. *We* built those complexes in Upper Silesia. If Gottleb and Amt D prove they're overrun with vermin we're blamed. Q.E.D. Of course that's not Tesch and Stabenow's fault.

STROOP: I agree, sir.

CRANACH: However, giving them another government contract so soon after the last might raise doubts as to our integrity.

STROOP: I agree, sir.

CRANACH: Is there anything you don't agree with, Herr Stroop?

STROOP: Unemployment. I'm near retirement. You can't please everyone, so I find it best to keep pleasing my superiors. But I do wonder, sir, if it's wise to dismiss Krupps's tender? The firm's shown undeviating loyalty to the Party since '33. Old Gustav Krupps was awarded the War Cross of Merit and Young Alfred's Party number's a low 89627. They have influence.

CRANACH: I'm not influenced by influence. Krupps've bad labor relations. They're only paying their foreign workers seventy pfennigs a day and refusing to build them a company brothel despite a UD 84763 directive.

ELSE *puts a cup of coffee on his desk and one on* STROOP*'s.*

In the old days, politicians were despised, administrators revered. Now politicians're sacrosanct and we've become the whipping boys of a public frustrated by wartime shortage and delays. They say we're divorced from the glorious reality of the National Socialist struggle. Our behavior must therefore be seen to be above reproach. The final decision's the Obergruppenführer's but this department'll recommend Tesch and Stabenow for the CP3(m) contract. *(HE drinks the coffee and grimaces)* I like my coffee weak but this is helpless.

ELSE: It's the new grain substitute. Secretly scented, *aromatically* flavored! Unique—no coffee, all aroma. Wait till you try the new Führer-make-him-happy-he-deserves-it cigarettes. Filtered bootlaces. One puff, you're deaf. . . . Two marks Herr Cranach.

CRANACH *grunts.*

For the bottle of schnapps Herr Wochner's bringing over. It's tradition to have a drink in the office on Christmas Eve.

CRANACH: I don't approve, but as it's tradition.

HE *opens a little purse, carefully takes out two marks and gives them to her.*

ELSE: I know the Führer-make-him-happy-he-deserves-it has given the nation a new set of holy days to celebrate, like the National Day of Mourning and the Anniversary of the Munich Putsch, but they don't quite take the place of Christmas. Two marks, Herr Stroop.

STROOP: When she was alive my wife was so fat she never had a clear view of her feet. She loved food and jolly Christmases, cutting up apples, baking white bread, covering the fruit trees with a cloth. Good eating, drinking, sleeping, without 'em it's just staying on earth, not living.

HE *gives* ELSE *the money.*

Two marks for schnapps. Sixty for butter. Fifty percent on income tax, no lights in the street at night, no heating during the day. I'm spending this Christmas lying in bed holding a candle in my hands, staring at the folds and edges.

ELSE: I thought of praying to God at Midnight Mass for better times, but I know the Führer-make-him-happy-he-deserves-it doesn't like anyone going over his head.

CRANACH: The State doesn't acknowledge God exists. If He did, I'm certain Adolf Hitler'd be notified before anyone else. Even so, concessions to Christ's birth've been made. Order 7334 Kd 10 grants a Christmas present of one pair of stockings for every woman and one tie for every man over and above the rationed quota. Stockings for every woman, a cravat for every man. National Socialism works!

STROOP: But there'll be more black-edged Q4928's posted this year than Christmas presents: "We regret to inform you your husband/brother/son/father has been killed in action defending the Fatherland."

CRANACH: The strain is beginning to tell. I see it daily in the *Morganpost* obituary notices. The bereaved're no longer observing the Reichsinnenminister's Decree 77/B1 of 5th April '42 that all such notices must be a uniform, ninety-six millimeters broad and eighty long. But I've measured some of the latest obits and most're over *two hundred* millimeters long and *one hundred and twenty* broad! When my son was killed I could've written things: "Fate has ended our waiting, our hope. We received the news our beloved son Joachim Cranach died from his wounds. All our joy buried in Russian earth . . . love him, mourn him, never forget . . . we live out the rest in grief . . ." and so on and so on. Instead I wrote, "In proud sadness we learnt our son Joachim Cranach was killed in action in the East, liberating the Ukraine from the Ukrainians. Send no flowers." That's under ninety-six millimeters broad, eighty long. Strictly in accordance with Decree 77/B1. What more to say. They pulled off his boots, dug a shallow grave and it was all over with.

ELSE: They're selling miniature "hero-graves" for four marks forty, at Kepa's, complete with tiny wreaths. Six for ten marks. Your wife might like one for her dressing table. (SHE *takes his empty cup*) Your son died at twenty-two, my mother lives, eighty-three and clinging fast. (SHE *collects* STROOP*'s cup and takes them to the cupboard*) All're dying, yet she survives with all the frail charm of an iron foundry.

CRANACH *(Opening a file)*: The German people've always preferred strong government to self-government. So why do they complain of too many decrees and regulations? It's one of the benefits of war. Usually our lives're so muddled that we don't know what we want, want what we don't want, don't want what we want. We're tormented by choice. Do you find it difficult to obey decrees and regulations, Fräulein?

ELSE *(Putting dirty cups in the cupboard)*: No, fortunately I'm a Roman Catholic and Roman doctrine forbids any kind of dissent. Obedience is regarded as a principle of righteous conduct. So I look on National Socialism as Catholicism with the Christianity left out.

CRANACH: We've had enough choices. We chose well because all choices're made for us. We've rules to live by which tell us what, when, where, how: no painful choices left to make except in sleep.

STROOP: German cheese gives me nightmares. I keep dreaming I'm punching Herr Gottleb in the face, though it's difficult from a kneeling position. The nightmares've got more frightening lately. I've started wanting to protest about conditions. I fight it but I can't resist. I must make my stand without the slightest "but." So I finally do it. I put a blank piece of paper into an envelope and send it to the

Reich Führer himself. Afterwards I feel so proud! It's terrible. I wake up trembling with fright. I must stop sleeping with my eyes closed.

CRANACH: You certainly can't afford to've nightmares Herr Stroop till you retire. You've taken a personal oath of loyalty to the Führer-make-him-happy-he-deserves-it. He'll know; he has devices . . .

HE *stops and sniffs suspiciously.* ELSE *and* STROOP *are moving to the filing shelves, but* HE *gestures to them to halt.* THEY *watch him slowly rise and move toward the door, sniffing the air loudly.* HE *pauses at the door for a moment, before flinging it open to catch* HANS GOTTLEB, *a chunky man with a Hitler moustache, crouching in the doorway, obviously listening at the keyhole.*

Gottleb, as I live and breathe!

GOTTLEB: Not for long if I can help it. (HE *straightens up and, gripping his briefcase, marches in, clicking his heels and jerking up his right arm in a Nazi salute)* Heil Hitler!

ELSE, STROOP *and* CRANACH *(Raising their arms):* Heil Hitler!

ELSE *and* STROOP *lower their arms but* CRANACH *and* GOTTLEB, *facing each other, keep theirs stiffly raised;* CRANACH's *arm is lower than* GOTTLEB's.

GOTTLEB: According to Hoflich of the *Schwarzes Korps* it's customary when Heiling Hitler to raise the right arm at an angle so the palm of the hand is visible.

CRANACH: Hoflich also wrote, "If one encounters a person socially inferior, when Heiling Hitler, then the right arm is raised only to eye-level, so the palm of the hand is hidden."

GOTTLEB: Socially inferior! Why you sclerotic pen-pusher, my brother's a close friend of Julius Streicher, Gauleiter of Franken.

CRANACH: Your sister too, I hear.

GOTTLEB: I warned Brigadeführer Glucks about you and your kind. He didn't listen. What gifts I've thrown before swine. You were seconded, didn't volunteer. Now you're a malignant virus in the healthy body of the SS—WVHA. You've no business here with your damn bureaucratic principles of promotion by merit and such. Merit, merit, I shit on *merit.* We old Party men didn't fight in the streets, gutters filled with our dead, to build a world based on merit. What's merit got to do with it? We weren't appointed on merit. Take merit as a standard and we'll all be OUT.

CRANACH: Gottleb, a man with a low forehead like yours has no right to criticize. Without more Upper Grade and Administrative Class officials who've risen on merit, Amt C&D'll collapse under the increased workload. 622.75 units per day're now being transported from all over Europe to Upper Silesia. We must've more trained civil servants to deal with 'em, not wild-eyed amateurs. Stand aside Gottleb and let us professionals do their job.

GOTTLEB: We scarred veterans're not going to be bypassed by you arse-licking, crypto-homo flunkies.

ELSE: Herr Gottleb, you haven't been reading *Das Reich*. This is Politeness Month. Everyone has to help restore gladness, kindness and courtesy to the German scene. The Party's sponsoring a contest to find the politest men and women in Berlin. Dr. Göbbels himself's presenting prizes to the most successful.

STROOP: "Even though you're German.
And it will come hard.
Just to learn to say you're sorry.
And win a week's supply of lard."

That won third prize. Two theatre tickets to *Sparrows in the Hand of God*.

GOTTLEB: Should be crushed. Like politeness. I shit on politeness. It stinks of philo-Semite decadence, foul mind curves there. Let Judah perish! Politeness'll undermine our whole society. You can't give orders lisping, "please," "please," "thank you," "thank you," and the New Order's built on orders. Politeness is anti-German. Bluff rudeness, stimulating abuse, is the true Aryan way, hard in the bone. We must tear out from ourselves, the soft, the liquid noxious juices, *ahh* . . .

HE *grunts with pain as* HE *attempts to lower his stiff arm which, together with* CRANACH's *is still raised in a Nazi salute; as* HE *pulls it down with his other hand,* CRANACH *wincingly does the same before crossing to his desk.*

We didn't need politeness when we shot and clubbed our way through the beer halls of Munich! Ah what days—sometimes I just want to be what I was, when I wanted to be what I am now. And we don't need politeness to crush the Bolshevik-Imperialistic half-breed armies in Asia and North Africa.

ELSE *and* STROOP *have resumed searching for files as* GOTTLEB *crosses to* CRANACH, *takes out a document from his briefcase and reads quickly.*

"All Section Heads WVHA (IV/QV) No. 44822/42 Obergruppen-führer Pohhl. Further to the implementation of the executive solutions agreed at the Wannsee Conference Sec L (IV/QU) No. 37691/42 the attached document 'General Instructions on Measures Sec. L (IV/QU)' is circulated herewith by hand and the signature of Department Heads is required on receipt of said copy." *(*HE *gives* CRANACH *a form to sign)* You'll like paragraph fifteen, Cranach. Just your style. (HE *opens the document at another page and reads)* "Future cases of death shall be given consecutive Roman numbers with consecutive subsidiary Arabic numbers, so that the first case of death is numbered Roman numeral I/1, the second Roman numeral I/2, up to Roman numeral I/185. Thereafter cases of death shall be numbered Roman numeral II from Roman numeral II/1 to 185. Each new year will start with the Roman numeral I/1." The dead talking to the dead. You bureaucratic tapeworms suck the color from life. Our work here's a crusade or it's nothing. We need images of light to fire the mind, words to set the heart salmon-leaping. 'Stead we're given Roman numerals followed by consecutive subsidiary Arabic numerals, Roman numeral I/1 to Roman numeral I/185.

ELSE *and* STROOP *join them with files.*

CRANACH: This is war, Gottleb, a million words've died on us. We no longer believe in a secure sentence structure. Neutral symbols've become the safest means of communication. I certainly endorse the use of coded symbols rather than consecutive numbering in recording cases of death. It's more concise and less emotive.

ELSE: In any case, Amt D II/3 is Statistics and Auditing, Herr Gottleb. We're Amt C 1—planning, costing and supervising of WVHA building projects.

GOTTLEB: Fräulein, you're a woman who could easily drive me to stop drinking.

STROOP: Deaths and paragraph fifteen isn't any of our business.

GOTTLEB: Ah, Stroop, still awake this late in the morning? Cranach, this office is only held together by the laws of inertia. Actually I've come over about the tenders for appliances CP 3(m) described in regulation E(5)—Amt D wants the contract to be given to Krupps AG for past favors.

CRANACH: Amt D wants? Amt D can continue to want. The contract'll be given strictly on merit. *Merit*, Gottleb, not on favors past, present or future.

GOTTLEB *(Taking out a memo)*: Confirmation of this request from Brigadeführer Glucks. Memo FC/867.

CRANACH *(Showing him a memo)*: Amt C operates independent of Amt D. Obergruppenführer's memo JN 72.

GOTTLEB *(Producing a second memo)*: JN 72 or not. I've got a 62 KG!

CRANACH *(Flourishing a second memo)*: And I've a 17Q!

GOTTLEB *(Producing a third memo)*: One 3H!

CRANACH: Two spades.

AUSCHWITZ

ELSE: Four no-trumps.
STROOP: I pass.
ALL: Root it out!

CRANACH waves STROOP and ELSE back to their desks.

CRANACH: There'll be no favors here. Thanks to favors received and given, bribery's become *the* organizing principle of the Third Reich.

GOTTLEB: You elongated, bespectacled rodent. Without bribery you could never attract the better class of people into politics. Bribery's the reward for those who helped the cause and now need help. Bribery's the one expression of gratitude people appreciate. But you're one of those stiff-arsed moralists who see a favor as an opportunity to show their piss-green incorruptibility rather than their gratitude. Damnable petit-bourgeois morality. I shit on morality. It stiffens the brain, dries out life's juices. I've seen it ruin thousands of good men in my time: morality, virtue, boredom, syphilis. Downhill all the way. Corruption has more natural justice to it, not based on your shit-spat merit or morality. Anyone can take his share if he's strong or weak enough. It binds all men together. That's the National Socialist way. Nature's way. All things come to corruption, our bodies too: corruption.

ELSE: But "this corruptible must put on incorruption and this mortal must put on immortality." First Episode of Paul to the Corinthians.

GOTTLEB: No priest-talk Fräulein! Fat-gutted clowns with their mitres and jewels and their Holy Trinity of rent, interest and profit. You ask 'em to do something religious and they take a collection. Two thousand years they've been preaching love and charity and when a continent of corpses've shown how bankrupt they are, some idiots still look at 'em and long for goodness. I shit on goodness! If there's a good God why is there old age and baldness, eh?

CRANACH: God or no God, corruption turns the best to the worst. If I granted favors out of fear or greed, I'd betray my son charred black and the other dead who fell asleep twenty-two degrees centigrade below. I'd betray all those good Germans fighting from Benghazi to the Caucasus, so that the enslaved millions of Europe can be free.

No one has noticed GEORG WOCHNER, a young man in a long, weighed-down overcoat, slip in.

WOCHNER: Heil Hitler!

ALL stand to attention and exchange Nazi salutes.

ALL: Heil Hitler!

WOCHNER (*Consulting a small notebook*): Amt C 1 (Building) December 24th. Herr Cranach. One bottle of schnapps. Six marks.

HE *opens his coat to show the right hand side is lined with bottles;* HE *removes one. As* ELSE *gets the money,* STROOP *hastily resumes work at his desk and* CRANACH *clears his throat.*

GOTTLEB: Count your days, Cranach! That's black market schnapps. You're dealing in blacks. And I have witnesses. This room's wired. (HE *shouts under the desk*) You hear that Winklemann? He's dealing in blacks! Blacks!

CRANACH *takes out the bugging device* HE *cut off and silently hands it to* GOTTLEB, *who stares.*

Destroying government property too. That's a serious criminal offense, Cranach. You'll be cropped— CROPPED. Regulation 47632/48 imposes the same penalties on buyers as well as sellers of black goods. We've just slaughtered a Bavarian butcher found guilty of illegal slaughtering; hung his carcass up till it turned black as the rest of his meat. I'll see you all hung up turning black, black, black! (*Chanting*) "Oh let the blood spurt from the knife."

ELSE *has paid* WOCHNER, *who ticks off the amount in his notebook, unconcerned.*

WOCHNER: Herr Gottleb, will you take your bottles now or should I deliver them to your office?

GOTTLEB: Give me two. You bring the rest. None of your dishwater bathmix now.

GOTTLEB *crosses as* WOCHNER *opens his coat again.*

CRANACH: Leak into another universe, Gottleb! You're up to your armpits in blacks!

GOTTLEB: Don't compare your case of blacks with mine. You only buy schnapps to drink, I to relax tired bodies, tight minds. (HE *gives* WOCHNER *money*) My men need compassionate leave, the same as other front-liners; I give it to 'em in a bottle.

WOCHNER: Five at six marks is thirty marks. Two marks short.

GOTTLEB (*Giving him two more marks*): I've been watching you, Wochner. (HE *mimes counting banknotes*) Licking your forefinger and thumb flick-

flick-flick-one-two-three-four-five. That's not the Aryan way of counting money. It's a sign of philo-Semite blood, counting money Panza-fast. Jew-blood, Jew-signs. Yes, their signs're everywhere if you've a nose for 'em. Biological proof of decadence. Prussian hair grows out spiky straight. But Czech moustaches all droop downwards. That's a sure sign they've got degenerate Mongol blood. Stroop! Give your face a blank expression so I can tell you're not thinking! Why aren't you in the army, Wochner?

WOCHNER: Just lucky, I have renal diabetes, cardiac murmur, crutch palsey, bat's wing lupus, Speighel hernia and Brigadeführer Glucks as an uncle. *(HE gives two bottles to* GOTTLEB*)* I'll leave the rest of your order in your office.

CRANACH: This one still has work to do.

HE *indicates the door, but* WOCHNER *does not move.*

ELSE: Herr Cranach, it's customary to offer the black schnapps supplier a drink to toast the Fatherland and victory.

GOTTLEB: No one'll toast victory here, Wochner, even the women're defeatist to a man. They only drink for pleasure; patriotism's dead. Come with me and I'll show you patriotic drinking, gut-heaving, bladder-bursting drinking, real German drinking.

CRANACH: As it's the custom. Herr Stroop, will you help Fräulein Jost with the bottle?

While ELSE *gets out the glasses from the cupboard,* STROOP *opens the schnapps.*

WOCHNER: Can I interest you in anything else? I carry a wide range of blacks from liberated capitals of Europe. *(*HE *opens his coat and takes various articles out of pockets on the left-hand side)* Silk scarves, Chanel perfume and toilet water, fifty marks. Fur muff, Paris label. Dutch butter. Pickled herrings from Warsaw, fifteen marks a jar. *(*HE *brings out a flat case filled with gold and diamond rings, which* HE *opens concertina-fashion)* Something cheaper? Confiscated wedding rings. Gold. For you, thirteen marks, and I'm not making a pfennig profit. Twelve? Ten? Any offers? Here's a novelty that's selling well, very risqué. Hammer-and-sickle badges. Every one guaranteed taken by hand from the body of a dead Russian soldier. Look their blood's still on some of them.

GOTTLEB *examines a badge.*

There's a human tragedy in each one of those badges. I'm practically giving them away.

CRANACH: Herr Wochner, this isn't an Afro-Oriental street market. Regulation AC 84/736(b) forbids these premises to be used for private business. Is this real silk?

HE *picks up a necktie as* GOTTLEB *scratches the dry blood off a badge and tastes it on the tip of his tongue.*

GOTTLEB: Russian blood? This isn't Russian blood. I've tasted Russian blood. I know about blood. We've given the world the salvation of blood. And it sends us trinkets, beads, worthless trash.

HE *throws the badge back as* STROOP *comes over with drinks for him and* CRANACH. ELSE *serves* WOCHNER, *who has moved slightly to one side.*

WOCHNER: Fräulein, I'm looking for a wife—anybody's wife. What would it take to make you fall in love with me?

ELSE: A magician. My father said, work hard and be a good girl. You can always change your mind when you're older. Now I'm older and it's too late. I've reached the age where I'm beginning to find sex a pain in the arse.

WOCHNER: That means you're doing it the wrong way.

CRANACH *(Raising his glass)*: A toast. To the Fatherland and Victory.

ALL: The Fatherland and Victory!

THEY *drink, stamp their right legs convulsively and gasp.*

WOCHNER *(Hoarsely)*: Good isn't it. Straight from the Hamburg boat.

GOTTLEB: Scraped off the sides. I can feel my toes exploding. Don't sip it like a virgin with lockjaw, Cranach. *(HE mimes)* Drink it in one, head back, mouth open wide so it doesn't touch your teeth and dissolve the enamel. *(HE crosses and examines the bottle)* Smooth. But you've got it wrong again, Cranach. "To the Fatherland and Victory" that's not a true National Socialist toast; the Gestapo could have a man's hanging testicles wired for less. I'll show you a true National Socialist toast. Listen. Learn.

Before CRANACH *can stop him* HE *fills his glass and raises it.*

A toast: to the Fatherland? *(HE drinks, stamps his leg convulsively and gasps)* Sm-o-o-th. *(HE immediately pours another glass and raises it)* A toast: Victory! *(HE drinks, stamps and gasps)* Sm-o-o-th. It's important to take

AUSCHWITZ

your time, Cranach. Doesn't the Fatherland merit a full toast? Doesn't our victory?

CRANACH: And doesn't he who is Victory itself? We've forgotten him. Let's drink to the man who made us what we are today.

Before GOTTLEB *can protest,* HE *opens one of* GOTTLEB'*s bottles.*

I know you'll contribute to this dedication, Gottleb.

GOTTLEB *scowls as* CRANACH *pours out the drinks.*

To the being who's given us a new center of being, around whose head the cosmic forces gather into a swelling new order.

STROOP: Who loves us and forgives all that's weakly human in us.

ELSE: Who knows no sacrifice he would not let us make to be worthy of him.

GOTTLEB: Who has laid the axe to the sacred trees, told the whole world, "Step out of our sunlight."

WOCHNER: Who turns the dross of pain into the gold of serenity.

THEY *all turn to the portrait of Hitler above the entrance and raise their glasses.*

ALL: The Führer—make-him-happy etc., etc.

THEY *drink, stamp their right legs and gasp hoarsely.*

Sm-o-o-th.

THEY *sing the Wagnerian choral opening of* Die Meistersinger von Nürnberg.

"As our Saviour came to thee, willingly baptized to be. Yielded to the cross his breath, ransomed us from sin and death. May we too baptized be, worthy of his agony. Prophet, preacher, holy teacher. Send us by the hand, home to Jordan's strand."

CRANACH: Wrong again, Gottleb. No sacred trees're axed. On the contrary, their roots're watered, the status quo preserved. National Socialism is part of the great conservative tradition. It is based on solid middle-class values. Just as the Führer-make-him-happy etc. embodies our hopes for "more" and our fear that when we get it, someone will try and take it away from us. Listen to him, speaking to the Reichstag May 21st '35. Noon. "As National Socialists we are filled with admiration and respect for the great achievements of the past, not only in our own nation but far beyond it. We are happy to belong to the European community of culture which has inspired the modern world."

GOTTLEB: Wrong again, Cranach. You only understood the words. But the sounds? What about the sounds? (HE *imitates the harsh nasal sound of Hitler's stabbing, lower middle-class, Austrian accent with its brutal, seductively hysterical, rhythms*) Szzztt nrrrr vrrr rrrchhhhh dddssss rrrrkkk rurrxxx ptsch nui KAAAA grrss iiiiichh R REECHTTT *RKK!*

A mighty chorus chants "Sieg Heil! Sieg Heil!"

Rrrrrrrkkk hhhh dddttss vvllkkk rrrchh . . . wrrrrkkk AAA! Ssrrt rrttt srrrr MPPFF gmuuuuttt cccHH dddrrr essskkkkk ZZZSWCH uuuuunn utt isssss KRR KRRKK SCHWEE SCHWRK SCHWRK sss uttu SCHWRK! SCHWRK! GROO SCHWRK!

THEY *all join in as the unseen audience roars* "Sieg Heil! Sieg Heil!"

Status quo, status quo, I shit on your status quo. Our world was dying of your status quo covered with status quo like horse mange. No air! No air! We flung the old order out of orbit, swept away the stiff-collars, monocles and cutaways, gave Germany social fluidity, permanent institutional anarchy. Before, our lives lacked the larger significance, he filled it with drama; there's always something happening in the Third Reich. He gave us faith in the sword, not in the Cross; that foul Semite-servility, that "other-cheek" brigade with their "Hit me! Hit me!" Our hand goes out to all men, but always doubled up. You middle-class bed-wetters squeak about mercy— that's decadence; hardness, greater hardness!

STROOP: The truth is, as Jews can be simultaneously scum and dregs, so National Socialism can simultaneously embody revolutionary and conservative principles and black and white the same color gray. That's the miracle of it. (HE *slumps into his chair*)

WOCHNER: The true miracle is that a man with renal diabetes, cardiac murmur, crutch palsey, bat's wing lupus and Spieghel hernia can prosper, not despite his afflictions but because of 'em. And I want to see another miracle, when this country's business'll only be business. Nothing'll stop us then, we'll be the paymasters of Europe. It'll be easy. No more uncertainties, we'll be able to judge a man's worth at a glance by his credit rating, know right from wrong, success from failure, by the amount of money in our pockets. Money's a necessity I've always placed just ahead of breathing.

CRANACH: Wochner, I shall ignore you with every fiber of my being. We Germans've always had the divine capacity for visions which transcended the merely commercial. That's why the Reichführer SS Heinrich Himmler himself, decreed that our first complex should be built in the forest outside Weimar, the very seat of German classical tradition. Didn't he leave Goethe's famous oak tree standing there in the middle of the compound and constructed the ramps, and block houses around it? You see, even in times like these, in places like that, for people like them, German culture is made available to all. We think transcendentally. We raise our eyes to the hills; the soul, the soul, the German soul! And you talk of money, credit ratings.

GOTTLEB: Materialistic filth! People spending money they haven't earned, to buy things they don't need, to impress neighbors who don't care. In the old days Wochner we'd've washed your mouth out with prussic acid. Our nation'll never descend to prosperity. I shit on prosperity. Hideous self-sacrifice is our way of life. You know nothing of sacrifice or suffering Wochner. What with renal diabetes, cardiac murmur, crutch palsey, bat's wing lupus and Spieghel hernia, you've had it too soft. Soft! Herr Cranach is right. You can only be ignored. (HE *takes another drink*) After a time this stuff grows on you, like leaf mold. Herr Cranach, I think we should examine memos FC/867, 62KG and 3H regarding CP3(m). If you're agreeable that is?

CRANACH *nods, crosses and sits at his desk.* GOTTLEB *stands beside him.* THEY *examine the papers together and drink their schnapps.* WOCHNER *shrugs and starts putting the goods back into his coat with* ELSE'S *help.*

WOCHNER: My fairest lady, may I offer you my arm and company tonight?

ELSE: I'm not fair, no lady, and I don't need an escort to see me home. I know men, when they're soft they're hard, when they're hard they're soft. I expect nothing from 'em, and that's what I always get— nothing. One of my fiancés once bought me a beautiful ring with a place for a lovely diamond in it.

WOCHNER: I had a fiancée but we broke it off on religious grounds. I worshipped money and she didn't have any.

ELSE: I've heard of your effect on women. Just being near you gives a girl hives.

WOCHNER: Women always judge with their bodies instead of their minds. I'll come for you tonight.

ELSE: "I'll come for you tonight." Act like a lover if you want to be one. Tell me, "the brightness of your cheek outshines the stars, one glance from your eyes outweighs the wisdom of the world." Woo me, say something beautiful.

WOCHNER: One jar of Kiel salt herrings. Two kilos of real coffee, four fresh eggs. One tin of skimmed milk.

ELSE: The answer's no. No. No. No.

WOCHNER: Three kilos of butter. Six of lard. One real woollen blanket. Three kilos of bacon.

ELSE *(Quickly)*: Three kilos of bacon plus the woollen blanket!

WOCHNER: I had Herr Sauckel's wife for three kilos of bacon. If I'd thrown in a woollen blanket I'd've got Herr Sauckel too. Only promise you won't talk of love while we make it. I desire you, enjoy you, utilize you. Love doesn't come into it. (HE *takes her hand*) I kiss your hand.

ELSE: Tonight it'll be all over, fortunately. Bring the goods with you or it's no trade.

WOCHNER *nods and turns to the others.*

WOCHNER: Gentlemen, I have to go.

CRANACH: In the end haven't we all.

WOCHNER *bows slightly and exits, his coat still weighing him down.* ELSE *pours herself another drink.*

STROOP: There were always as many women available when I was young as there are now. But what I hate about life is there's always a new lot enjoying 'em. There's nothing sadder than an old roué with nothing left to rue.

CRANACH: Was Wochner ever in the Hitler Youth? Tough as leather, swift as whippets, hard as Krupp steel. Somehow I can't see him sitting round a campfire singing the "Horst Wessel" song and dreaming of being a Gauleiter like any normal German boy.

GOTTLEB: Wochner's time's short. Brigadeführer Glucks won't be able to save him. I've seen to it. Certain Party officials know about his filthy empire of blacks—and they want their share. Any moment now that tide-mark won't be the only thing around his neck.

ELSE: Please, not until after I've finished my business with him, Herr Gottleb.

GOTTLEB (HE *opens his other bottle*): To please you Fräulein, I'll let him enjoy Christmas. It never hurts to show a little compassion and warm the knife before you stick it in. (HE *pours her another drink*) This schnapps must be stronger than I thought. You're beginning to look attractive, Fräulein, in an elementary sort of way. Why aren't you married? The Führer-make-him-happy etc. promised every woman in the Third Reich a husband, dead or alive. A woman should be in her own home, behind a spinning wheel, weaving heavenly roses.

ELSE: The whole of Germany is our home and we must serve her wherever we can.

AUSCHWITZ

GOTTLEB: And you've no children. We must all do our part for the perpetuation of the Nordic race. I've been a virile lover, thirty years, man and boy. The boy's worn out, but the man's still active.

ELSE: I've tried, but Karl was killed in Norway, Horst in the Belgian Ardennes, Kurt and Josef taken in the taking of Greece and Crete, Fritz assaulting Tobruk, Edgar capturing Kiev. All great victories, but death didn't seem to know that, made no distinction pro or contra. Left me standing at the altar whilst my mother survived.

CRANACH: You could still have had children without benefit of. And no stigma. Reichsminister Lammers' ruling, memo QBX 54738 that extramarital motherhood was not a reason for initiating disciplinary measures against female members of the civil service.

GOTTLEB: We've replaced hypocritical bourgeois morality with honest National Socialist immorality.

ELSE: Veneral satisfaction outside wedlock's a mortal sin, unless forced and without pleasure. I can't commit mortal sin, cut myself off from God's light, grace, my last end.

GOTTLEB: Jew talk! You've a good childbearing pelvis, Fräulein. But just look at yourself. I know the Party's ideal woman is one of Spartan severity, but you go too far. Without those glasses, that hairstyle, why you'd be beautiful. Here, let me show you.

HE *takes off her glasses, then removes the comb keeping her bun in place.*

Don't worry, I've got very delicate hands. . . . Just let it fall out . . .

ELSE*'s hair tumbles down,* SHE *shakes it free.*

There, there, you see, Fräulein . . . why you look . . .

SHE *glances up;* HE *shudders.*

Worse!

ELSE *grabs the comb and starts putting her hair back up.*

ELSE: If we're ever alone on a desert island, Herr Gottleb, bring a pack of cards.

STROOP: When we were kids, we used to take a stick and hit each other over the head. Even the games were different then. I liked to be domineering, but I could never find anyone who wanted to be submissive.

ELSE *has fixed her hair back into a bun and puts her glasses on.* GOTTLEB *points triumphantly.*

GOTTLEB: There, I was right. The hair, the glasses, it makes all the difference. Why, now you look almost beautiful, Fräulein Jost.
ELSE: But this is exactly the way I was before!
GOTTLEB: And not a moment too soon.

CRANACH *stands up, sways slightly, and sits again.* ALL *are getting progressively more drunk.*

CRANACH: Gottleb, I've studied these memos and I still can't grant special favors to Krupps AG.
GOTTLEB: I understand perfectly Cranach. I don't agree with what you say and I'll fight to death your right to say it. I can't be fairer than that. Have another drink. (HE *pours himself and* CRANACH *another drink*)
CRANACH: I don't want to be unfair, Gottleb. If you wish the Reichführer SS Heinrich Himmler himself to renew the case I'd've no objection.
GOTTLEB: Ah, the Reichführer's a truly great man, trying to recreate the pure Aryan race according to Mendel's laws. His commitment to the community's total, TOTAL. "If ten thousand Russian women die digging a tank ditch, it interests me only as far as the tank ditch is completed for Germany."
CRANACH: But he also said, "We Germans're the only people with a decent attitude to animals." I don't understand why he has such a bad reputation.
GOTTLEB: I met him once in person. He was sitting at a large black table with a bottle of mineral water and Obergruppenführers Jeckeln, Kaltenbrunner and von Herff. They were all staring into space, forcing a traitor in the next room to confess, purely by exerting their collective Aryan wills. It was called an exercise in concentration. Of course the SS're usually more physical in their approach. But this time they were dealing with a cross-eyed, bearded dwarf.
CRANACH: An intellectual?
GOTTLEB: Yes, the subtle method can sometimes be very effective with intellectuals. Of course if they turn out not to be intellectuals, you can always go back to basics; put the needle in the record and separate the soul from the wax with traditional whips, cold chisels and such.
ELSE: Tell me, do fully uniformed men actually believe they can force someone to tell them the truth by will power alone?
GOTTLEB: If the will's truly Aryan. Aryan will cuts through steel plate, thirty meters thick. It's pure light, burning light. I'll show you. You've no intellectuals here, so we'll have to use old Stroop—there's a full moon tonight but it won't make him any brighter. Right, Stroop?

STROOP, *slumped in his chair deep in thought, nods absently.*

GOTTLEB: We'll make him confess the truth. Fräulein Jost, Herr Cranach, concentrate there on his bald spot. There. . . . Concentrate . . .

CRANACH: No. I can't let one of my staff risk speaking the truth out loud in public.

GOTTLEB: It won't hurt him. He's amongst friends. Now concentrate . . . three Aryan minds converge . . . burn into his brain . . . h-a-r-d . . . the truth . . .

GOTTLEB, CRANACH *and* ELSE *stare fixedly across at the top of* STROOP's *head. Jaws tighten, eyes bulge in the tense silence. Finally,* STROOP *opens his mouth and belches.* THEY *continue concentrating.* STROOP *suddenly clutches his head, lets out a low moan and rises unsteadily from his chair.*

STROOP: Clara Bow's panties. Willy Frisch and Lilian Harvey and the hair from Adolph Menjou's moustache. Oh, the glories of man's unconquerable past. Hans Albers' tights! His legs were too thin for him to play Hamlet, alas poor Yorick, one fool in the grave.

CRANACH, GOTTLEB *and* ELSE: Root it out. Root it out.

STROOP: No, it's the truth. It was different then. The sky never so blue, the snow never so white. I was remembering a Christmas I spent in the country. Every house with evergreens decorated with stars. A man pulling a cart heaped with holly. A girl herding geese through a gate. A little boy listening at the bedroom door to the music and dancing below.

ELSE: When I was a girl, Mother used to take me to afternoon dances at the Vaterland. They hung the hall with Chinese lanterns in the summer and the girls were given posies of violets. Mother'd sit knitting and Father'd read the "B.Z. Zum Mittag" and I danced to the music of "Madam Judl and Her All Ladies Viennese Orchestra."

Lights down slightly. There is an illusion of swaying Chinese lanterns overhead as STROOP *bows to* ELSE *and dances her solemnly round the office as* CRANACH *and* GOTTLEB *hum a Strauss waltz.*

CRANACH: Our garden had carnations of all colors, nasturtiums, snapdragons, Madonna lilies, monthly roses. Mother loved flowers so, she said they never tried to borrow money. How long the summers were then, how bright the sun. Smell the jasmine round the arbor walls.

Without stopping the dance, HE *takes* STROOP's *place as* ELSE's *partner while* STROOP *hums with* GOTTLEB, *who is crying. The dance ends and* CRANACH *escorts* ELSE *back to her desk.*

GOTTLEB: My mother was a saint. She was born to laugh; instead her whole life was spent crying and saying goodbye. My father ran off with a waitress. Three brothers killed West Front 1918, when we were stabbed in the back. She raised six, always telling me I had to sleep faster, she needed the pillows. Fifty years on her knees scrubbing for Jews and Bolsheviks. From a person to a nonentity, face worn to the bone. "What's dying?" she asked. "What I've had in life was worse." Yet she was gentle as water, so good, birds perched on her outstretched hand. (HE *sings, sobbing*) "I see your eyes at sunset's golden hour. They look on me till night's first stars above. You speak to me across the silent land. From out the long ago, Mother I love . . ."

GOTTLEB'S MOTHER, *a little old lady, head wrapped in a black shawl, hobbles on.*

GOTTLEB'S MOTHER: Son, son, I need food.
GOTTLEB: Mother, don't bother me now, can't you see I'm singing. (HE *sings*) "I hold your hand as through the world I go. And think of your sweet face gentle as a little dove. Your presence fills each throbbing hour of life. Oh heart of long ago, Mother I love . . ."
GOTTLEB'S MOTHER: But, son, I haven't eaten for three days.
GOTTLEB: Didn't I give you a new pair of shoes for your birthday?
GOTTLEB'S MOTHER: Three days without food!
GOTTLEB: How did you get past the guard dogs? Mother, you climbed over the wall again. (*Singing*) "God keep your memory fragrant in my soul. And lift my eyes in thankfulness above. Until I stand beside you at the last. And hold you in my arms, Mother I love."
GOTTLEB'S MOTHER: Food! Food!

SHE *turns and staggers off.* GOTTLEB *passes a hand over his eyes. Lights come full up.*

GOTTLEB: Had no time for her then, the Party came first, last and always. Too old, too late to share it. But the song's true, the pain real, despite . . . (HE *raises his glass*) My mother.

THEY *all drink; as* THEY *pour another glass each,* GOTTLEB *sways over to* CRANACH.

I was wrong about you, Viktor, you've got Aryan qualities. So've you, Fräulein Else, and even you Heinz, or can I call you Stroop. (HE *clasps* CRANACH) I need new friends, I keep eating up the old ones. Let's be friends.

ELSE: Why not? I've always found it easy to be friends with men I dislike physically.

STROOP: I haven't made any friends since I was in my forties, after I realized they couldn't save me.

CRANACH: You're right, Gottleb—Hans. Friendship's a reciprocal conciliation of mutual interests. We're natural allies, dedicated to building the best. On the personal level too we've much in common. We both earn twenty thousand marks a week, only they don't pay us it. Without us, the machine grinds, halts, and it all spills out.

THEY *put their arms around each other.*

Salt of the earth . . . brother in arms . . . have another drink.

GOTTLEB: We should've been friends before. I blame our Sturmbannführers. Towers of jelly, not a healthy fart amongst the lot of 'em. When we came to power I thought we'd build gold pissoirs in the streets. Instead they do it in their diapers. They run bowel-scared so they set Amt C against Amt D, D against B. The place is alive with hate-beetles. And Brigadeführer Gluck's the worst. Brigadeführer! He wouldn't make a first class doorman for a second class hotel, he's about as sharp as a billiard ball; why're my superiors always my inferiors? In the old days it was bowlegged turds with their university degrees and diplomas lording it; dead fish stinking from the head.

CRANACH: Academics, the higher education breed, as useful as two left feet, trying to imagine what the flame of a candle looks like after it's been blown out. Never liked 'em.

GOTTLEB: Book-readers! They read *books.* We showed 'em books. Books is nothing! I've burnt ten thousand books in a night, reduced 'em to a pile of ash—well, they're easier to carry that way. Now we've got a new bunch of snot-pickers up there giving us orders. I can give orders 'stead of taking 'em. MARCH! SHOOT! DIE! Our day to crow it in the sun. MARCH! SHOOT! DIE! That was the promise and the dream. (HE *pulls off his moustache*) We was robbed again. MARCH . . . SHOOT . . . DIE . . .

STROOP: I was ruined when I was twelve. I found a fifteen thousand mark note in the gutter and I spent the rest of my life with my eyes fixed on the ground, always looking down instead of ahead. If I could've seen where I was going it would've been different. I was young, strong, hard. They couldn't've stopped me. I'd've had a new uniform with bright buttons and boots up to the calf. Leather boots to step on fat faces, boots, boots, marching up and down again left-right, left-right, *crunch, craa* . . . (HE *raises his rigid legs and smacks them down savagely as* HE *goose steps frantically around the office until* HE *cramps up and has to hobble painfully back to his chair)*

ELSE: For two thousand years Christians've worshipped the Cross and made women like me carry it. If I hadn't had a bad case of Catholic conscience, I could've been mistress of Silesia by now. When I was in the Ministry, Gauleiter Hanke wanted what I had. I said he couldn't have it, it was Lent. So he took a pimple-faced shop girl from the Wittenbergplatz. Prussian blockhead. His idea of style was mirrors in the bedrooms, fountains in the hall, and bull-necked SS men serving tea in white gloves. White gloves! Oh what taste and elegance I could've shown him. *(SHE sweeps around, acknowledging imaginary guests with gracious smiles and nods)* A luxury villa in Dahlen, dining every night at the Horcher or driving to the Furst von Stollberg in the Harz Mountains. I could've set the tone for the best society. Instead we have Frau Göbbels rushing up to the wife of the Italian Minister, shouting, "Is that dress real silk?"

STROOP *(Giggling)*: You know what Frau Emmy said to Reich-Marshal Göring at their wedding reception. "Why've you got on your tuxedo and medals Hermann, this isn't a first night."

ELSE: She's given up membership of the Church, she's lost faith in the resurrection of the flesh.

THEY *gather round laughing.*

CRANACH: Don't laugh. It's an offense to make people laugh. Jokes carry penalties. So don't. Have you tried the new Rippentrop herrings? They're just ordinary herrings with the brain removed and the mouth split wider.

Shrieks from ELSE *and* STROOP, *while* GOTTLEB *roars and slaps his thigh in delight. Their laughter quickly grows louder and more hysterical.*

GOTTLEB: That'll get you five years hard labor, Viktor. Here's one carries ten: my dentist is going out of business. Everyone's afraid to open their mouths.

ELSE: The only virgin left in Berlin is the angel on top of the victory column—Göbbels can't climb that high.

GOTTLEB: I sentence you to fifteen years, Fräulein.

ELSE: A German's dream of paradise is to have a suit made of genuine English wool with a genuine grease spot in it.

GOTTLEB: Another fifteen.

STROOP: We can't lose the war, we'd never be that careless.

GOTTLEB: Twenty years hard.

STROOP: The time we'll really be rid of the war is when Franco's widow stands beside Mussolini's grave asking who shot the Führer?
GOTTLEB: Thirty.
CRANACH: Listen, listen, what do you call someone who sticks his finger up the Führer's arse?!
GOTTLEB: Heroic.
CRANACH: No, a brain surgeon!
GOTTLEB: That's DEATH.

CRANACH, ELSE *and* STROOP *collapse in hysterical laughter. But it dies away as* THEY *become aware that a suddenly sober* GOTTLEB *is staring balefully at them.*

CRANACH: You're not laughing, Hans.
GOTTLEB: But I am inside, *inside.* (HE *stamps around triumphantly*) I have you strung up and out, Cranach! I waited and I won it. You didn't realize I'm abnormally cunning, like most fanatics. Death's mandatory for all jokes, good or bad, about our beloved Führer-make-him-happy-he-deserves-it. No more talk of not giving Krupp AG that CP3 (m) contract. I'll have you in front of People's Court Judge Rehse in a day, sentenced and hanging from piano wire by the end of the week. Job, family, life, lost in one, Cranach. And the rest of you're going under. . . . "His sacred arse . . . a finger up it . . . brain surgeon." Filthy! Filthy!
CRANACH: Sacred ass . . . finger up . . . brain surgeon? You've been drinking, Gottleb! I never tell jokes. Everyone knows I've no sense of humor.
ELSE: Nobody has in Amt C, the atmosphere isn't conducive.
CRANACH: I know you want Krupps AG to get the CP(m) contract and us professional civil servants out. But you go too far in treating the Führer's arse—bless-it-and-make-it-happy-it-deserves-it as a joke. Every part of the Führer's superhuman anatomy is treated with awesome respect in this office. We shout "Heil Hitler, Heil Hitler, Heil Hitler" every morning. We worship him as a flawless being, a divinity, and you talk of his arse.
GOTTLEB: *I* don't, Cranach, *you* do . . .

The OTHERS *gasp and shake their heads in horror.*

Lies, shit-drizzle of lies. But I expected this.

HE *opens his briefcase on the desk and takes out a small tape recording machine: the* OTHERS *look puzzled.*

It's the latest example of Aryan technological genius. A magnetic tape recording machine, just developed by Army Intelligence. A masterpiece of German ingenuity. The magnetization on the tape induces electrical currents in the coil, which are then amplified and reproduced, recreating the original sounds. Soon every home'll have one wired to a central control. Then every word spoken'll be noted and banked, no more secret words, only secret thoughts. And one day those too'll be taped. What a day that'll be. I switched it on when you started making jokes. You look ill Cranach, and you Stroop. I'll play it back, see if you think it's still funny. Somehow I don't think you'll laugh this time around, jokes've a way of dying too. (HE *starts to wind back the spools on the machine*)

STROOP: I'm an old man, my legs don't bend so easy. I let the flies settle and the days burn out like matches. Herr Cranach did say something about arses and fingers. He said it, I didn't. . . . I'm only repeating . . . you don't think I . . . how could. . . . Heil Hitler! Heil Hitler!

ELSE: I heard Herr Cranach too. I'd have to swear it for my Mother's sake. She's a grand old lady over eighty now. Once met the Kaiser, more or less. I've been nonpolitical for over thirty—twenty—years, so whoever it was it wasn't me! Heil Hitler! Heil Hitler!

GOTTLEB: I like it! I like it! I'm peeling you naked to the center. I like it! I like it! Oh, I like it!

CRANACH: I'm sure we all said things. I believe you even mentioned it'd be heroic touching up the Führer—MAKE-HIM-HAPPY-HE-DESERVES-IT. Bad schnapps talking, not a good German. We're all in this together.

GOTTLEB: Old lies, I shit on old lies. Here's something you'll hear beyond your death. The truth!

CRANACH, ELSE and STROOP *brace themselves.* HE *switches on the tape recorder to hear a cacophony of high-pitched screeches, muffled squawks and clicks.* CRANACH, ELSE *and* STROOP *exchange looks, while* GOTTLEB *smiles complacently.*

GOTTLEB: You can't lie your way out of that! (HE *leans closer to the recorder and repeats words only* HE *can hear on the tape*) "What do you call someone who sticks his finger up the Führer's arse . . . ?" Disgusting! Disgusting . . . ! "No, a brain surgeon." (HE *switches it off*) Ipso facto. Hang him.

CRANACH: For what? It's just noise. Not one human voice. It doesn't work.

GOTTLEB: It doesn't work? The latest product of German technological genius and you say it doesn't work. That's anti-German slander. You could get another ten years on top of your death sentence for that. You don't hear anything because you don't want to. But I hear voices, clear as bells.

CRANACH: That nobody else can hear. If you had more brains, Gottleb, you'd be in an asylum. Fräulein Jost, Herr Stroop, did you hear anything?

THEY *both shake their heads.* GOTTLEB *rewinds the spools.*

GOTTLEB: I'm not surprised. Women never listen, they haven't the glands and that old fool's half dead and completely stupid. But you can't get round hard facts. Listen. (HE *switches on the tape recorder again, which plays exactly the same noise)* NOW tell me you can't hear anything . . .? "Finger" . . . "arse" . . . "brain surgeon. . . ." The Gestapo'll take that as evidence. (HE *switches off the recorder)* Especially when it's confirmed by your own staff. Fräulein Jost, Herr Stroop, you've already sworn he made the joke. Now it's your duty to swear his life away for the Fatherland. 1937 Civil Service Code, paragraph 6. No matter how humble his station in life, every German enjoys equal opportunity before the law, to denounce his social superiors. I appeal to your patriotism, or better still, your greed and envy. (HE *rewinds the spools)* Remember informers inherit their victim's job as a reward. (HE *crosses and pours* STROOP *a drink)* Stroop, if you tell the truth and say you hear Cranach's voice on the tape, you take over his position. Think of it. Head of your own department at sixty-four. That's fantastic progress, for someone with your obvious limitations.

STROOP: Will I be able to sign memos, have the largest desk, two phones, lose my temper and no one have the right to answer back?

GOTTLEB: All yours, just tell the truth. (*Pouring* ELSE *a drink)* And you Fräulein, from Acting Secretary Grade III (Admin) to Permanent Secretary Grade I with increased salary and pension, and permanent use of the first floor Grade I executive washrooms.

ELSE: I'm told each toilet seat's individually covered with an organdie doily, capped with a gilded swastika. Some women've stayed in those washrooms for days.

GOTTLEB: Shithouse decadence! It killed my father! But it's all yours if you tell the truth, hear Cranach's voice. Listen. LISTEN.

HE *switches on the recorder again and* THEY *listen hard.*

STROOP: Yes . . . sounds behind the sounds . . . laughter . . . a voice.

ELSE: Faint . . . faint . . . what does it say?

GOTTLEB (*Slowly)*: "What do you call someone who sticks his finger up the Führer's arse?"

ELSE *and* STROOP (*Repeating slowly*): "What do you call someone who sticks his finger up the Führer's arse?"

GOTTLEB: "A brain surgeon."

ELSE *and* STROOP (*Repeating slowly*): "A brain surgeon."

There is a click. CRANACH *has switched off the machine.*

GOTTLEB: Too late, Cranach. I've witnesses now. They heard. Who's guilty, Cranach? The punished man, the punished man!

HE *produces a children's Christmas toy squeaker and blows it repeatedly at* CRANACH.

CRANACH: Fräulein, Herr Stroop, the joke's on you, not on the tape. Give him that finger and he'll want the whole hand. (HE *pours* ELSE *and* STROOP *a drink from his bottle*) Fräulein, he won't let you see a Grade I salary, pension or toilet seat. You're marked dead meat, cold water. And you, Heinz. You'll never become Department Head. It'll be Gottleb's thirty pieces reward for denouncing me. But he can only get it if you lie about me and the Führer-make-him-happy-he-deserves-it famous arse. I know you won't lie. Over the years we three've formed an abiding relation, working together, grieving together when your wife died, Heinz and your mother didn't, Fräulein. The best way to help ourselves is by helping each other. The times're sour, we've lost the true meaning of things, but I know I can still find integrity and trust amongst my friends.

GOTTLEB: "Integrity," "trust," "friends." Whenever I hear noble sentiments I reach for my wallet to see if it's been lifted. Your friends're selling you Cranach, because I can give 'em something better than "integrity," "trust," "friendship."

CRANACH: So can I, Gottleb—"security." Fräulein, Herr Stroop, you measure out your days classifying, documenting, numbering. It's always the same, but always within your capabilities. Sometimes you're bored, but never anxious for you know tomorrow'll be the same as today. If you denounce me it'll never be the same again, only the same as outside, full of choice and change, violence and blood. Are you going to throw away all this security on the word of a man who every hour he's out of prison is away from home? He's not one of us. He isn't safe!

ELSE: No, Herr Cranach. I have to tell the truth. No matter who it hurts. A so-called joke about the location of the Führer's mighty brain-make-it-happy-it-deserves-it was told in this office.

GOTTLEB: Now it falls, it falls!

ELSE: By you, Herr Gottleb!

STROOP: You said he needed a finger surgeon! We all heard you Gottleb. Filth! Filth!

GOTTLEB: He said it, I didn't. . . . I was only repeating . . . you don't think I . . . how could . . . Heil Hitler . . . wheezle-gutted, chicken-breasted vomit! In the old days every good German was an informer, now you can't rely on anyone to betray the right people. The true Aryan spirit's gone forever. I don't need white-livered, crow-bait.

CRANACH: You do, Gottleb. Without them you've got nothing. *(HE switches on the tape)* Nothing but laughter. They'll laugh you out, Gottleb, just as we're laughing you out.

Laughing loudly, ELSE, STROOP *and* CRANACH *produce children's toy squeakers, put on Christmas paper hats and advance triumphantly on* GOTT-LEB, *who defends himself by also putting on a paper hat and whipping out his toy squeaker.* THEY *blow furiously at each other. But* GOTTLEB *is outnumbered.* HE *backs away, claps his hands over his ears and collapses in a chair.* CRANACH *switches off the recorder, while* ELSE *and* STROOP *continue jeering.* GOTTLEB *takes off his paper hat.*

GOTTLEB: I'm tired in advance. All these years fighting. The forces of reaction're too strong. Pulled down by blind moles in winged collars. Your kind can't be reformed, only obliterated. As you build 'em we should find room for you in one of our complexes in Upper Silesia: Birkenau, Monowitz or Auschwitz.

ELSE *and* STROOP *stop jeering.*

That's where I should be too. Out in the field. Not stuck behind a desk in Orienburg, but in the gas chambers of Auschwitz, working with people. Dealing with flesh and blood, not deadly abstractions: I'm suffocating in this limbo of paper. Auschwitz is where it's happening, where we exterminate the carrion hordes of racial maggots. I'd come into my own there on the Auschwitz ramp, making the only decision that matters, who lives, who dies. You're strong, live; you're pretty, live; you're too old, too weak, too young, too ugly. Die. Die. Die. Die. Smoke in the chimneys, ten thousand a week.

CRANACH, ELSE *and* STROOP *look disturbed.*

STROOP: What's he say? What's he say?

CRANACH: Too much. Hold your tongue between your fingers, Gottleb, there're ladies present.

ELSE: I only type and file WVHA Amt C 1 (Building) to WVHA Amt D IV/5 your reference QZV/12/01 regulation E(5) PRV 24/6 DS 4591/1942.

STROOP: We only deal in concrete. We're Amt C 1 (Building). Test procedure 17 as specified structural work on outer surfaces of component CP3(m) described in regulation E(5), what's CP3(m) to do with life and death in Upper Silesia? Everybody knows I'm sixty-four years old.

GOTTLEB (*Rising*): You know extermination facilities were established in Auschwitz in June for the complete liquidation of all Jews in Europe. CP3(m) described in regulation E(5) is the new concrete flue for the crematoriums.

CRANACH, ELSE *and* STROOP *sit.*

CRANACH: Who knows that?

ELSE *and* STROOP: We don't know that.

GOTTLEB: You don't know that only knowing enough to know you don't want to know that. Future cases of death must be given consecutive Roman numbers with consecutive subsidiary Arabic numbers, numerical I/1 to I/185. If you could see the dead roasted behind Roman numerals I/1 to Roman numeral XXX/185 you'd run chicken-shitless, but you haven't the imagination. Even if you read of six million dead, your imagaination wouldn't frighten you, because it wouldn't make you see a single dead man. But I'll make you see six million! I'm going to split your minds to the sights, sounds and smells of Auschwitz. Then I'll be rid of you. You'll go of your own accord. You piss-legs haven't the pepper to stay in WVHA Amt C knowing every file you touch's packed tight with oven-stacked corpses. No way then to hide behind the words and symbols. You won't be able to glory in it like me, seeing the night trains halting at the ramp behind the entrance gate, between Birkenau and the Auschwitz parent camp. Don't you see the searchlights, guard dogs, watch towers, men with whips? And at the far end, Crematoria I and II, belching sticky-sweet smoke and waiting for the new concrete flues, CP3(m). Don't you see the trains carrying three thousand prisoners a time, eighty to a wagon built to hold thirty? They've been traveling five days without food or water so when the doors're open they throw the corpses out first, the sick fall next, stinking from typhus, diarrhea, spotted fever. Hear the screaming? They're being beaten into lining up five abreast to march past the SS doctors. Those fit to work go right, those unfit, the old, sick, and young go to the left for gassing. Mothers try to hide their babes, but the Block Commanders always find 'em. "What's this shit?! This shit can't work!" They use the newborn babes as balls, kicking 'em along the ramp shouting, "Goal! Goal!"

ELSE *sobs,* STROOP *and* CRANACH *cry out in protest as they clasp their heads in pain.*

You see! They're there, behind those files there, stripped, shaved, tatooed on their left arms 10767531. Two thousand living in blockhouses, built for five hundred; primitive conditions for Europe's primitives. Work till you die, on a quarter loaf of bread and one bowl of soup made of potatoes, and old rags. Look there, see the labor gangs stagger our through the morning mists, to start their twleve-hour shift in Krupps's fuse factory, skin peeling back from their bones. No malingerers here, if sick, they're allowed one lick of an aspirin hanging on a string, two licks if they're really ill. Life expectancy four months. Some do survive and have to be killed off with ben-zine injections, dying, in those files, for being too strong or too weak. Amt C like Amt D's only concerned with dying. Dying by starva-tion, despair, crowbar, bullet, axe, meathook, surgeon's knife. Roman numerals LXX/27 to XC/84, dying by chloral hydrate, phenol, evipan, air that kills, Roman numeral CXI/30 to CLXII/67. Trou-ble makers die hardest, hanging from window frames, hot radiators, see Roman numeral XXX/104; with iron clamps round temples; screwed tight, skulls craaaack, brains slurp out like porridge. "Corpse carriers to the gate house at the double!"

ELSE, CRANACH *and* STROOP *stagger up, shaking and moaning.*

We need more plants like Auschwitz, manufacturing and recycling dead Jews into fertilizing ash. We've already reached a peak output of 34,000 dead gassed and burned in one day and night shift. A record Belsen, Buchenwald, Dachau or Treblinka can't touch. And it's all due to the new gas chambers and crematoriums. You help build 'em so you should be able to see 'em plain. They've been made up to look like public bath houses. "Our Wash and Steam'll Help You Dream." The dressing rooms've signs in every European language, "Beware of Pickpockets," "Tie Your Shoes Together and Fold Your Clothes," "The Management Take No Responsibility For Any Losses Incurred." Oh we're clever, we're clever. Don't you see how clever? It helps calm those marked down to die as they go naked along carpeted passeges to the communal washroom. Fifteen hundred a time.

There is the reverberating sound of a steel door shutting up stage. CRANACH, STROOP *and* ELSE *whirl around to face it, clamping their hands over their ears.*

Now see, see 'em packed, buttock to buttock, gazing up at the waterless douches, wondering why the floor has no drainage runnels. On the lawns above, Sanitary Orderlies unscrew the lid shafts and Sergeant Moll shouts, "Now let 'em eat it!", and they drop blue, Zyklon B hydrocyanide crystals changing to gas in the air as it pours down and out through false shower heads, fake ventilators. What visions, what frenzies, the screaming, coughing, staggering, vomiting, bleeding, breath paralyzed, lungs slowly ruptured *aaaaah!* See it! See it!

Twisting frantically to escape the sound of his voice, CRANACH, ELSE *and* STROOP *gasp, cough and scream in panic.*

Children falling first, faces smashed against the concrete floor. Others tear at the walls hoping to escape. But see, they're falling too, flies in winter, rushing to the door, shrieking, "Don't let me die! Don't let me die! Don't let me die!", the strongest stamping the weakest down, all falling still, at last, a solid pyramid of dead flesh jammed against the washhouse door, limbs tied in knots, faces blotched, hands clutching hanks of hair, carcasses slimy with fear, shit, urine, menstrual blood they couldn't hold back. You see it now! Look! There! There!

CRANACH, ELSE *and* STROOP: We don't see! We don't see!

GOTTLEB *(Pointing up stage)*: LOOK. Mind splits, death house door slides open . . . SEE.

As the sound of the gas chamber door being opened reverberates, the whole of the filing section slowly splits and its two parts slide apart to reveal a vast mound of filthy, wet straw dummies; vapor—the remains of the gas—still hangs about them. They spill forward to show all are painted light blue, have no faces, and numbers tattooed on their left arms. CRANACH, STROOP *and* ELSE *stare in horror and* GOTTLEB *smiles as two* MONSTROUS FIGURES *appear out of the vapor, dressed in black rubber suits, thigh-length waders and gas masks. Each has a large iron hook, knife, pincers and a small sack hanging from his belt. As* THEY *clump forward,* THEY *hit the dummies with thick wooden clubs. Each time* THEY *do so there is the splintering sound of a skull being smashed.*

GOTTLEB: The Jewish Sonderkommando Sanitation Squad. They go in after, to see no one's left alive and prepare the bodies for the fire ovens.

AUSCHWITZ

Slipping and sliding, the SANITATION MEN *use their iron hooks to separate the dummies.*

They have to work fast, there's always another train-load waiting. *Faster! Faster!* New Sanitation Squads are brought in every three months and the old ones're sent to the ovens, all used up. *Faster! Faster!* Part of their job is to recover strategic war material for the Reich.

The FIRST SANITATION MAN *starts tearing at the mouth of a dummy with his pincers, accompanied by a loud, wrenching sound.*

Gold teeth. They're extracting gold teeth from the corpses. That's why they're called the "Gold diggers of 1942." Root it out. Root it out! . . . Quicker, don't take half the jaw bone!

While the FIRST SANITATION MAN *mimes putting the teeth into his sack, the* SECOND SANITATION MAN *gouges a dummy's face with his knife.*

Glass eyes. This way we've thousands of spare glass eyes ready for empty German sockets. *Faster scum, you want to join the others in the fire pits?!*

The FIRST SANITATION MAN *quickly cuts off a dummy's finger and puts in in his sack.*

That's better. It saves time when you're collecting wedding rings to slice off the whole finger. *Faster scum! Faster! The ovens! The ovens! More coming. More coming.* SEE. See what's behind your files?!

As the SANITATION MEN *rip, slice and gouge with increasing frenzy amid the noise of breaking bones and tearing flesh,* CRANACH, ELSE *and* STROOP *jerk their heads from side to side and whirl around to avoid looking.*

CRANACH: I see it! I can't fight 'em. I couldn't say "no" to them. This isn't the time to say "no." I've just taken out a second mortgage!
ELSE: I see it too! But what can I do? I'm only one woman. How can I say "no"? This isn't a good time for me either to say "no." Mother's just bought a new suite of furniture!
STROOP: Yes, I see it! But they'll stop me growing roses, wearing slippers all day. I'm peeing down my trouser leg. I'm an old man. You can't expect me to say "no." I couldn't say "no," how can I say "no" to them? It's a bad time to say "no." I'm retiring next year. I'd lose my gold watch!
GOTTLEB: *Faster garbage! Faster!*

Using their iron hooks, the SANITATION MEN *stack the torn dummies in neat piles.*

They're laying out the meat for the fire ovens. It's baking time. That's a sight you must see, see, see!

The OTHERS *fall on their knees, facing away.*

4,500,000 killed and roasted. You'll smell 'em every morning you come into the office, crisp flesh done to a turn, all senses confirm, feathers torn from the wing.

ELSE *covers her eyes,* STROOP *his ears,* CRANACH *his mouth.*

You'll find it hell 'less you get the hell out. So run. Hide. Find somewhere to hide. The sky's falling. This is men's work. *Faster! Faster!*

HE *crosses, yelling at the* SANITATION MEN. CRANACH *takes his hands from his mouth.*

CRANACH: Fight. Fight. Can't let him win. We're Civil Servants, words on paper, not pictures in the mind, memo AS/7/42 reference SR 273/849/6. Writers write, builders build, potters potter, bookkeepers keep books. E(5) Class I and II, L11, L12, F280/515 your reference AMN 23D/7. "Gas chambers," "fire ovens," "ramps," he's using words to make us see images, words to create meanings, not contained in them; then nothing means what it says and our world dissolves. Words're tools. CP3(m) is CP3(m). Two capitals, an Arabic numeral and a bracket round a small letter "m," the rest is the schnapps talking. 4,500,000 dead, no yardstick to measure, one four, one five, six noughts, brain can't encompass. *(HE gets up)* Memo Amt C1 (Building) to Amt D1 (Central Office). Your reference EC2Z 5LZ. Our reference F68. We merely operate policies embodied in existing legislation and implement decisions of higher authority. Copies to Amt A (military administration) Amt B (military economy) Amt W (SS economic enterprises) . . .

HE *helps* ELSE *and* STROOP *up.*

Get up, horizontal positions diminish the genius of the German people, we must always be vertical and hierarchial. It's all in the mind. He was lying. I could tell, he used *adjectives.* We merely administer camps which concentrate people from all over Europe. Are we going to let the wet dreams of an obscene buffoon like Gottleb drive us out? He said it, it's all imagination, and hard facts leave nothing to the imagination. We're trained to kill imagination before it kills us. So close mind's door, shut out the light there. Concentrate on what's real, what's concrete. Concentrate and repeat: Component CP3(m), described in regulation E(5) serving as Class I or Class II appliance shall be so constructed so as to comply with relevant requirements of regulations L2(4) and (6) L8(4) and (7).

ELSE *and* STROOP: Component CP3(m) described in regulation E(5) serving as Class I or Class II appliance shall be so constructed as to comply with relevant requirements of regulation L2(4) and (6) L8(4) and (7) . . .

The steel door of the gas chamber is heard slowly closing and the two sections of filing cabinet begin to slide back into position, blocking off the dummies and the SANITATION MEN. GOTTLEB *rushes back down to* CRANACH, ELSE *and* STROOP.

GOTTLEB: You can't shut it out, not word play, dream play, I've been there! It's *real!*

CRANACH, ELSE *and* STROOP *(Chanting)*: Future cases of death shall be given consecutive Roman numbers with consecutive subsidiary Arabic numbers. The first case Roman numeral I/1 the second Roman numeral I/2 up to Roman numeral I/185. Thereafter the cases shall be numbered Roman numeral II from Roman numeral II/1 to Roman numeral II/185 . . .

The steel door is heard shutting with a final clang as the two filing sections are rejoined in their previous position. The dummies and SANITATION MEN *have vanished from sight behind them.*

ELSE: Sanctus, Sanctus, Sanctus. Benedictus Deus!

STROOP: All gone "phoof," nothing disturbing left. It's a triumph.

GOTTLEB: Of mongoloid reasoning, I'll take you there . . . !

CRANACH *picks up* GOTTLEB'*s briefcase,* ELSE *his file and* STROOP, *while quickly finishing the last dregs, his schnapps bottle.* THEY *thrust them at him.*

ELSE: Knowing you Herr Gottleb makes it hard to believe all souls're equal in the sight of the Lord. Go break a leg.

STROOP: Drown yourself, it's funnier.

CRANACH: Krupps AG won't get the contract in Upper Silesia and you won't get us out of Amt C. You're a man with both feet on the ground

Gottleb, until they hang you; I'll send you a rope with instruction. You're OUT.

GOTTLEB: The final degradation, these old Party hairs, pissed on by secret Semites, obvious mediocrities. That's what's finally spoiled National Socialism for me, having to share it with people whose lack of imagination would diminish the Colosseum and the Taj Mahal by moonlight. I'd rather be a bad winner than any kind of loser. I can stand anything but defeat!

CRANACH, ELSE *and* STROOP: Root it out!

GOTTLEB *gives a yell as* ELSE *opens the door.* CRANACH *and* STROOP *grab his arms and throw him out. As* HE *lands in the corridor with a crash,* ELSE *slams the door shut. The* THREE *grin delightedly and congratulate each other.*

ELSE: I'll put in a RLS/47/3 to E6 (Cleaning and Maintenance) to have this office fumigated.

CRANACH: Give it priority. Now perhaps we can get back to work. There's still a war to win.

As THEY *move back to their desk the door suddenly opens and* GOTTLEB *pops his head in.*

GOTTLEB: I've still one more throw, the best and the last.

HE *deliberately sticks his Hitler moustache back on his upper lip.*

HAAA. Top that!

Before anyone can react, HE *quickly withdraws.* CRANACH, ELSE *and* STROOP *resume work.*

STROOP: That man could've done terrible things, overrode recognized procedures, ignored official channels, created precedents. You saved the department, Herr Cranach. I'm proud to've been able to help.

ELSE: We may not be much, but we're better than Gottleb. This time it didn't end with the worst in human nature triumphant, meanness exalted, goodness mocked. The other side has its victories. It's a Christmas present we'll remember, thanks to you, Herr Cranach.

CRANACH: Thank you, Fräulein. In centuries to come when our complexes at Auschwitz're empty ruins, monuments to a past civilization, tourist attractions, they'll ask, like we do of the Inca temples, what kind of men built and maintained these extraordinary structures. They'll find it hard to believe they weren't heroic visionaries, mighty rulers, but ordinary people, people who liked people, people like them, you, me, us.

ELSE *and* STROOP *look at him, then all* THREE *march down to sing at the audience with increasing savagery.*

CRANACH, ELSE *and* STROOP *(Singing):* "This is a brotherhood of man. A benevolent brotherhood of man. A noble tie that binds, all human hearts and minds. Into a brotherhood of man. Your life-long membership is free. Keep a-giving each brother all you can. Oh aren't you proud to be in that fraternity. The great big brotherhood of man." Sing! Everybody sing!

Lights go down and an unseen chorus joins the finale in the darkness.

EPILOGUE

ANNOUNCER'S VOICE: Stop. Don't leave. The best is yet to come. Our final number. The Prisoners Advisory Committee of Block B, Auschwitz II, proudly present as the climax of this Extermination Camp Christmas Concert, the farewell appearance of the Boffo Boys of Birkenau, Abe Bimko and Hymie Bieberstein—"Bimko and Bieberstein!"

Introductory music. Applause. A follow spot picks out two hollow-eyed comics, BIMKO and BIEBERSTEIN as THEY enter dancing, dressed in shapeless concentration camp, striped prison uniforms with the yellow Star of David pinned on their threadbare tunics, wooden clogs, and undertakers' top hats complete with ribbon. Carrying a small cane each, THEY perform a simple dance and patter routine, to the tune of "On the Sunny Side of the Street."

BIEBERSTEIN: Bernie Litvinoff just died.

BIMKO: Well if he had a chance to better himself.

BIEBERSTEIN: Drunk a whole bottle of varnish. Awful sight, but a beautiful finish. Everyone knew he was dead. He didn't move when they kicked him. He's already in the ovens.

BIMKO: Poke him up then, this is a very cold block house.

BIEBERSTEIN: They're sending his ashes to his widow. She's going to keep them in an hourglass.

BIMKO: So she's finally getting him to work for a living.

BIEBERSTEIN: The camp foreman kept hitting me with a rubber truncheon yesterday—*hit, hit, hit.* I said, "You hitting me for a joke or on purpose?" "On purpose!" he yelled. *Hit, hit, hit.* "Good," I said, "because such jokes I don't like."

BIMKO: According to the latest statistics, one man dies in this camp everytime I breathe.

BIEBERSTEIN: Have you tried toothpaste?

BIMKO: No, the dental officer said my teeth were fine, only the gums have to come out.

BIEBERSTEIN: Be grateful. The doctor told Fleischmann he needed to lose ten pounds of ugly fat, so they cut off his head.

The music has faded out imperceptibly into a hissing sound. The follow spot begins to turn blue. THEY stop dancing.

BIMKO: I'm sure I've got leprosy.

BIEBERSTEIN: Devil's Island's the place for leprosy.

BIMKO: It's good?
BIEBERSTEIN: It's where I got mine.
BIMKO: Can I stay and watch you rot?

They cough and stagger.

BIEBERSTEIN: I could be wrong but I think this act is dying.
BIMKO: The way to beat hydrocyanide gas is by holding your breath for
   five minutes. It's just a question of mind over matter. They don't
   mind and we don't matter.

THEY *fall to their knees.*

BIEBERSTEIN: Those foul, polluted German bastardized . . .
BIMKO: Hymie, Hymie, please; what you want to do—cause trouble?

THEY *collapse on the floor, gasping.*

BIEBERSTEIN: To my beloved wife Rachel I leave my Swiss bank account.
   To my son Julius who I love and cherish, like he was my son, I leave
   my business. To my daughter I leave one hundred thousand marks
   in Trust. And to my no-good brother-in-law Louie who said I'd never
   remember him in my will—Hello Louie!
BIMKO: Dear Lord God, you help strangers so why shouldn't you help
   us? We're the chosen people.
BIEBERSTEIN: Abe, so what did we have to do to be chosen?
BIMKO: Do me a favor, don't ask. Whatever it was it was too much. . . .
   Hymie you were right, this act's dead on its feet.

The spot fades out.

BIEBERSTEIN: Oh mother . . .

THEY *die in darkness.*

END OF PLAY

Replika

A Performance Scenario

Józef Szajna

translated by E.J. Czerwinski

Playwright's Note

The name *Replika* does not simply mean repetition of an historical event. Perhaps it is more like a history lesson. From the Holocaust to the mass suicide of madmen by nuclear explosions is only a step away. Through *Replika* I warn our times and indict power and violence. Power can never be right: the rights of man must always overpower power. I dedicate *Replika*, on the one hand, to all those murdered by fascism; and, on the other hand, to all those governing today as a pledge of honor, obligating them and others after them to uphold that pledge, that such horror will never happen again.

—Józef Szajna
Warsaw, 1987

Replika
A Performance Scenario

The following scenario was written and published as an author's program note at the time of the American premiere of Replika *in 1975.*

On the concrete floor odds and ends, the scraps of civilization, are scattered—mannequins, wheels and shoes, old, badly battered stovepipes, torn newspapers and sacks, ropes, canvas and plastic—all covered with peat and earth resembling a huge refuse-dump. The mysterious, motionless mound bulging in the middle of the hall begins to show signs of life after a few moments.

Self-exhumation

The little mound begins to erupt, emitting smoke; something starts to stir inside. In silence someone tears up paper; a hand slowly emerges, clawing for a chunk of bread. Seizing it, the hand swiftly disappears, trembling with fear of losing it. One can see that the entire mound pulsates and undulates in rhythm of a chewing organism. Again the earth subsides and a hand emerges; soon another comes into view. Both hands seek each other, meet and lock firmly. Then a leg appears; after a while, another. Finally people extricate themselves. They seem in a way simple and coarse, dressed in gray sacks, barefooted, with their hair cropped. The people, frightened and blinded by the daylight, slowly accustom

149

themselves to the space. They rise from the ground to their knees. They become participating heroes in the mystery that is about to take place. They address the audience offering them the earth. Lumps of peat fall through their fingers. They pass the peat like sacred hosts to the others who in turn pass it on.

The Uncovering of Fellow Men

Out of the warm mound the actors excavate puppets. Here the puppets imitate life. Death will be played by an actor. The actors try to bring the puppets back to life: they find them among the people. They are entirely preoccupied with their activity. They have uncovered the puppets and are now carrying the "Pregnant One," a crippled woman covered with sacks. With effort they attempt to set her on her feet; they appeal to the audience for help. The actors find it impossible to steady the unstable puppet. They speak to her familiarly, as if she were someone close and dear to them. The actors treat the puppets as their partners in the play. The actors themselves are in a way relics of the dead, living reminders of those who managed to survive. Single words—"help," "the eye," "look"—break the silence.

A Child's Remembrance

The actress finds a blind child. She recognizes and accepts the tragedy of the puppet-creatures as if it were her own tragedy. She disentangles remembrances of the child from the puppet's rags: a broken comb, a pocket-mirror, a toothbrush. She tenderly strokes its face. Besides the one-eyed pregnant woman there is also a puppet signifying "Mother-grandmother" with disheveled gray hair which is rocked by the actor. The puppet flies over the heads of the spectators. The actor plays with it, cherishes its memory and finally hangs it up in the little altar, as though wanting to sanctify it.

The Birth of Superman

A sharp noise awakens the representative of automatism, a terrorist and usurper of power whose terrifying screams silence the others into obedience.

Golgotha

Now the excavated hurriedly bring in and set up a piano. They assemble a sculpture made up of artificial limbs and a willow-like tree. A monument to the usurper is created by the hands of the oppressed. The piano is white and scorched, as though it were taken out of a fire. Nearby the actors hang sacks full of shoes, swing them pendulum-like, run about, mutter something, whisper in different languages, repeat single words: "the eye," "mother."

Of Dust and Ashes Man Is Born

Yet only one person is as strong as a superman, the exponent of totalitarianism born to rule. The usurper armed with a pipe marks time with his nailed boots. He is the last to rise from the ground. He is power here. To the exhausted he throws motorcycle wheels. The people catch these wheels. They groan while carrying them. They run around the common grave, the mound. On the verge of exhaustion they put on gas masks and glasses like those worn by the blind—the dark glasses of their lives. Off-guard, they have involuntarily become the penal colony of common serfdom. Putting the wheels away, they assemble a plastic composition, "Man and the Wheel." Only tired panting is heard in the otherwise still scene.

Confession and Penance for Sins Uncommitted

"The mock-up of horror" is put on the trunk of the puppet. It is a relic of something that has remained of the altar. Perhaps it is only a picture of a saint, here serving the purpose of collective confession. The women seem to snivel, they sing litanies, they light the candles. Something bordering on a pagan ritual takes place: the devil-usurper dispenses absolution with a hammer.

Our Replika

The superman suddenly appears with a hissing fire extinguisher, resembling a machine gun. A ballet with pipes changes into a battle. Accompanied by the noise of clashing pipes, a spacial ballet-composition is created in which the actors participate. The death of the superman is followed by a group-bath. The hiss of the fire extinguisher cools the atmosphere. Smoke covers the ravaged earth. The candles go out.

Requiem

Now the pipes perform the function of sleep-inducing instruments. Apparently on the verge of exhaustion, the actor has lifted the "Guerrilla" and attempts to support himself on the puppet he has dragged in. In the puppet's holster he finds a handful of coins which he throws among the people. He rests along with the wounded soldier. The two resemble each other.

Epitaphs and Apotheoses

A long series of shots. The actors bring in a long roll of old photographs. They spread them out, displaying them to the audience, dragging the photographs across the hall, carpet-like. They use them as a shroud to cover the mound, as though it were a common grave out of which they have arisen. The music dies out. The photographs are trampled down by the boots which fall out of the sacks. The boots pace the distance, dividing it into the lives of the lost millions. The image of the lost and forgotten is completed by setting into motion a colorful tune-producing top. Its movement does away; in this way a spatial composition is created—*Replika*.

Ghetto

Joshua Sobol
adapted by Jack Viertel

Playwright's Note

On various festive occasions our tradition demands that we *remember*. On the first night of Passover, which is the celebration of the freedom of a nation born of slavery, every adult participating in the feast is invited to tell the story of the Exodus in as much detail as possible. In other words, everyone is encouraged to reimagine the past, to revive it for his children by telling it as if he had lived it himself. History should be a constant and permanently-living presence, the fruit of creative and imaginative memory. Maybe because it is the only possible way to assume it and yet to go on living, to survive.

Characters

SRULIK, puppeteer, singer
DUMMY
KITTEL, SS officer, saxophone
    player (he also plays
    Dr. Paul)

GENS, head of the ghetto
WEISKOPF, director of a tailoring
    factory
CHAJA, female singer
KRUK, director of the library

The Acting Troupe, who also play:
HASID, a palm reader
DR. WEINER, a young doctor
DR. GOTTLIEB, an old doctor
JUDGE
RABBI
WOMAN

GRODZENSKI, a young smuggler
JANKEL, a young smuggler
GEIWISCH, a young smuggler
ELIA, a young smuggler
HEIKIN, a klezmer clarinetist

DESSLER, chief of the ghetto police
LEWAS, officer of the Jewish police

JEWISH PROSTITUTES, JEWISH POLICE, GESTAPO OFFICIALS.

Time/Place

The play takes place in the mind of Srulik as he recollects the Wilna ghetto during 1941-43.

Adapted from a literal translation by Kathleen Komar and as used for the first American production at the Mark Taper Forum, Los Angeles in October, 1986.

The Play

Ghetto

ACT ONE

*The living room of an apartment in Tel Aviv. 1984. A bourgeois home,
typically orderly and clean. A one-armed* MAN *sits in an easy chair, wearing a bathrobe.* HE *speaks with the difficulty and confusion of old age.
His name is* SRULIK.

SRULIK: The last performance? I don't want to talk about it. No, I don't
remember anymore. It was a long time ago . . . . Well, some things
I remember, but what's the point? It was on the evening before Kittel
murdered Gens. Gens was the head of the ghetto. Exactly ten days
before the liquidation of the ghetto. That was the last performance.
A full house! Of course. It was like that at every performance. The
audience came right up to the last days of the ghetto. People who
were loaded up and sent away in trains the next morning, still put
on their best clothes the evening before and came to our theatre
performance.

But as for what happened on the stage—that's all gone now. I'm
the only one who could remember it, and I'm . . . (HE *shrugs, as if
to say "hopeless"*)

We had arranged a competition for plays about life in the ghetto.
We got lots of plays. Everyone wrote: Katrielka Broide, Liebele
Rosenthal, Hirshke Glick, Israel Diamantman. Everyone wrote for

155

Joshua Sobol

us. Wonderful plays. Songs too! (HE *sings*) "Frozen toes and frozen fingers frozen to the bone!" All hand-written, all gone now. Life in the ghetto. I mean, we lived in a world—a mad world—where people disappeared and their clothing stayed behind.

(Suddenly struck by his own words) Yes! The clothing! *Di Yogenesh in Fas.* I still have a few songs from that satirical revue. *Di Yogenesh in Fas.* That's Yiddish for "chasing around in a barrel" because the theatre was so small. But do you get the pun? "Di-yog-en-ez"/Diogenes? Diogenes, the Cynic philosopher? He lived in a barrel and so did we. He roamed the world carrying a lantern in broad daylight looking for justice and truth. And in our little barrel? The ghetto? Did we have justice? Truth? We had a chase. A manhunt. Chasing around in a barrel. Of course, I'm no Diogenes . . .

But for a time I thought I saw . . . really saw what was happening. And we had a number in that show about clothes. "Finish it quickly!" No. "Disappear." Hmm. "Finish up quickly! Something, something disappear!" I get confused . . . "Finish it up! Today you're here, tomorrow . . . disappear . . ."

A great rumbling and banging is beginning to swell behind him.

I don't want to talk about it!

With a stunning crash, the walls of his apartment collapse, the apartment vanishes, and we're faced with a bare stage. At the rear wall is a tremendous, chaotic mountain of clothing.

The explosion of the apartment leaves us in a dark, undefined space. Then we hear the clatter of keys, the shooting of a bolt, and a man enters. HE *is dressed in underwear, but* HE *takes from the pile of clothing a German officer's uniform and puts it on. As* HE *does so, the stage fills with* OTHERS, *dressed in rags and sorting through more rags. The German officer,* KITTEL, *finds a machine gun and a long black case, and walks among the crowd shining a flashlight from place to place.*

KITTEL *(Observing the mess)*: Chaos!

WEISKOPF, *a mousy little man dressed in rags walks up behind him.* KITTEL, *ignores him.*

Light! Get some light on in here! Separate 'em! Sort 'em! Keep moving!

WEISKOPF *throws a switch. Industrial light goes on.*

SRULIK *(To the audience, as the scene materializes around him.* HE *is young now, and has both arms)*: That's Kittel. I was there too. We had to sort the clothes that came in.

KITTEL: More light!

HE *moves to the group of ragged* PEOPLE *pawing disconsolately through the clothes, indicating different areas for different piles of clothes.*

Men's. Children's. Wet. Dry. We've got truckloads outside. Move!

The PEOPLE *separate into* TWO GROUPS. ONE *sorts, the* OTHER *brings in more piles from outside.* KITTEL *stands in the middle of all this, indifferent.* CHAJA, *a young woman, appears and approaches.* SHE *shivers with cold and pulls the sheet* SHE'*s wearing around herself tighter. Her hair is tangled and unkempt. Her feet are bare and filthy.* SHE *approaches* KITTEL *and stands, watching the* WORKERS *and* UNPACKERS. KITTEL *shines his light in her face.*

CHAJA: May I . . . please . . . a pair of shoes.

KITTEL: Come.

HE *points to the spot in front of him.* SHE *moves to him, frightened.*

You need what?

CHAJA: A pair of shoes.

KITTEL: If you knew where these shoes had been, you'd stay barefoot.

A pause.

Please. Help yourself. *(To* WORKERS*)* Again! Pile 'em again!

CHAJA *hesitates. Then* SHE *goes to a pile of shoes and begins to try some on.* KITTEL *spots her and hits her with his flashlight beam. The* WORKERS *stop and watch.* CHAJA *finds a pair, puts them on and starts to run.*

KITTEL: Halt! *(Pointing to the spot in front of him)* Come!

CHAJA *returns.* HE *points to her sheet.*

Take it off.

SHE *complies. Beneath,* SHE *wears only a torn-up slip.*

You need a dress.

CHAJA *shakes her head.* KITTEL *points to the mound.*

Take a dress!

SHE *goes; takes a dress.*

Put it on!

SHE *does.*

(*To* WORKERS) What are you staring at? This isn't a show.
A coat!

SHE *goes to the coat pile, picks one up quickly.*

Hat!

SHE *moves to the hat pile.* SHE *takes a beret, but doesn't put it on. Again* KITTEL *points to the spot in front of him.*

Come!

Defeated, SHE *goes to him.* HE *shines the light in her face.*

Hold your head up! Fix your hair! Put on the hat!

SHE *complies in something like panic.*

Not bad. With a little effort, you people can really be first-class. Turn.

SHE *turns, the reluctant model.* HE *looks at her belly quizzically.*

What's that? (HE *points the tip of his gun to the slight swelling in her belly*) What is that? A baby? Do you have any idea what happens to Jews who get pregnant?

SHE *is silent.*

Do you?! Come! Wait!

CHAJA *takes another step toward him.* HE *puts a hand on her belly.*

What is this?

CHAJA *takes a small bag from under her dress.* KITTEL *holds out his hand.*

Let's have it.

CHAJA *hands it to him.*

A pound of beans! (KITTEL *turns over the bag. Beans fall out and cascade across the stage)*

Black market? Who sold you this? I want names!

CHAJA *is silent.*

No names? So. You stole a pound of beans. (HE *looks piercingly at her for a moment)*

In a whirlwind KITTEL *grabs* CHAJA *and pulls her up to the pile of clothing.* HE *turns and crosses downstage, cocking his gun as he moves.*

Hands up!

SRULIK, *who has been carrying clothes to the pile, runs to him. In his hand* HE *holds a life-sized dummy, who is completely beside himself. The* DUMMY *screams at* KITTEL *while* SRULIK *tries to silence him.*

DUMMY: Stop! Halt! *Arrêtez!* Whoa! For God's sake, hold your fire!
SRULIK *(To the* DUMMY*):* Cut it out, Ignatz, he's got a gun.
DUMMY: Oh, terrific! She's about to be blown to bits and you're pissing in your pants.
SRULIK *(To the* DUMMY, *a well-worn routine):* Well at least I know how!
DUMMY: So much for chivalry! Whatever happened to the days of yore, when damsels in distress were rescued by knights in shining armor?
SRULIK: So get a knight. I'm a Jew.
DUMMY: You don't have to brag about it.
SRULIK: Who's bragging? I'm trying to stay alive.
KITTEL: Hold it! Who are you?
DUMMY: He stole the beans.
KITTEL: Is that right?
SRULIK: Would you take evidence from a dummy? He's pathological!
DUMMY: Pathological?! I'm not even Jewish!
KITTEL: That's enough!
SRULIK: You heard the gentleman. That's enough.

DUMMY: He was speaking to you!

SRULIK: No, you.

DUMMY: No, you.

SRULIK *(To* KITTEL*)*: You see, I'm helpless. He's driving me crazy. I can't get rid of him.

DUMMY: He's quite right Herr Kittel, but he's got it backwards. I can't get away from him.

SRULIK: Yes, you can!

KITTEL: *Shut . . . up!* Or I'll tear your head off. *(To* SRULIK*)* Did you give her the beans?

SRULIK: If I had beans they'd be in *my* stomach. Besides, this woman's not a thief. She's an artist. A great artist.

DUMMY: Yes, she's an artist. And besides . . . *(Sotto voce)* He *loves* her.

SRULIK: Before the war, she was a star. Now she hasn't worked in months. She'll starve. I turn to you only because you are an artist too.

DUMMY: Ass-kisser! Kittel *hates* ass-kissers!

KITTEL *(A satisfied laugh)*: How true, how true. *(Suddenly serious,* HE *roars)* You! Get a scale.

All work ceases. PEOPLE *gather round.*

Juden! Achtung! You all have exactly one minute to find every bean she stole. A pound of beans and not an ounce less. Go!

A massive bean hunt; a scale is produced. EVERYONE *crawls around the stage, retrieving beans.* KITTEL *looks at his watch.*

STOP!

ALL *freeze.*

. . . On the scale!

EVERYONE *puts the remaining beans on the scale.* CHAJA *checks the scale.*

CHAJA: Eleven ounces.

KITTEL: Five ounces short. Well, well . . . you now have a choice. Careful here. Think. This? *(HE points to the gun in his hand)* Or this? *(HE points to the long black case* HE*'s been carrying)*

CHAJA *(SHE points to the case)*: That.

KITTEL: Ah, hah. Yes, indeed. *(HE takes out an object from the case.* HE *whirls on the crowd holding a saxophone as* HE *would hold a machine gun.* HE *laughs.* HE *puts it to his mouth and plays a few bars of Beethoven's Ninth Symphony)* Do you know that one?

CHAJA *nods.*

Well, by all means, let's try it.

KITTEL *plays.* CHAJA *opens her mouth but no sound comes out.* HE *stops.*

According to this Jew, you're a singer. A great artist. If he lied, then tomorrow morning, you're both off to Ponar where you will be stripped, marched to the pits, and shot. I hope that's sufficient inducement. Now sing!

SHE *opens her mouth wider, but still nothing comes out.* SHE *points to her throat.*

CHAJA: My throat is dry . . .
KITTEL: Well, why didn't you say so?

HE *gives her his flask.* SHE *takes a gulp and gives the bottle back.*

CHAJA: Thank you. If I could sing one of our songs instead . . .
KITTEL: S'il vous plait, Madame!
CHAJA *(Sings "Shtiler, Shtiler" [Be Still]):*
    Be still, be silent, be a shadow, softly draw each breath
    The day of wrath is here, my child, we're in the house
        of death
    Your papa's vanished like the wind and I with anguish burn
    And pray that, like the wand'ring wind, he one day will return
    The past's a fading fantasy, the present inky black
    Our single road leads to Ponar with no road leading back
    The world has turned its face away, we're banished, battered
        and reviled
    But still, be still, we may yet live, my child

    I saw a woman on the street whose manner was bizarre
    Some people spoke in whispers of her children and Ponar
    This is the winter of our souls, the blackest hour of night
    But nature's timeless wheel must turn and bring a new day's light
    Then there will come another time before your eyes grow old
    For us a warmer season when our foes will feel the cold
    We'll greet your papa at the door, we'll be a fam'ly as before
    And you will sing out loud forevermore—forevermore.
KITTEL: My God you really are an artist. Jesus, look at this. *(*HE *rubs his eye with a finger)* Real tears. Well. That experience, in my opinion, is worth an ounce of beans. I mean . . . tears are easy. What about

the other four ounces? You can't find work at your trade, so how do you propose to pay? You're all artists, yes?

DUMMY: Yes sir. All artists. At your service, sir!

KITTEL: Well. Interesting. Prove it to me. Prove your art is worth four ounces of beans. You'll get your opportunity. But watch out. I'm no fool. Don't play me for one.

HE *turns and goes.* EVERYONE *exits after him except* CHAJA, SRULIK *and, of course, the* DUMMY.

CHAJA *(To* SRULIK*)*: How can I thank you?

DUMMY: How do you think?

SRULIK: Don't be silly. You don't need to thank me.

DUMMY: Hypocrite!

SRULIK: I'm just happy you're still alive.

DUMMY: Give the man a shovel!

CHAJA: But you risked your life for me.

SRULIK: Well, my life. What's it worth, really?

DUMMY: In beans?

SRULIK: After all, when you get right down to it, who am I? A puppeteer from the Meidim Theatre. An actor, not much of a man.

CHAJA: I think you're a very brave man.

DUMMY: Brave?! Are you kidding? Did you see him trying to muzzle me? Chajale! I'm the one who saved you.

CHAJA *(Stroking the puppet's head)*: You're cute.

DUMMY: Oh, my. Mmm . . . that is *heaven.* Do you know how long it's been, since somebody stroked me like that. Would you like a backrub? I could—

SRULIK: Enough! You ought to be ashamed of yourself.

DUMMY *(Confidentially, to* CHAJA*)*: He's insufferably jealous. *(To* SRULIK*)* Now go. Sit over there.

SRULIK: Where?

DUMMY: There.

SRULIK: Here?

DUMMY: *Further!* And don't bother us! *(To* CHAJA*)* You do love me, don't you.

CHAJA: How could anyone not love you, *mazik?*

DUMMY: And I love you, too! From the moment I saw you, my heart leapt. And I . . . you must be hungry. And here I am making idle chit-chat. *(To* SRULIK*)* Get her some food!

SRULIK: Food?! Where from? I'm starving.

DUMMY: Hah! What's in your pocket, then?

SRULIK: My pocket? Lint. (HE *turns his pocket inside out. It's empty)* Not even lint.

DUMMY: The other pocket, *gonif.*

SRULIK: Oh the *other* pocket. Well . . . *(HE finds a carrot)* I must have forgotten . . . I, uh . . . please, take it. *(HE gives her the carrot)*

CHAJA: And what will you eat?

DUMMY: Don't worry about him! When it comes to carrots he's a bottomless pit.

SRULIK *takes a second carrot from his pocket.*

SRULIK: *Bon appétit.*

THEY *eat in silence a moment. Then* SRULIK *speaks, getting up his courage.*

Do you . . . have a place to sleep?

CHAJA: Under the stairs.

DUMMY: Well, come to our place. We have an enormous blanket.

SRULIK: What a suggestion!

DUMMY: You think it's any fun snuggling up to you at night? You're all bones, and it's freezing at our place. Chajale, I only meant we could, you know, bundle up together. For warmth. Is that a sin?

CHAJA: No, it's no sin, you little rascal, not in this world. I'm cold at night, too. All right, let's go!

CHAJA, SRULIK *and* DUMMY *sing* "Hot Zich Mir Di Shich Zerissn" *(Dance, Dance, Dance).*

CHAJA:
Frozen toes and frozen fingers
I'm frozen to the bone

DUMMY:
But what's the good of freezing
When you're freezing all alone

So dance, dance, dance
A little dance with me
Let's do a sultry tango
It'll warm us up, you'll see

CHAJA:
Not a penny, not a crust
Nor twig do I possess

DUMMY:
But with you beside me
I remember happiness

So kiss, kiss, kiss
Share a little kiss with me
And maybe we can reinvent
What kissing used to be

SRULIK:
Colored papers, pink and yellow
Yellow saves your life
I've got my yellow papers
But I haven't got a wife

DUMMY:
So marry, marry, marry me
Love's not beyond recall

SRULIK:
And maybe we will live
To see tomorrow after all.

CHAJA *exits.* SRULIK *looks around the stage like a professional appraiser.* GENS *appears and calls out to him.*

GENS: So? What do you think?
SRULIK *(Dubiously)*: Well, it's a place . . .
GENS: Did you count the seats?
SRULIK: I counted.
GENS: Six hundred seats!
SRULIK: I counted.
GENS: And have you had a look around at the stage?
SRULIK: It's a stage.
GENS: This place, I give to you. Take it and create the Ghetto Theatre here. Not just plays: discussions, lectures . . . concerts. Culture!
SRULIK: Culture. Well, yeah, why not?
GENS: Clean the place up. I need an inventory—what's here, what you need—a list.
SRULIK: When do you need it?
GENS: Yesterday.

A HASID *enters.*

HASID *(Calling toward* GENS*)*: Your honor, your honor! Mr. Police Commissioner, sir!
GENS: What do you want?
HASID: I want to read your palm. Give me your hand, I'll give you the future. Your hand please!
GENS: What is this? A sideshow? Get a job.

HASID (*Suddenly trancelike*): This summer will change your life forever.

GENS: Wait, wait, wait. How do you know that?

HASID (*Businesslike again*): I do ears, too. But it is in the palm that all of the details lie. Your palm, sir.

GENS: Oh, for God's sake. (*Giving over his palm*) Make it quick, I'm busy.

HASID (*Trance routine again*): Ah hah. Do you see it? Do you see it?

GENS: What?

HASID: Three changes into eight. Can you see that?

GENS: What if I can?

HASID: Well, it's obvious. Three represents the third letter, which is Gimel. Eight is the eighth letter, which is Chet. You do see that?

GENS *is silent, impatient.*

Well, Gimel is G, like Germany, and Chat "Ch" which is like Cherut—that means independence and freedom. You will deal with the Germans with independence, and lead us to freedom. There will be a great revolution. But before that, you will take command of the ghetto. You will lead us to freedom.

GENS: Great. You have dates for this event?

HASID (*Staring at* GENS's *palm intently*): In three more time periods.

GENS: Three more time periods? . . . What the hell does that mean?

HASID: Could be three weeks, three months . . . even three years.

GENS *laughs. The* HASID *sticks out his hand for payment.*

Three marks, please.

GENS: What?!

HASID: Three marks.

GENS (*Paying*): Go find some decent work. You peddle the future around the ghetto, you'll starve.

HASID: Another thing I noticed in the future is an acting company . . .

GENS: You were listening!

HASID: And, I'm an actor. (*The* HASID *pulls off his wig and beard*) You want comedy, tragedy? "Has a Jew not eyes? Has a Jew not hands? If you prick us do we not bleed?" . . . (*Sings*) "So dance, dance, dance, do a little dance with me."

GENS: Alright, alright. Go dance over there.

GENS *pushes the* HASID *upstage and looks to* SRULIK.

You'll find a place for him, yes? Now, we were saying . . . will the place be all right?

CHAJA: The place is fine.

SRULIK: But it's the time, Jakob. Three weeks ago fifty thousand Jews were murdered on this spot. The blood's not dry yet and you want us to create theatre here? It's not the time.

GENS (*Goes to a door at the side of the stage*): Not the time, you say. (*GENS opens the door and calls out*) Let 'em in! Now!

> MEN and WOMEN *are shoved into the room: the acting company.* THEY *look around, dazed, frightened, blinking.* SRULIK *stares at them dumbfounded, as if seeing ghosts.*

SRULIK: Lionek, my God. No, no it's all right. You're safe. It's me. Umma . . . I was sure you were dead.

CHAJA (*Spots* HEIKIN *and runs to embrace him*): Heiken, my klezmer. You're alive.

> HEIKIN *embraces her, in a daze.*

SRULIK: Where . . . Jakob . . . where did you find them all?

GENS: Living in garrets, working in forced labor, hiding in root cellars, Srulik. These were the ones I could still save.

> CHAJA *has been running from person to person as the room fills with* ACTORS, *showing off* HEIKIN, *who still looks about blindly.* GENS *hands him his clarinet.* HEIKIN *stares at it in disbelief, but can't bring it to his lips.*

CHAJA: Heikin, please. For me.

> HEIKIN *stares at her balefully.* SHE *begins to sing "Ich Benk A Heym"* (*I Long For Home*) *for him.*

CHAJA *and the* ACTING COMPANY (*singing*):
> When you are young,
> Yes, young and strong,
> You long to try your wings.
> You leave your home,
> Your childhood nest,
> Forsaking childhood things.
> But when old age draws near,
> Scenes from your past appear
> And, oh! What feelings rise,
> From those forgotten ties,
> From childhood scenes
> When seen through older eyes.

I long to see my home once more.
Is it the way it was before?
The weathered porch, the slanting stairs,
Four walls, a table and some chairs,
My poor old home.

I long to know them once again,
The things I took for granted then
The songs I sang, the dreams I dreamed
Are more enduring than they seemed.
I miss my home.

I hear a breeze
As gentle as a sigh,
Recalling a mother's lullaby.

HEIKIN *begins to play, and the* ENSEMBLE *sings.*

ALL:

Though not of brick nor made of stone,
A stronger home I've never known.
As strong as steel, as light as air,
Built from my mother's loving care.
I long for home!

I long to know them once again,
The things I took for granted then.
The songs I sang, the dreams I dreamed
Are more enduring than they seemed.
I miss my home.

I hear a breeze
As gentle as a sigh,
Recalling a mother's lullaby.

CHAJA:

Though not of brick nor made of stone.
A stronger home I've never known.
As strong as steel, as light as air,
Build from my mother's loving care.
I long for home!

The ENSEMBLE, *momentarily uplifted, is lifeless again.*

SRULIK: Jakob, this is not going to work.
GENS: Tell me, Srulik, what these men and women have in common.
SRULIK: They're artists!

GENS: Artists? Pathetic! What they have in common is no work permits. Also no food rations. They're next in line for Ponar—that's what they have in common. You want that on your conscience? *(Gradually working himself up)* The right time for theatre, the wrong time for theatre. You intellectuals amaze me. When all this is over I can hear you telling your grandchildren: "Even though police chief Gens tried to force us to perform on the site of the massacre, I refused." The pride! The moral conviction! Well, look at them, Srulik! Look in their eyes! If you make them into an acting company on this spot, I can get them yellow work permits—and bread. And butter—and potatoes. And soap! A half ration of soap for every one of your "artists."

ALL *(Ad lib in whispers)*: A half ration!

GENS: That's right, for each of you. (HE *marches back and forth like an officer dressing down his troops)* But there's more . . . . As a troop of Jewish actors, you can make a difference! Look around! Our self-esteem is in the sewer. People walk the streets staring at their shoes—if they have shoes to stare at. You can change all that—give them back their self-respect. That's what I want: show them they have a culture—a language, a powerful inheritance: an inner life. Nu? Begin the rehearsal! In three weeks, I want to see a play! A performance!

SRULIK: With all due respect, Mr. Gens, what are we supposed to rehearse? What kind of a play?

GENS: Do I ask you how to run the ghetto? How should I know what kind of play? Something good, something funny, something cultural. Whatever will make us feel like men again. You know what I mean— you're artists!

SRULIK *and the* ACTORS *exit. As* THEY *go,* GENS *and* WEISKOPF *remain. Across the stage, in the library,* HERMAN KRUK *appears.*

WEISKOPF: Mr. Gens! Mr. Gens!

GENS: You, too. You, too! Go rehearse.

WEISKOPF: Mr. Gens, I'm not an actor.

GENS: So who the hell are you?

KRUK *speaks, as if dictating, far from the actual scene.* GENS *and* WEISKOPF *remain motionless while* KRUK *dictates.*

KRUK: That's Weiskopf. A few weeks ago he was a nobody, a *vonce* with a tailor shop. Who could know what the war would make of this man? In a few weeks—the king of the ghetto. A man to keep your eye on . . .

WEISKOPF: If you could spare me just a minute or two, Mr. Gens . . . you won't regret it.

GENS: I hope not.

WEISKOPF: Do you know how many first-class tailors we have in the ghetto?

GENS: Tailors?

WEISKOPF: And sewing machines? How about sewing machines?

GENS: Sewing machines . . .?

WEISKOPF: Take a look. *(Giving* GENS *a small notebook)*

GENS: What is this?

WEISKOPF: I made a few inquiries. Tailors . . . seamstresses . . . machines . . .

GENS: A list. With names, addresses . . .

WEISKOPF: I went from room to room.

GENS: But what for?

WEISKOPF: Have you seen the trains, traveling from the Russian front to Germany?

GENS: I don't understand.

WEISKOPF: Do you know what their cargo is?

GENS: How should I know?

WEISKOPF: Uniforms. Torn, bloody German uniforms. And why are they sent from the Russian front all the way to Germany?

GENS: I imagine . . . to be put back in shape.

WEISKOPF: You can appreciate the crucial point. We are next door to the Russian front here in the ghetto. Hundreds of tailors, seamstresses, sewing machines. . . . It's *meschugge*, no?

GENS: And you think the Germans . . .

WEISKOPF: Approval on the spot. We'll erect a giant uniform repair factory. Instead of sending the stuff thousands of miles, burning coal, losing time, stopping up the tracks, they can deliver the uniforms here. Good for them, good for us.

GENS: And every tailor, every seamstress, will be indispensable. . . . How many can you use?

WEISKOPF: We could begin with, say, a hundred. Later we'll raise it to a hundred and fifty. I've picked out a spot.

GENS: A hundred and fifty families, kept alive indefinitely. Come to my office tomorrow morning.

WEISKOPF: Tomorrow? What happened to today? If we work through the night, tomorrow morning you'll lay out the whole program for the Germans—precise figures, just the way they like it—and we're in business.

GENS *(Regards* WEISKOPF *for a moment)*: I like people like you. What's your name?

WEISKOPF: Weiskopf.

GENS: Come into my office, Mr. Weiskopf—Mr. Factory Director.

THEY *exit. Across the stage,* KRUK *dictates, leafing through some documents and letters.*

KRUK: An interesting chapter in the life of the ghetto. An interesting case. Weiskopf. (HE *picks up a letter from his desk and reads*) "January 17, 1942. On Sunday, January 18, you are cordially invited to the premiere performance of the new Ghetto Theatre. On the program: dramatic scenes, songs, music . . ." (HE *turns to his invisible secretary*) Put this in capital letters: YOU DON'T PERFORM THEATRE IN A GRAVEYARD.

A rush from all sides of the stage. MEMBERS OF THE RESISTANCE *scurry about, leafleting and postering the stage with* KRUK's *slogan: YOU DON'T PERFORM THEATRE IN A GRAVEYARD.* THEY *exit, leaving* KRUK *where* HE *was.* GENS *enters the library, carrying a poster* HE *has ripped from the wall.*

GENS: Herman Kruk? (HE *holds up the sign*) I know who did this. I know everything that happens in the ghetto. Everything. Why this slogan?
KRUK: Why this invitation?
GENS: Every important person in the ghetto was invited. You run the library.
KRUK: And did you really think I'd come to your vaudeville show?
GENS: What have you got against theatre?
KRUK: The invitation is an insult.
GENS: Insult?
KRUK: A personal insult. (*Pause*) In any other ghetto, perhaps. There might be some entertainment, even some fun. One should always try to live in the presence of art—if possible. But here? In the middle of the tragedy of Wilna? In the shadow of Ponar? Of the seventy-six thousand Wilna Jews, how many are left? Fifteen thousand.
GENS: Sixteen thousand.
KRUK: A theatre? Now? It's shameless!
GENS: All right. Let's talk about shame. On Saturday, September 6th, 1941, the Germans herded us into the ghetto. Hell on earth. People were driven through the rain; wagons stranded in muck. And what did you see? Books. Books slipping from people's hands, into the mud. While our people stumbled through the streets as if they were drugged, Herman Kruk made a book collection. Next morning, you opened this library. Well, for that I salute you. Relax, Herschel, I don't expect anything in return. Look, let's face it, you're a socialist,

a Bundist. I am a Zionist, a revisionist. Worlds separate us. Jakob Gens didn't fish any books out of the slime. I admit it. *I pulled human beings out of the slime.* I found them clothing and food, and I forged them into an orchestra and a theatre troupe. I've given them back their jobs, and I'll get them work permits. Heikin, the klezmer? I took him out of forced labor. I took a pickax out of his hand and gave him back his clarinet. Is that a crime? *(A pause.* HE *fishes the invitation to the theatre opening off* KRUK*'s desk)* This is no invitation. It's an order. You and your friends, Bundists, socialists, leaders of the workers' union, all of you, will be at the theatre.

KRUK *(Regards* GENS *for a moment, struck by his ferocity)*: Why is this so important to you?

GENS: Solidarity. Everyone in the ghetto must agree that we are one people. A great, brave people, a creative force through history. I'm going to unite the ghetto. Everyone, everyone—without exceptions. It's not a matter of choice anymore.

KRUK: I don't think you'd miss us. After all, the Jewish police, the foremen and brigadiers of the forced labor groups—you'll have a distinguished crowd. Plus whatever guests you've invited from the outside— German staff officers and their wives. I gather our famous chanteuse is feverishly looking for a few *Deutsche lieder* to add to the program, in case the Germans—heaven forbid—should want a few songs from the Fatherland.

GENS: Look, we can continue this little discussion the day after tomorrow. In the meantime, I expect to see you at the theatre.

KRUK: Enjoy it. Play up to the Germans any way you want to. The workers' union has decided to boycott. None of us will join this concert of crows.

GENS: In that case, Mr. Kruk, your workers' union is hereby dissolved.

KRUK *(Outraged)*: What?!

GENS: Forbidden.

KRUK: It's the only Jewish organization in the ghetto that was democratically chosen!

GENS: Aye-aye-aye—*Vusszugstute*, Herschel.

KRUK: What are we, Jakob? Nothing more than your own personal kingdom? And this theatre is your Versailles? We refuse to take part in this revisionist farce!

GENS: You think you can play party politics with me? Listen to me, Kruk: One more poster like this, you go straight to Ponar.

KRUK *(*HE *dictates again)*: The boss of the ghetto has ordered the dissolution of the only democratically elected group we have: the workers' union. It seems the workers have been playing partisan politics. Just to make sure he is clearly understood, he has also threatened to send Kruk and his comrades to Ponar.

GENS: History will judge which one of us helped the Jews more in this catastrophe, Kruk. Write *that* down in your diary. *(HE leaves)*

KRUK: I write, I write. What else is there to do? *(Dictating again)* We are living through such a dismal time that people can no longer recognize the true nature of the world around them. They don't want to see. They can't see. And the sad truth is, as long as we are made helpless by fascism, it is our duty to write. That's why my notebook will see all; it will hear all; it will be the mirror and conscience of this catastrophe.

During KRUK's *monologue, the* ACTORS *and* MUSICIANS *become visible on stage behind him.* CHAJA *sings "Wei Zu Di Teg" (Crazy Times). It is a rehearsal.*

CHAJA *(Singing)*:
Oy, little ones . . .
What times we live in!
Life grows harder day and night . . .
Cruel, crazy times . . .

Times of hydroplanes and Dreadnoughts!
Times of iron, steel and lead!
Ships that sail beneath the water!
Trains that rumble overhead!

Oy, it's all topsy-turvy!
Nothing is the way it was before.
Once the world was simple;
Now I don't understand it anymore!

The future's a puzzle,
The present's a maze!
Confusion and madness
Disfigure our days!

The future's a puzzle,
The present's a maze!
Confusion and madness
Disfigure our days!

ALL:
Oy, it's all topsy-turvy!
Nothing is the way it was before.
Once the world was simple;
Now I don't understand it anymore.

*Oy, little ones . . .
What times we live in!
Life grows harder day and night.
Cruel, crazy times . . . *(Repeat three times*)*

Oy, it's all topsy-turvy!
Nothing is the way it was before.
Once the world was simple;
Now I don't understand it anymore!

Oy, it's all topsy-turvy!
Nothing is the way it was before.
Once the world was simple;
Now I don't understand it anymore!

At the end of the song, WEISKOPF *swings onto the stage with elan.*

WEISKOPF: What is it with the moaning and groaning, people?
SRULIK: Weiskopf, this is a rehearsal.
WEISKOPF: Life is a rehearsal. Hard times? Nu? When do the Jews ever
   have it easy? Suffering makes us strong people. Take me for exam-
   ple. Who has better grounds to moan and groan than Weiskopf?
   Before the war I was a Schneider with nine tailor shops; nothing
   much but it was mine. Then the Germans came and squeezed us
   into the ghetto. No more shop, no more nothing. Kaputt, my whole
   life, into the toilet. Could I have cried? And how I could have cried!
   But no! I said to myself: Why are you called Weiskopf? Weiser Kopf.
   Wise head. All brains. (HE *taps himself on the head*) So. I took my little
   Jewish brains and said to myself, Weiskopf, you have lost your store.
   Are you kaputt? Sure! And if you lose your head what? Double kaputt
   you'll be. But you have your brain, and as long as they don't remove
   it with a scalpel, you'll stay alive! So you've got a brain, why not
   use it? I looked around me: A ghetto—walls, walls, walls, walls.
   Closed up tight. But always: always always always there is a way out.
   And who found it? *(Triumphant) Weiskopf!* So before the war what
   am I? Just a nebbish with a shop. And today what do you see before
   you? The director of a tailoring factory—the largest in the district!
   A hundred and fifty Jews work for me. And who are my partners?
SRULIK: The Germans!
WEISKOPF: The Germans give *me* contracts. It's a great big business and
   all it does is grow. Each morning I wake up to a bigger income, and
   does that make me stingy? Do I hoard it? The opposite, my friends:
   I'm very generous. If someone comes to me with a good cause, I'm
   open handed; five thousand rubles I give, minimum. I'm free with

my money and everyone should know it. I'm not ashamed of what I do. My way is the only way! I set an example for the community! I am an ordinary Jew, but we Jews, we're gifted. If you would follow my example, instead of kreching and moaning, we would have a productive ghetto, and they would find us indispensable, the Germans. And once we're indispensable, we stay alive.

KITTEL *emerges from the pile of clothing.* HE *has a large case in each hand.* HE *puts them down and applauds* WEISKOPF's *speech.*

KITTEL: Bravo, Weiskopf, bravo! I like you. And when I like someone, he stays alive. (HE *goes to a* GIRL *and slaps her*) Doesn't anyone say *shalom aleichem* around here?

EVERYONE *stops and greets him.*

I'll let it go this time because I took you by surprise. I didn't come through the gate. So no one could send out the warning—"Kittel is in the ghetto." (HE *laughs*) Be careful, though. Kittel doesn't use the gate. Kittel slithers into the ghetto like a snake. You dig a tunnel to hide yourself, Kittel reaches out to grab you. You take an idle stroll down the street, Kittel strikes from an attic window. Don't hide in the basement. Kittel is already there. (To SRULIK, *suddenly*) What is in the cases? The wrong answwser will cost you more than you can pay.

SRULIK (*Pointing to one case*): The gun.

KITTEL (*Opening the case*): The gun. Very good. (HE *gets it out and loads it. Then to* CHAJA) And in the other one.

CHAJA: The saxophone.

KITTEL: Well, let's see. (HE *opens the case*) The saxophone. The gun and the sax! Haaa! (*Suddenly cutting and threatening*) Why do I love you Weiskopf? Why?

WEISKOPF: I'm productive.

KITTEL *laughs.*

And I make a contribution to the war economy.

KITTEL: And who made you productive?

WEISKOPF: You did.

KITTEL: I . . . (HE *smiles, then becomes enraged*) . . . can't stand ass-kissers. (*To* SRULIK) Why can't I?

SRULIK: Because you're an artist.

KITTEL: I'm an artist. And what do artists invariably love?

SRULIK: The true, the good, the beautiful.

KITTEL: Did you hear that, Weiskopf? The true, the good, the beautiful.
I didn't make you productive, *you* made you productive. All I did
was create the climate for you, so that a previously hidden tendency
in your Jewish character could emerge full-blown. I mean, this mad
energy you Jews possess, Christ almighty. I look at the Lithuanians
trudging through the streets; Jesus, what scum they are. We should
be wiping *them* out, not you. What a mistake. No wit, no spirit—
they're the walking dead. Then I slither into the ghetto, and it's
another world. Raw energy is spilling out into the street, it's a sight.
It's beautiful. You probably didn't even notice; I mean, those who
live in paradise take it for granted. Yes? But for me . . . the cafes,
the shops, the sense of people doing business . . . the spirit! When
you run out of real food you chop up some beets and call it caviar.
Sauerkraut juice becomes champagne—so it's champagne and caviar
every night. Combine that Jewish spirit with German soul, and
something great will be born. Did you ever dream you'd come so
far Weiskopf? Tell the truth now!

WEISKOPF: Never.

KITTEL: So. The good, the beautiful and the true. All right, we've covered
the good and the beautiful, now for the truth, without which there
is no real art. A question, Weiskopf. The true answer lies at the
essence of your Jewishness, and it is a question of truth. Let me remind you, Weiskopf . . . (HE *gestures to the two cases at his feet*) The gun,
the saxophone. (*Picking up the gun*) Now, Weiskopf, what is the difference between partial liquidation and total liquidation? That is
the question.

WEISKOPF *looks at him, thinks. Tension builds.*

WEISKOPF: If you kill fifty thousand Jews but not me, that's partial liquidation. If you kill me, that's total liquidation.

KITTEL: Bravo! Very nice, Weiskopf, absolutely on the mark. The wit!
The sting! No one but a Jew could think of such an answer. Well,
forget about the gun, this is hardly the time for the gun. It's time
for the saxophone. I'm telling you, when the ghetto is liquidated,
I'm going to have a piano set up right by the gate, and while you
march to the trains, I'll play Schumann. "Scenes from Childhood,"
I think. Or "Carneval"? (HE *muses*) Well. I'll tell you what I'm doing here. Ah! The orchestra?

The MUSICIANS *step forward, warily.*

Gentlemen! To your instruments!

The MUSICIANS *move hesitantly to their instruments.*

The reason I came . . . is Gershwin. Can you imagine? All of a sudden I had this hankering for Gershwin. Funny, isn't it? These pigs at the Ministry of Culture in Berlin have banned him. "Death to jazz," they shout. So, when the simple urge for a bit of Gershwin begins to get to me, where am I supposed to go for satisfaction? Ah, the ghetto. Your Mr. Gens told me you had a jazz band, and that's why I'm here. (HE *looks over the* BAND, *missing someone*) Where's your vocalist? There's a singer here, she owes me two ounces of beans . . .

CHAJA *steps forward out of the group and stands face to face with him.*

Mademoiselle. Well, let's see if you can pay your debt. (HE *leaps onto the improvised podium, and directs with his saxophone*)"Swanee"! Do you know it? You must! Everybody—"Swanee"! Alright, I'll make it simpler for you. Sing it in Yiddish.
SRULIK: We'll have to . . .
KITTEL: Now!

The BAND *launches into "Swanee."* CHAJA *gives it all* SHE*'s got, fighting for her life.* KITTEL *moves between the* ACTORS, *sax in hand, and orders them to dance.* THEY *improvise a jazz number to "Swanee."*

CHAJA *(Sings "Swanee"):*
　　Ich bin avek fun dir a lange zait
　　Ich benk noch dir, ich gai ash oiss
　　Ch'ob a gefil, du libst mir fil
　　Swanee, du rufst mir oiss.

　　*Swanee, wi ich lib dir
　　Wi ich lib dir
　　Main taire Swanee,
　　Ich shenk di ganze velt
　　Zu zen noch ein moll D-I-X-I-E
　　—Ven now my mamee warten oif mir
　　Davwen far mir
　　Dort bai der Swanee
　　Di fremde weln mir nisht zen shoin mer
　　Ven ich kum zu dem Swanee mer . . . (Repeat *)

*Swanee
Swanee
Ich kum zurick zu Swanee
Mammy
Mammy
Ich will zurick a heim! *(Repeat *)*

KITTEL: Ladies and gentlemen, I thank you! What a unique artistic experience. Not perfect, of course. The choreography was a bit . . . how can I say it . . . ragged? And a touch . . . heavy-handed. In jazz, the body must be light, utterly relaxed. (HE *dances a bit to demonstrate, singing his own accompaniment.* HE *stops; turns to* CHAJA) And the vocal? Not bad at all. I'd say you have a bright future in front of you. In a few years you could sink your teeth into—what—*Porgy and Bess?* Or even *Carmen.* As for today's performance, let's call it an ounce of beans on the Kittel scale. A magnificent score. *(Turning to* WEISKOPF*)* Look at them, Weiskopf, they can't step out on stage in these rags! You may donate the costumes from your treasure-house, yes? And make it lavish, Weiskopf. Extravagant.

WEISKOPF: Only the finest.

KITTEL: Good man, Weiskopf. Don't forget: I'll be there.

KITTEL *starts to leave without his gun and saxophone.* WEISKOPF *runs and picks them up.*

WEISKOPF: Mr. Kittel . . .?

KITTEL *(To* EVERYONE*)*: And the rest of you—remember: Kittel can turn up anywhere—anytime, anyplace. Lift up a rock, Kittel is coiled underneath. Kittel, the snake.

HE *laughs, and disappears, without the cases, into the orchestra pit. Two* GESTAPO OFFICIALS *run in and grab the cases from* WEISKOPF *and exit.*

WEISKOPF: Okay, okay, people, let's get going. Come and get it. Take what you need, whatever you want. *Meine* is *deine.* Any cut, any size, any amount. The one thing we have in abundance is clothing. Everything sorted, everything stacked. Help yourselves, try it on for size. (WEISKOPF *grabs a dress from the pile and hands it to* CHAJA) Here Chajele! Try it on. Slips, suits, cloaks and coats. The finest workmanship, the latest styles. From Lodz. (HE *holds up a little girl's dress by mistake)* Children's wear?

A *momentary shock-wave, as the* ACTORS *realize what this clothing is.* WEISKOPF *tries to cover, dropping the dress quickly.*

Well, it's not a children's theater. What do you need in fabrics? You
want wool, you want corduroy? What do you want, rags? Of course,
you need rags, for a play. Rags I also have no shortage of. And professional stuff? Whatever your play calls for: police, judges, doctors—I
got cloaks for Hasidim, caftans for rabbis in genuine velvet. And
for ladies and gentlemen of leisure, the finest tweed suits from Man-
chester, and haute couture from Paris. Wait, wait! What about
uniforms? The Polish cavalry I got in heavy supply. Uniforms of
brave heroes, some from Warsaw, some from Danzig, men who
galloped on horses with fixed bayonets and met the tanks of the German army. Can you imagine what these uniforms looked like when
they turned up in my shop?! Like from a sausage grinder! The blood,
the bullet holes—and now? Take a look I beg you. Like new. Their
past life has been erased with an invisible weave. Step into them and
step right out on stage. You don't want Polish uniforms, how about
German? Believe me they don't look so much better than the Poles
when they get here from the front. If these uniforms could talk, my
God, the tales they'd tell! I'll tell you, you should see the action in
our laundry when these uniforms come in, *that* you could make a
play from. Real drama! Germans and Poles chasing each other in
the wash kettles, fires blazing in the ovens, the muck and filth that
comes boiling over and runs across the floors and out into the sewer.
An entire world fogged over with chlorine, grease and steam. What
a battle! And then you should see the repair shop! An enormous
tailoring station, a hundred and fifty sewing machines rattling away
around the clock—RAT - TAT - TAT - TAT - TAT—it sounds like a
railroad station. And all for you! The theatre company! Ladies and
gentlemen, help yourself, whatever you don't see, just ask. There
is no shortage of clothing here!

The ACTORS *have dressed.* TWO *are dressed as* DOCTORS GOTTLIEB *and*
WEINER, ONE *in a rabbi's caftan, and* ONE *in a judge's robes. A* WOMAN
has dressed herself in rags, and immediately turns screaming to WEISKOPF.

WOMAN: Mr. Weiskopf, Mr. Weiskopf! They've arrested my husband.
WEISKOPF *(Still lost in thought)*: Don't worry, please. It'll all work itself out.
WOMAN: Work itself out? They caught him with five pounds of flour,
and locked him up in Lukischki.
WEISKOPF: I said, be calm. It will work out.
WOMAN: But he's a diabetic. Without insulin he won't last a week.
Everyone says, you're the only one—
WEISKOPF: Please, I'm talking now. I was right in the middle of—
WOMAN: I have to come up with twenty thousand rubles *today*. If I don't
pay them—

WEISKOPF: I beg your pardon. Do you know who you're talking to?

WOMAN: Weiskopf! But there's so little time! From Lukischki they send them straight to Ponar, and—

WEISKOPF: My good woman. Why is my name Weiskopf? You can go home now. *It will all work out.* I'll speak to my German before the day is out. Weiskopf will never give up. (HE *exits regally*)

Another ACTOR, *who will later play* DOCTOR GOTTLIEB, *immediately waltzes on behind him, doing a dead-on imitation.*

GOTTLIEB: I'll speak to my German! Weiskopf will never give up! Weiskopf will never shut up, Weiskopf will never wake up!

WOMAN (SHE *looks around, confronts the* JUDGE *and the* RABBI, *still in character*): We should kiss Weiskopf's shoes! He gives carloads of food to the poor. He gets people out of jail. . . . We should kiss Weiskopf's shoes I say!

SHE *hands* WEISKOPF'*s shoe to the* RABBI. HE *passes it to the* JUDGE.

JUDGE: Well, there's no legal precedent for shoe-kissing, but in these extraordinary circumstances, I'll make an exception.

RABBI: Yes, an exception should be made. This man Weiskopf may not be a scholar, but in view of his amazing generosity and . . . ah . . .

ALL: Power . . .

RABBI: Power! He should immediately be elevated to a honored place in our council.

JUDGE: Next case! (*Slams shoe*)

Music. GOTTLIEB *and the* WOMAN *move over to the others.* GOTTLIEB *quickly dons his doctor's coat and falls asleep. The* WOMAN *becomes a nurse. What's left on stage is a set-up for vaudeville scene: five characters dressed in exaggerated stereotype.*

WEINER: Rabbi. Your Honor. Dr. Gottlieb. I'm glad you're here. The situation is desperate.

RABBI: So what else is new?

JUDGE: Who is this guy?

RABBI: Dr. Weiner.

JUDGE: Oh! Dr. Weiner. Well, introduce yourself.

WEINER: I'm Dr. Weiner—in charge of the ghetto hospital, and here is my problem. I've got too many diabetics and not enough insulin. In three months all the insulin in the ghetto will be gone, and all our diabetics will die. Now, some could live long, full lives, others are already old and dying. I have to give out the insulin. You're the moral pillars of the ghetto. You tell me: do we have the moral right to . . . ah . . . choose . . .

JUDGE *and* RABBI: Gesundheit!

WEINER: Do we have the right to select?

ALL: What?

WEINER: Select . . .

ALL: WHAT?

WEINER: Select.

ALL: Oh! Select. . . . WHAT?!

WEINER: Cut off insulin to the old and dying, and allow the fittest to survive? Or do we condemn them all to death?

A long silence. It grows oppressive, then embarassing.

JUDGE *(Finally)*: That's a good question. All right, the case is clear. You want to know whether you can condemn specific people to death. As a judge I can give you a judicial answer: Sure. But not just anybody. Only in cases where the crime carries the death penalty. So I ask you: What is the nature of the crime of these old diabetics? The answer is: They're accused of being seriously ill. Proof? Plenty—blood sugar count, lab tests, occasional coma.

ALL: Guilty, guilty, guilty.

JUDGE: But, I make a concerted search of every law book in my library, and nowhere do I find serious illness listed as a capital crime. I'm sorry, Doctor.

RABBI: There is a passage in the Talmud which relates to this theme. Maybe. It's hard to tell, but let's give it a try. An enemy attacks a city and demands, let's say for the sake of argument, twenty hostages. By the death of the twenty, the city will be saved. Now, the Talmud asks: Should one deliver the hostages or not? And the Talmud answers: Maybe. If the enemy presents a list of names, then those people should be delivered so that the city may be saved. But, if the enemy does not give a list of names, then not one man may be delivered to the enemy. Better that the whole nation should be destroyed than that anyone should have the power to decide who lives and who dies. That leaves us with a big question: Who is the enemy here, and who makes the list?

WEINER: The list? Here's the list. *(HE produces the list)*

EVERYONE *dives for cover.* HE *chases them around the room with the list.*

Here. Each patient and his medical history. Name, age, legal status. Occupation, contributions to the community. Look!

JUDGE: Get away from me with that list!

RABBI: I don't want to see! I don't want to know!

WEINER: Listen to it! Who gets the insulin? Here's a seventy-eight-year-old widow, no children, critically ill. And here a thirty-six-year-old father of three with a law degree—should I name names?

JUDGE *and* RABBI: No names! Never name names.

RABBI: What's the point of your list! God alone gives life, He alone may take it back. Can you tell me who will live through the night . . . if any of us? Human beings don't know. Human beings have no right to know! Only God.

KITTEL *(Offstage)*: Gens! Gens! Gens! (HE *pops up from the corner of the stage and calls out*) Gens! Oh, there you are. You've got to help me Gens. I've got a problem of logic here—you're the only man who can untangle it. A man and woman get married, right? They have a child. Have they added to the race or not?

GENS: Not ultimately, no.

KITTEL: Good. Very good, Gens. So far, excellent. Now, they have a second child. Have they added to the race yet?

GENS: No. Two parents, two children . . .

KITTEL: Right. Of course. Now: three children.

GENS: Well, three children . . . that, ah . . . that would be an increase.

KITTEL: Three children is an increase! Exactly as I thought. Thank you, Gens. The Führer, you realize, has ordered an immediate stop to the natural propagation and increase of the Jewish race. Which means that the third child . . .

GENS: Is excess?

KITTEL: Precisely the word. Excess. I knew I could count on you, Gens, to solve the problem with that exquisite logic I've come to expect. Right! Now: selection of the third child—let's get to it, Gens. One mother, one father, two children. The third child, out. Move it, Gens.

HE *tosses* GENS *a cane with a bent knob on top.* GENS *stands on a platform and conducts the selection.*

GENS: Father, mother, child, child. Father, mother, child, child. Move it! Double time! Father, mother, child, child . . .

Music is heard in the distance. As GENS *works,* KRUK *comes downstage and dictates.*

KRUK: Eight rows ahead of me were five people: husband, wife, and three children. Now what? Gens counted them like this:

KRUK *and* GENS: Father, mother, child, child, child.

Joshua Sobol

KRUK: The youngest boy, a twelve-year-old, he smacks with the cane and knocks him back off to the side. The rest of the family he shoves into the group that lives. The family stands open-mouthed among the chosen survivors, wailing: "Our child is lost, taken from us by a Jew; Jakob Gens has murdered our child!" Rage sweeps through the crowd. They surge forward, whispering, "Gens, the Jewish Jew-killer. The traitor." Only abject terror keeps them in check. Meanwhile, another family moves past his cane: a mother, a father, a child. Gens counts: "One father, one mother, one child. . . ." He stops, turns to the father, and shouts: "You idiot! Where the hell is your twelve-year-old?" The father begins to stutter uncontrollably, denying the existence of a second child, but Jakob Gens, the Jewish Jew-killer, won't hear of it. He smacks the man with the cane, shrieks at him, creates a complete uproar of protest. In the midst of this chaos, Gens grabs the stray twelve-year-old, the third son of the other family, and pushes him at the bewildered father: "Schmuck! Here's your son, for God's sake keep track of him!" The child goes with the new family, and the family stands among the survivors. And Jakob Gens, the Jewish Jew-killer, saves another child.

Lights down on KRUK. *The white curtain goes up again, reintroducing the* DOCTORS, *the* RABBI *and the* JUDGE, *in the pose where we left them. But something has changed. Their vaudeville costumes have been replaced by realistic clothes, and their jovial style has vanished as well.* THEY*'re sober, serious.*

RABBI: Look Dr. Weiner. It just can't be. We are neither legally nor morally authorized to decide who lives and who dies. It's God's decision. God and God alone.

WEINER: With all due respect, Rabbi, what world are you talking about? Surely not the world *we* live in—the world of the ghetto. God has deserted us here. Men decide everything here. Everything! And what you shrug and call the will of God, is the will of a group of evil men.

RABBI: That's blasphemy.

WEINER: What keeps us going? Hope. Hope that—what—that the Red Army will march in here and liberate the ghetto while we're still alive to appreciate it. Hope! That's all we have. (*Producing insulin ampule*) And this ampule here, for the men and women who live by it, contains the little word, "perhaps." It's hope in a bottle. In a little bottle of insulin is more hope for these men and women than all your principles could give them. For the others, the ones we call "hopeless cases," what's the point? If that day of liberation comes, what will it mean to them? It's too late for them. Heaven has nothing to say about these things anymore.

RABBI: Blasphemy!

WEINER: Look, Dr. Gottlieb. You're older than me, you have far more experience. Say something!

GOTTLIEB: I'm sorry. I'm walking out of this meeting as a protest. I won't stand for discrimination against the ill. No matter how ill.

WEINER: Are you suggesting I should become a robot? A medicine dispensing machine that sees nothing, feels nothing—is that your idea of ethics?

GOTTLIEB: You're on your own. I wash my hands of it; you're a monster of medical science. Selection among patients? It's Nazi medicine!

WEINER: I am a monster?! You condemn them *all* to death. You walk away from your responsibility to humanity and let them die? And you call me a Nazi?!

GOTTLIEB *looks from the* JUDGE *to the* RABBI *and back again. Without a word, the three of them turn and depart, leaving* WEINER *alone.*

What are you walking out on? Me, or your conscience?

GENS *steps into the hospital basement.* HE *has a bottle in his hand, and is drunk.* HE *mumbles past* WEINER.

GENS: Father, mother, child, child. . . . Father, mother . . . *(HE waves at* WEINER *and collapses on the pile of clothes)* How come you stay here, Doctor? *(Pause)* Why not just . . . take off? Go join the partisans for God's sake. You even look Polish. You've got the forged documents, I *know* that. *(Self-mocking)* "Gens knows everything that's going on in the ghetto!" Sure, sure, sure. On top of everything else, you *sound* like a Pole. One hundred percent Warsaw Pole. What's keeping you, for God's sake; there's no future in the ghetto, y'know. So?

WEINER *remains silent.*

Go on. Join the partisans. Get out!

WEINER: I'm afraid.

GENS *(HE laughs, mirthlessly)*: What, you're staying here because it's so safe?

WEINER: I'm afraid of deciding.

GENS: But you have the courage to stick around here.

WEINER: Here in the ghetto, I never decide anything. I go from day to day, not responsible, not responsible. I let it happen. Day after day you let it happen. In the ghetto there is nothing more beautiful than the philosophy of passivity.

GENS: There's no future here, you know that very well.

WEINER: What about you, Mr. Gens? You could leave anytime. What are *you* doing here?

GENS *(With the insolence of a drunk)*: My place is here. With my people.
I stand with the Jews in the ghetto. I won't flee into the forest.
WEINER: Flee? You know the partisans aren't running away. Whoever
goes into the forest goes to fight. They're heroes.
GENS *(Sits bolt upright. His drunkenness vanishes)*: Hear me! There are many
forms of resistance, my good Doctor. You want gun running and
sabotage? Go to the forest. Don't bring it here in the ghetto.

WEINER *tries to object, but to no avail.* GENS *is gaining power as* HE *speaks.*

Don't play dumb, Dr. Weiner. Are you blind? Don't you understand
what the Germans have in mind? Blowing our bodies to bits? That's
easy. They can have any one of us they want. No, Dr. Weiner. They're
after our souls. They're trying to get inside—reach down our throats,
to the essence that's inside. Our souls. And that must never happen. This is the ultimate test of Jewish history: they'll lose the war,
of course, that's a matter of time. But they could lose the war and
still conquer the Jewish spirit, still infect us with their deadly sickness.
Do you see? Can you understand? That's what the Resistance can
never prevent out there. We have to protect our spirit, our essence
in here, in the ghetto. And to do that, we have to save those who
are strong. Physically, spiritually strong. Selection! We have no
choice. The sick, the weak, the hopeless ones: let them go. They're
a sacrifice. So much for insulin. *(Pause)* What will our children, our
grandchildren think? Will they be able to justify our actions in their
minds? Can they possibly understand the world we had to survive
in? Well, it's not my problem. I stay here. I've got to save what there
is to save. (HE *slugs from the bottle, and goes off mumbling)* There's no
future in the ghetto. No future. That's why I stay.

SRULIK *crosses downstage. Blackout.*

END OF ACT ONE

ACT TWO

Four young gutter rats climb through a hole in the ghetto fence, maneuvering a coffin with them. THEY *are* LIEB GRODZENSKI *and his henchmen,* JANKEL, GEIWISCH *and* ELIA. GENS *shines a flashlight on them.* THEY *freeze in its beam.* GENS *recognizes one of them.*

GENS: Halt! Good God. Leibele Grodzenski?

GRODZENSKI: Evening, chief.

GENS *(Pointing to the coffin)*: What the hell is that?

GRODZENSKI: They buried a man in the cemetery outside, so we're bringing back the coffin.

GENS: Through a hole in the wall? Has the gate disappeared, what?

GRODZENSKI *(Thinking fast)*: It's a short cut.

GENS *(Cuffing* GRODZENSKI *good-naturedly)*: What the hell is in that coffin Grodzenski? You running guns for the Resistance?

GRODZENSKI: Who, us? Transport illegal firearms into the ghetto? You gotta be kidding, chief . . .

GENS: All right, all right, so whaddaya got? Salami? Coffee? What? Sugar?

GRODZENSKI: A ghost, chief. The ghost of a dead man, that's all.

GENS *(Trying to lift one end of the coffin)*: This ghost has rocks in his pockets.

GRODZENSKI: Well, there are ghosts and ghosts, right, chief . . .

GENS: I can't have it, Lieb. You can't do this in public and expect to get away with it. You be at my office tomorrow morning at nine AM. I want a five thousand ruble contribution to the juvenile delinquents home. In cash. Is that clear? Call it a tax.

GRODZENSKI: Three thousand rubles, sure chief, sure . . .

That's all GENS *can take.* HE *collars* GRODZENSKI.

GENS: You don't negotiate with me, friend! You're under arrest.

GRODZENSKI: Wait, chief, wait. Tomorrow morning, nine AM. Five thousand rubles. For juvenile delinquents. No problem, chief. You have the word of Leib Grodzenski.

GENS: Too late. You spend the night in a cell while your friends dig up a ransom. You'll have some time to think it over, Momser. Next time you'll think twice before you tangle with Jakob Gens.

GENS *pulls him out. The* OTHERS *remain, look on in disbelief.* JANKEL *and* GEIWISCH *are talkative.* ELIA *lurks in the shadows.*

JANKEL: Nu? What, do we follow him? You want to go spring him, what?

GEIWISCH: That's a nice idea. Your five thousand rubles or my five thousand rubles?

JANKEL: Oh, yeah. That's a problem. Well, you know what? Maybe we should make—a plan.

GEIWISCH (*Looks at him incredulous, then defeated*): We'll wait here for our contact to come from Weiskopf. When he collects the goods, he'll give us the dough, and we'll spring Leib from the can.

The TWO *of them settle down on the coffin and roll cigarettes.*

JANKEL: That was a good plan.

GEIWSICH: It wasn't that complicated.

ELIA, JANKEL *and* GEIWISCH (*Singing "Isrulik" [They Call Me Izzy]*):
Come buy my fine tobacco
Or buttons for your shirt.
A lower price you'll never have to pay!
Thank heaven for the ghetto:
Where life is cheap as dirt!
A penny lets me live another day!

> They call me Izzy,
> A kid right from the ghetto.
> Always busy,
> I hustle all day long.
> In my pockets,
> Less than nothing;
> My only assets:
> A whistle and a song.

A coat without a collar,
Galoshes but no shoes;
There's room inside my pants for two or three.
And if you think that's funny,
Well, mister, I got news:
I'll teach you not to laugh at guys like me!

> They call me Izzy,
> A kid right from the ghetto.
> Always busy,
> I hustle all day long.
> In my pockets,
> Less than nothing;
> My only assets:
> A whistle and a song!

I wasn't born an orphan
Or raised by hearts of stone.
My parents loved me just as yours loved you.

But they were taken from me.
Since then I'm on my own
And like the wandering wind, I'm lonely too.

> They call me Izzy,
> A kid right from the ghetto.
> Always busy,
> I hustle all day long.
> In my pockets,
> Less than nothing;
> My only assets:
> A whistle and a song!

> They call me Izzy,
> A kid right from the ghetto.
> Always busy,
> A smile from ear to ear.
> Still it happens,
> All too often
> When no one's looking,

Sudden stop. Slowly.

> I wipe away a tear.

JANKEL: Hey! Shh. Someone's coming.
GEIWISCH: From Weiskopf. Our contact.

The HASID *enters.*

HASID: Good evening, boys, how are you?
GEIWISCH: You come from Weiskopf?
HASID: I can read your palm.
GEIWISCH: Oh, for God's sake! Get the hell out of here!
HASID (*Moving to* ELIA, *the third gangster*): Ah hah! What's this? The coming week will bring a fundamental change in your life.
GEIWISCH: I said beat it!
ELIA: Hold on a minute. How do you know that? You haven't even looked at my palm.
HASID: I do ears, too, but it is in the palm that all of the details lie.

ELIA *wrestles with his better judgement for a moment, but* HE's *hooked.*

ELIA: Okay, okay! Read my palm.

The HASID *looks at his palm.*

HASID: Very interesting. Very interesting. Your palm is made up of eight and three. Chet and Gimel are at war, yes? In your hand, Chet conquers Gimel. Chet is like Cheruth—freedom, independence. Gimel is like Germany. Therefore, in your hand, freedom and independence will win out over the Germans. In three more time periods.

ELIA: In what? What is that—"three more time periods"?

HASID: Could be three weeks, three months, three years . . . *(Extending his hand)* Thirty rubles please.

ELIA: What about three seconds?

HASID: Well, if it's three seconds that will be forty rubles!

ELIA: Here, take it.

> HE *sticks a knife into the* HASID's *gut. The* HASID *gasps.* ELIA *drags him a few steps, pulls out the knife, and the* HASID *collapses in a pool of blood.* ELIA *rifles his pockets.*

GEIWISCH: My God, Elia you're crazy! What the hell did you . . .

> ELIA *stands up with a fistful of money.*

ELIA: Crazy, eh? A thousand, two, six, *ten thousand rubles!* Crazy is right.

GEIWISCH: Stash it in the coffin! Quick!

> THEY *open the coffin lid. A* FIGURE *wrapped in a shroud sits bolt upright. The* THREE GANGSTERS *gasp. Then the shrouded* FIGURE *stands and climbs out. The* THREE *scream and scatter. The* DEAD MAN, *now alone on stage, starts to unwrap his shroud. It's* KITTEL. *At that moment,* KRUK *enters the library and starts to dictate.*

KRUK: This is the second murder and robbery in the ghetto. There's no doubt now that the perpetrators are members of the ghetto underworld. According to my sources, the crimes are tied to the flourishing black market here. The ghetto elite acquire whatever their taste dictates, and the underworld keeps the goods flowing to those who can pay.

> KITTEL *throws the shroud into the coffin and removes a thick book.* HE *puts on a pair of horn-rimmed glasses, sticks the book under his arm and is thus transformed into a new character—*DR. PAUL. HE *enters* KRUK's *library.*

DR. PAUL: Do I have the honor of addressing Mr. Herman Kruk?

KRUK: Indeed. And to whom, may I ask—

DR. PAUL: My name is Dr. Paul. I'm from the Rosenberg Foundation. For the investigation of Judaism without Jews? It's a pleasure. You have heard of us.

KRUK: I've heard the name . . .

DR. PAUL: The foundation, Mr. Kruk, works with scholars and experts in all areas of Jewish culture, sending them into specially chosen ghettos to conduct our research. Our goal is to document the intellectual, spiritual and religious components of your culture, and separate the chaff from the wheat, so to speak. We're after the essence of Judaism—in terms of artifacts. Then, when we've collected certain cultural objects we send them to the Central Institute in Frankfurt.

KRUK: I see.

DR. PAUL: It's a difficult task, and it must be completed soon, before the transmitters of your rich heritage, ah . . . cease to exist. I have been given the great honor of being sent to Wilna, and I hope that you and I can develop a close working relationship, as befits a couple of scholars embarking on a noble, arduous task. I've heard much about you—your mind, your abilities. No doubt you've heard nothing whatever about me. Allow me to give you my most recent work.

HE *gives* KRUK *the book* HE'*s been carrying.* KRUK *leafs through it.*

KRUK: Investigations of the Talmud . . .

DR. PAUL: Precisely. The Jerusalem Talmud. That's my particular area of expertise. I'm ashamed to admit that I still haven't mastered Aramaic. But I've begun. I've even done some work on the Babylonian Talmud.

KRUK: And how, may I ask, did you find me?

DR. PAUL: I used the method of Rabbi Jochanaan Ben Sakkai. But in reverse.

KRUK: I beg your pardon?

DR. PAUL: I was speaking metaphorically. The Rabbi escaped the occupied city of Jerusalem, as you no doubt know, on the eve of the temple's destruction. He was carried out in a coffin by four of his students. And I have entered your ghetto—the Jerusalem of Lithuania, to employ another metaphor—by the same method. Wouldn't you like to sit down?

KRUK: Thank you.

DR. PAUL: As your great poet Bialek said: "As man *schtejt*—*redt* man, as man *sitzt* . . ."

KRUK: "*Redt sech* . . ."

DR. PAUL *laughs.* KRUK *joins him uneasily, then stops.*

How does it happen . . .

DR. PAUL: How can a goy like me converse so easily in Yiddish? Do you think the question offends me? Or did you take me for a Jew? Even in Jerusalem they thought I was Jewish. Well. The Arabs did. I almost got killed in the pogroms of '36. The kids—Arab street gangs— pummeled me. I'm only here today because the Jewish fighters from the Haganah saved me. Good men, nice fellows. (HE *chuckles as if at the memory of them, then his laugh turns threatening*) Were you there? In Jerusalem?

KRUK: No.

DR. PAUL: What a shame.

KRUK: I've never even been to Palestine.

DR. PAUL: Shame on you.

KRUK: I wouldn't say that. I'm no Zionist.

DR. PAUL: Communist?

KRUK (*After a moment to consider*): I *was* a communist.

DR. PAUL: You were a founding member of the Polish wing of the International Communist Party, as a matter of fact.

KRUK: So. You know all about me.

DR. PAUL: Does it embarrass you, this . . . episode . . . in your political life.

KRUK: Embarrass me? (*A pause*) Not at all. I mean, during the October revolution all of us were drunk with enthusiasm. I really thought—I really *knew*—that the revolution meant the end of all injustice, the end of persecution—even of Jews.

DR. PAUL: But you left the party. *Before* Stalin's excesses made it fashionable.

KRUK: Long before. Stalin had nothing to do with it. I left because the Jews in the party were vilifying their own heritage. It was outrageous.

DR. PAUL: And that bothered you. Even though you're not a religious man.

KRUK: My atheism has no more to do with it than Stalin did. It's just incomprehensible to me that Jews would spit on their own beliefs. The self-loathing, at the time I just couldn't understand—

DR. PAUL: . . . But now you do. Understand, I mean.

KRUK: That's right. Thanks to the Germans.

DR. PAUL (*Looks at him a moment*): Now *I* don't understand.

KRUK: It's the circumstances that allow us to see ourselves so clearly. I mean, when Jews like that Gestapo-agent Dessler, and his henchman Lewas routinely storm around the ghetto beating up Jews to show the Germans how friendly they can be, what am I supposed to think? When the Jewish police invite German officers to the Jewish council building to have a party, get drunk together, sing songs together, invite in a truckload of Jewish whores for the night, I suddenly understand just how deeply Jewish self-hatred is rooted.

DR. PAUL *(Regards him with apparent sympathy)*: Yes. I see. But you're a socialist, right? A Bundist, as you people call it? A believer in the Diaspora. Jews wandering the world, as opposed to a Jewish state.

KRUK: That's right. Does that seem odd to you?

DR. PAUL: After everything that has happened to you, you still believe that socialism in the Diaspora would allow for the survival of Jewish culture?

KRUK: Absolutely. Maybe not in my lifetime, but someday.

DR. PAUL: You remind me of a Hasidic legend. A king had a fight with his son, and threw him out of the castle. Then he thought better of it, and sent a messenger out to find him. He said to the messenger: "Go seek my son, and ask him what he'd wish for if he had three wishes." The messenger found the son living in filth, clothed in rags, and put the question to him. And the son said: "Three wishes? Bread, clothing, and a place to sleep." The messenger reported back to the king, and the king said: "My son has forgotten that he's a prince. If he'd remembered who he was, he would have only had one wish— to come back to the castle. With that, all his other wishes would also have come true. He would have had food, clothing and far more than shelter. My son is really lost forever." So you see? You dream of native cultural riches for a people wandering the world? Why fight for a few priviliges among people who don't want you when you could go back to the castle? In Palestine you could have it all. You wouldn't have to walk around in rags *hoping* that one day—"not in my lifetime"—good would triumph over evil.

KRUK: Are you a lobbyist for the Zionists, Dr. Paul? Allow me a question. What did you do in Jerusalem?

DR. PAUL: Allow me a question, Mr. Kruk: I know you deplore the way Gens uses people like Dessler and Lewas to control the ghetto. Strong-arm tactics and—

KRUK: Gens does what he can under the circumstances you created.

DR. PAUL: Are you defending these characters? Believe me, I don't like them any better than you do. All they want to do is mimic us, look like us . . . but what they look like is a horrifying caricature— something you might see in a funhouse mirror. I, for one, don't enjoy staring at such things. This slavishness will get them nowhere. You, on the other hand, are different. You go your own way. You have good instincts, Mr. Kruk. *(Confidentially)* Listen: I know you were in the underground in '20 and '21. During the anti-Semitic riots you behaved heroically, I know all that. Suppose I told you Gens's days are numbered? He and his henchmen are no good to us anymore, and we'd like to put you in their place. You could hand-pick the people you'd work with. Carte blanche.

KRUK: Are you joking? I wouldn't take a job offer from you!

DR. PAUL: Not even if you crown Gens by your refusal?

KRUK: *Nebuch!* Heaven protect me from a king who depends on *your* favor. And as for the Hasidic legend, you've got it all wrong. The son understood the situation perfectly. He wished for what he needed: Men aren't at home because of any particular soil—they're at home with their heritage, with their traditions. *That's* the loss they must guard against. Without culture, they lose their identity.

DR. PAUL: Very well. If you side with the Diaspora, you leave the future of Zionism to the Genses of this world. *They* don't turn down offers of power. Not from us, not from anyone.

KRUK: What people do in the ghetto, Dr. Paul, may have nothing to do with their behavior in Palestine. Palestine's another world.

DR. PAUL: Permit me to disagree. I've been there, you haven't. I'm also familiar with the leaders of the same Zionist movements that Gens and Dessler subscribe to. I know whereof I speak. *(Pause)* I admire *your* brand of Judaism, Mr. Kruk. *Your* Judaism might stand a chance of creating a balance between our two peoples. I regret that you won't assert it, just at the moment when you might gain some political influence. You might have corrected a terrible historical injustice.

KRUK: What balance? What historical injustice? What are you talking about?

DR. PAUL: Well, never mind. We'll discuss it another time. *(HE stands up, hands KRUK a list)* In the meantime, I need these books wrapped. I have to send them to Frankfurt. Artifacts, as I said. In addition, I have a less tempting job offer, one that you'll hardly find tainted, though. I need a report on the sect of Karaites in Wilna. In Berlin they want a scientific opinion as to whether the Karaites belong to the Jewish race of not.

KRUK: Of course they're Jews, but . . .

DR. PAUL: You're not above making such a report?

KRUK *stares at him. In the background, the noise of a crowd.* DR. PAUL *and* KRUK *stand.*

DR. PAUL *(Points to the noise)*: You see? Those are the *other* Jews. They understand power. Those are the faces in the funhouse mirror. You think I enjoy looking at them? *(HE laughs a bone-chilling laugh and disappears)*

GENS, *the* JUDGE, DR. GOTTLIEB, DESSLER *and* LEWAS *enter. The latter two are dressed as ghetto police.* THEY *lead the three condemned gangsters,*

ELIA, JANKEL *and* GEIWISCH, *who are tied together. A wooden frame is shoved onstage by* TWO ACTORS *dressed as butchers. On the upper crossbar are three meathooks, each dangling a hangman's noose. Three stools are placed under the hooks.*

GENS *(Calls out)*: Your Honor!

JUDGE: The Jewish court of the Wilna ghetto, in its session of June 4th, 1942, has reached a verdict in the case of Jankel Polikanski and the brothers Itzig and Elia Geiwisch. The accused are found guilty of the murder of actor and palm reader Joseph Gerstein on the night of June 3rd. Having been found guilty of this murder, the three are sentenced to death by hanging.

GENS *(Trying to remain sympathetic)*: Your Honor, members of the Jewish Council, police officers, ladies and gentlemen. Of the seventy-six thousand Jews who once populated Wilna, sixteen thousand, thank God, are still alive. It is the duty of these remaining Jews to be upright, hard-working and honest. For those who do otherwise, we have no comfort. We must investigate and prosecute all criminal cases within the ghetto, and carry out the sentences with our own hand. We have no choice . . .

KITTEL *enters and stands near* GENS. THEY *greet each other with a look. Suddenly* GENS *is a transformed man, aggressive and blunt.*

The execution of the three convicted slayers—Jews who murdered Jews—will be carried out in the courtyard of the old slaughterhouse, at number nine, Butcher's Street. The sentence will be carried out by the Jewish police, whose duty is to protect life, law and order in the ghetto. *(To the* POLICE*)* Gentlemen: your duty!

DESSLER *and* LEWAS *lead the condemned* MEN *to the gallows.* GENS *raises his cane, and gives the signal by sharply dropping it.* KRUK *dictates.*

KRUK: The rope around the neck of Jankel Polikanski broke, and Jankel fell to the ground. He was still alive. Gens, citing the oldest traditions of judgment, wanted to pardon him. Kittel, looking like a Roman Caesar, turned thumbs down . . . and Jankel was hanged again.

KITTEL *(Moves to center stage, raises his arm to speak, and pulls a sealed notice from his pocket.* HE *ceremonially breaks the seal, unfolds it, and reads)*: On this solemn and impressive demonstration of orderly self-rule by the Jews of the Wilna ghetto, which has been carried out flawlessly in every respect, I hereby declare: Whereas the Wilna ghetto leader-

ship is about to embark on an important new task; and Whereas
the present Judenrat is an unwieldy and slow-moving body, now
therefore, the Jewish Council is hereby dissolved. In its place I name
Jakob Gens as the autonomous and sole leader of the Wilna Ghetto.

Applause.

He will be assisted by Mr. Dessler, as police chief and Mr. Lewas
as chief guard of the gate.

Applause.

GENS *(Raising his hand, like* KITTEL *did)*: Thank you. In honor of this change
in ghetto leadership, I invite the police chief and other public officials to a celebration. And I make a solemn promise to all of you:
The new ghetto leadership will do everything, everything in its power
to promote well-being and security in the community. I thank you.

KITTEL: I accept your invitation to the celebration if—if—you can
guarantee good music, and a first-rate show. It will be a great honor
to see your unforgettable chanteuse again. I still have a small bill
to settle with her, perhaps we can do some business at your celebration. (HE *puts his proclamation away, turns to go, then turns back for a moment)* One other thing. In honor of this event, I will waive one of
our strictest regulations. For the celebration—and only for the
celebration—you may once again bring flowers into the ghetto.

HE *goes. A jazz* BAND *appears and strikes up a cheerful number. It's not
a real band, but the ragged* ACTORS *who we met earlier with their instruments, spruced up a bit for the occasion.* WEISKOPF *sweeps on stage,
very much the successful businessman in authority. During his next speech,
his instructions are followed, causing a riot of activity.* WEISKOPF *himself
runs to and fro, the happy despot in the midst of his prosperity. At the end,
the stage is utterly transformed.*

WEISKOPF: Flowers! For God's sake more flowers! It's a once in a lifetime
event, I want to see a riot of colors. Petals, blooms—everywhere.
(To a pair of ACTORS *carrying a buffet)* Look, the cold buffet can go over
there, and the roast chicken over here. *(To some* COOKS *setting up the
food)* No, no! The gravy next to the chicken, what is it with you people? You've never been to a dinner party before? Shlemiel. All right
now. (HE *turns, looking for something)* Wait a minute, where's the *cholent*?
What the hell happened to the *cholent*? What, are you gonna serve
it for desert? Get it out here!

More COOKS *emerge with a huge stewpot.*

Okay. Now the bar, the bar . . . the bar can go there. No, wait. Better idea. Divide the bottles up among the people and they can drink all they want.

WAITERS *begin to place bottles on tables.*

Open 'em up! Open 'em up! I want it lavish—leftovers we can donate. We'll show these pigs we know how to celebrate. What happened to the kvass? *(To an idle* WAITER*)* Hey, you! Shmuck! Bring the kvass. *(To another)* And you! Didn't I say open all the bottles? Don't talk to me about waste, it's my money, right? Is it your money? No, it's my money, I'll spend it my way. Besides, it's business. I mean what the hell, *shmeikel* these pigs today, tomorrow the orders start rolling in. I'll bring in a hundred times what I'm spending today. Today's nothing. Especially the way it looks now—who the hell is responsible for this?! All right, all right, the orchestra goes here and the stage . . . (HE *turns to the makeshift platform where the entertainment will take place)* My God, the stage! Who the hell arranged this place? What is this, poverty theatre? This is supposed to be a "Follies," not a tragedy—who thought this up? Oh, what the hell, strew the damn place with flowers, who'll notice? *(Shouting off)* Another truckload of flowers! *(Under his breath)* I'll kill that Srulik, where does he find these set decorations?

To the STAGEHANDS *as* THEY *work with the flowers.*

I want it gorgeous. Gorgeous and plush, like a bower in heaven. Their eyes should pop out of their heads when the lights come up. Their eyes should pop out and they should never find them! May the plagues of the Pharaohs and the trials of Job befall them! *(Going a bit mad now)* And the food—gorgeous too! And with a smell—they should eat like no tomorrow. Seconds, thirds, stuffed from head to heel! Plug 'em up at both ends and may the worm of Titus dance a tango in their brains. *We'll pleasure them to death!* Rice, meat, roast chicken and gravy! Cake! And kvass, kvass, kvass! Build up the pressure, tangle their guts till their asses explode! Strangle 'em on their entrails and feed 'em to the dogs! *(Looking around, in a sweat)* Magnificent! Spectacular! Brilliant! Orchestra ready? *Play!*

The stage is unrecognizably lavish. The ORCHESTRA *strikes up. The guests enter:* GENS, DESSLER, MUSACHKAT, KITTEL, *two* GESTAPO OFFICIALS, *three* JEWISH PROSTITUTES, SRULIK *and his* DUMMY, *and* CHAJA, *in a spectacular evening gown.* WEISKOPF *receives the guests, offers drinks and hors d'oeuvres. While* THEY *eat and mingle,* CHAJA *sings "Friling" (Springtime). During the song, the orgy begins. Dancing, drinking, eating. The* PROSTITUTES *move through the* CROWD *offering their favors freely.*

CHAJA *(Singing):*
I wander through alleyways, lost and distracted
Until I arrive at the wall.
The weather is warm and the breezes are gentle
But I don't feel April at all.
I stand there and listen to laughter and street sounds
That come bubbling in from outside.
Your face is before me wherever I go
And it's almost a year since I cried.

> Springtime
> Where is my loved one?
> Why do the birds sing up there in the trees?
> Springtime
> There's music in the flowers
> But till I join you I won't hear the melodies.

I pass our old house ev'ry morning at six
On the way to my long daily grind.
The doors are all padlocked, the windows are shuttered
Like me, it is deaf, dumb and blind.
Each night I am drawn to the same shady corner
We'd meet there each day, way back when.
But why do I go there? I guess I can't help it . . .
Tonight I will go there again.

> Springtime
> Where is my loved one?
> Why do the birds sing up there in the trees?
> Springtime
> There's music in the flowers
> But till I join you I won't hear the melodies.

I peer in dark waters, the face that's reflected
Is someone I no longer know.
Wherever you are, be it earth or in heaven
Or hell, that's the place I will go.
I wander through alleyways, lost and distracted
My odyssey's practic'ly through
And spring will be warm in the April of Aprils
When I'm reunited with you.

Springtime
Where is my loved one?
Why do the birds sing up there in the trees?
*Springtime
There's music in the flowers
And when I join you I will hear the melodies.   *(Repeat *)*

When the song is done the AUDIENCE *applauds.* KITTEL *raises his hand and there is silence.* HE *moves to* CHAJA.

KITTEL: Close your eyes.

SHE *does.* KITTEL *pulls a long string of pearls from his pocket and places it around her neck. Amazed admiration from the* CROWD.

Now open them.

CHAJA *(Discovering them)*: Oh!

KITTEL: Unfortunately, they're only pearls. But if you knew where I'd gotten them . . .

CHAJA *tries to take them off, but* KITTEL *stops her.*

Now, now. She who begins with shoes ends up with pearls. But you still owe me three ounces of beans. Well, two and a half, counting that last song.

DUMMY: Careful Chajele, your price is dropping.

KITTEL *(Leaves her and moves to* SRULIK *and the* DUMMY*)*: And how's our little wooden friend? Still taking chances?

DUMMY: Taking chances? Please. It's just ordinary, run-of-the-mill chutzpah.

KITTEL: Ha! Chutzpah, you say. A great Jewish tradition. Let's hear a little chutzpah, if you dare.

DUMMY: All right, but . . . my, my, Herr Kittel, you don't look too well.

KITTEL: It's nothing. A little headache.

DUMMY: A headache. Well, by all means, I'd prescribe head baths. A miracle cure guaranteed to eliminate all pain.

KITTEL *(Not understanding)*: Head baths?

DUMMY: Stick your head in the water three times and pull it out twice.

KITTEL *laughs and* EVERYONE *joins him. Suddenly* HE *stops.* EVERYONE *stops. Tense silence. Then* KITTEL *laughs loudly again.*

DUMMY: Do you know why a German laughs twice when he hears a joke?

KITTEL: No, why?

DUMMY: Once when he hears it, and once when he gets it!

KITTEL (*Laughs once, goes silent. Then laughs again, goes silent again, ominously*): So. That's chutzpah. Very good. I bet you wouldn't dare to take it one step further.

DUMMY: How much do you bet?

SRULIK (*To the* DUMMY): What?! Cut it out.

DUMMY: You cut it out. We could get rich here. (*To* KITTEL) All right. You can put up fifty thousand rubles, and I'll wager my life.

KITTEL (*Reaches in his pockets and comes up with some paper money*): I'm a little short . . .

WEISKOPF (*Butts in, forcing a wad of bills on* KITTEL): Please, Mr. Kittel, be my guest.

KITTEL: Do you have a pen, I'll give you an IOU.

WEISKOPF *pats his pockets for a pen.*

DUMMY: What does he need an IOU for? Germans always give back, it's in their character. You took Krakov—you gave it back. You took Stalingrad, you gave it back. Germans give *everything* back—you'll pay Weiskopf back every penny, of course!

The proceedings come to a dead, stunned halt. KITTEL *stares at the* DUMMY. *A horrified silence.*

KITTEL (*Handing the money to* SRULIK): Here. You win. This time.

SRULIK: No, please . . . he didn't mean . . .

DUMMY: Shut up and take it. A thief who steals from a thief is no thief.

KITTEL (*Sharp, angry to* SRULIK): *Es reicht.*

Another dead, mortifying silence. WEISKOPF *breaks in with a bottle of cognac.*

WEISKOPF: Some cognac, Mr. Kittel, please. You've never tried a finer. Exquisite French cognac . . . only the best for you.

HE *forces a glass on* KITTEL. *Both* MEN *drain their glasses in a single swallow.*

KITTEL: Aaahhh! Paree! Paree! That reminds me of Paris. Paris . . . Paris. Very nice, yes.

SRULIK *quickly orders the* ORCHESTRA *to strike up some French music.* CHAJA *begins to sing a chanson. The party has now begun to deteriorate into a debauch, crushed flowers and clothing litter the stage, and many empty liquor bottles.*

WEISKOPF (*To* KITTEL): I'm in a position to make you a fantastic offer.

CHAJA (*Sings "Parlez-moi d'Amour"*):
Parlez-moi d'amour
Redites-moi des choses tendres.
Votre beau discours
Mon coeur n'est pas las de l'entendre.
Pourvu que toujours
Vous répétiez ces mots supremes:
Je vous aime.

Parlez-moi d'amour
Redites-moi des choses tendres . . .

KITTEL *is now dancing suggestively with* CHAJA *as* SHE *sings. The* COMPANY *interrupts her with "Mir Lebn Eibek," carrying her away from him.*

ACTING COMPANY (*Singing*):
Mir lebn eibek, ess brent a velt.
Mir lebn eibek, on a groshn gelt.
Un oif zepukenish alé sonim
Voss viln unz farshvarnz unzer ponim—
Mir lebn eibek, mir zeinen do!
Mir lebn eibek, in yeder sho.
Mir viln lebn un derlebn
Shlechte zeitn ariberlebn.
Mir lebn eibek, mir zeinen do!

At the end of the song WEISKOPF *calls for silence.*

WEISKOPF: Ladies and gentlemen! I have good news. Mr. Kittel and I have just closed the most tremendous deal in the history of laundry! We will take in four hundred railroad cars of uniforms in need of repair. Work for everybody! But there's more: I've just received word—I'm afraid I can't reveal my source—that I am to have a meeting with Göring himself! I will travel to Berlin to work out a five-year contract between the German army and the factory. We will build a new place—a gigantic plant with all new machinery and equipment for making uniforms, fatigues, combat boots, dachrician—everything for the modern soldier. The success story continues! So . . . to your health! L' chayim.

ALL: L' chayim!

KITTEL: Prosit!

ALL: Prosit!

EVERYONE *drinks. The orgy gets further out of control.* KITTEL *sees* GENS *standing alone, observing.*

KITTEL: Gens! Gens!

GENS *goes dutifully to* KITTEL. KITTEL *lays a hand on* GENS*'s shoulder, and walks with him.*

What's your problem, friend? You're not enjoying this party.
GENS: I'm having a wonderful time.
KITTEL: Please! Dessler is having a wonderful time. Muschkat is having a wonderful time. Lewas is having a wonderful time. You are standing like a stone. You never have any fun. You know how to throw a party, but you have no idea how to enjoy one. And do you know why? Because you're an asshole, Gens. You want to *use* a party. You want to make sure we're fraternizing in a useful, productive way. You want favors. You want to prove something. I just want you to have a wonderful time. How does the song go? You know the song: "I want to be happy, but I can't be happy . . ."
GENS: ". . . till I make you happy too." I'll do my best.
KITTEL: It's not hard! Look, I'll help you.

KITTEL *raises his hand. Immediate silence.*

Ladies and gentlemen! I have good news. You'll all be very proud. I've decided to expand the empire of our friend Gens. I hereby annex the Oschmany ghetto. From this moment on—with the aid of the Jewish police and the honorable Mr. Dessler, the Jews of Oschmany are your subjects.

Applause. DESSLER *stands and bows.* KITTEL *raises his hand. Immediate silence.*

There is one . . . small . . . thing. As you may know, there are four thousand Jews living in Oschmany. Unfortunately, that's two thousand more than we need. So, this evening, a battalion of the Jewish police, under the direction of Dessler . . .
DESSLER: Yes, sir!
KITTEL: We will conduct a selection process. Of course, we could send our own people or Lithuanians, but our presence in the ghetto always upsets you people so much. No need for unnecessary panic. Your people speak Yiddish, the population will stay calm, and the job can be done smoothly. *(Issuing an order)* Police officers. Attention!

The JEWISH POLICE *rise, untangling themselves from the* WHORES. THEY *are stripped to their underwear.*

Ah. How convenient. You see, everything works out for the best. To celebrate the Oschmany plan, you will get new uniforms. Russian officers' uniforms, complete with caps and coats, leftover from the Czar's army. We found them in the Wilna warehouse. Bring on the uniforms!

A GERMAN SOLDIER *brings fresh uniforms. The* JEWISH POLICE *dress.* ONE *of the* WHORES *distracts* KITTEL, *who collapses on top of her for a quickie. As* HE *paws her,* GENS *stand over them.*

GENS: Excuse me. Uh . . . pardon me, Mr. Kittel. Out of four thousand people, more than half have got to be productive.

KITTEL *(Distracted, but listening)*: You think so?

GENS: Absolutely. According to our experience, no more than one thousand are really unproductive.

KITTEL: Is that so? Really? All right, make it one thousand.

GENS: Well, wait, wait. Let's suppose that in the selection process, we discover that there are only eight hundred who are really unproductive.

KITTEL: Take it easy, Gens. Productivity is a vague concept, I don't need to tell you that. A Jew can prove anything he wants to, yes? Is an eighty-year-old man in a wheelchair productive? *You'd* connect a generator to the wheel chair and claim he's making electricity when he rolls off to take a shit!

GENS: All right, all right. Look, that brings up age, and age is very clear. What would you say to a selection of all Jews eighty and older.

KITTEL *(Looking* GENS *straight in the eye)*: Seventy.

GENS: Seventy.

KITTEL: But a minimum of seven hundred.

GENS: No fewer than five hundred, no more than seven hundred.

KITTEL: Listen, Gens, what's a hundred head more or less between you and me? Call it six hundred and we'll shake on it.

GENS: Six hundred. Deal.

KITTEL *turns to the* POLICE, *who are now in uniform and armed with truncheons.*

KITTEL: Nice. Very handsome. We'll send along eight Lithuanians from the Ypatinga militia. You hand over the old people, they'll do the rest. Dessler!

DESSLER: Yes, sir!

KITTEL: The troops are at your command!

DESSLER: Yes, sir! Thank you, sir!

KITTEL: Would you care to address the troops, Dessler?

DESSLER: Gentlemen! MOVE! We have been given an order, and we will execute it to the letter! Every detail. Any questions? All right then: Left face! Division, march! Left-right, left-right . . .

THEY *march off in front of* DESSLER, *when* HE *is almost off,* GENS *shouts after him.*

GENS: Dessler! Get back here!

DESSLER *returns.*

You're about to do a filthy job. There's no choice, I understand that. You needn't jump at it like a famished dog in front of these butchers.

DESSLER: We're doing it, aren't we? You think it matters *how* we do it? You think your broken heart buys you anything? We're none of us going to heaven, Gens, and you gave the order. You stay here and drink—I go out into the field and do the job. Don't you preach morality to me!

DESSLER *wheels and departs.* GENS *spits after him.*

GENS: Scum! (HE *upends a bottle of cognac*)

KRUK *appears and dictates.*

KRUK: Four hundred and ten old and sick Jews were selected and penned together in the square in Oschmany. An old Jew began to sing *"El Moleh Rachamin,"* and everyone started to cry. Some of the Jewish police, who had rounded up the elderly, broke into uncontrollable wailing. The 410 were driven six miles out of town, and the eight Lithuanians went to work, liquidating the throng while the seven Jewish police from Wilna stood by. The action was overseen by Dessler, Nathan Ring and Mosche Lewas—all Jews. The three of them were armed with pistols. During the entire process, selection and extermination, the seven Jews and eight Lithuanians consumed one hundred bottles of vodka and schnapps. The Jewish Council donated a baked lamb for the event. When it was all over the astounded citizens of the Oschmany Ghetto lined the streets in dumb incomprehension and stared at the departing Jewish police. One of the policemen, Isaak Auerbuch, was seized by hysteria during the selection process and had to be given emergency medical treatment. Another, Dressin, began to sing:

"We came to warm your heart,
Good night, we now depart."

GENS *(Drunk, lurches forward and speaks to* KRUK*'s voice)*: Kruk—no, no, no, listen—Kruk is an honest man. A courageous man. He tells the truth, and not many people want to hear it. He's all right. Fearless. Many of you think just the way he does, I know it. I know it. You think I'm a traitor, you wonder what the hell I really want out of all you upright, innocent people. After all, it's me you're talking about, isn't it? I'm the one who has your hiding places blown up, right? Gens! Well, Gens has his own way of hiding Jews from the butchers. I wheel and deal, right? I'm a monster, right?! Well, for me only one thing counts. Not Jewish honor. Jewish life! Jewish lives. If the Germans want a thousand Jews from me, they *get* 'em! Because if we don't do it their way, they'll march in here and take a thousand Tuesday, and a thousand Thursday. And a thousand Saturday. And ten thousand next week. You people are all saints, I know! You don't dirty your fingers. Gens gets down in the mud and wrestles with the pigs. And if you survive, then you can say: Our conscience is clear. But me? If I live through this I'll walk through life dripping shit, blood on my hands, and I'll turn myself over to the Jewish tribunal and say, "Look at me! Everything I did I did to save as many Jews as I could. To save some, I led others to their deaths with my own hands. And to preserve the consciences of many, I had no choice—I plunged myself into the sewer, and left my conscience behind." A clean conscience for Jakob Gens? I couldn't afford one!

END OF ACT TWO

ACT THREE

The PEOPLE *slowly start to awaken and clean up the orgy. As* THEY *do this* CHAJA *sings a Yiddish version of "Friling."*

CHAJA *(Singing)*:
Ich blondzshé in geto
Fun gessl zu gessl
Un ken nit gefinen kein ort;
Nito iz main liber
Wi trogt men ariber,
Mentshn, o zogt chotsh a vort.
Ess loicht oif main heim izt
Der himl der bloyér—
Voss zshé hob ich izt derfun?
Ich shtei vi a betler
Bai jetvidn toyér
Un betl, a bisselé zun.

Friling, nem zu main troyer,
Un breng main libstn,
Main trayen zu-rik.
Friling, oif dainé fligl bloyé,
O nem main harz mit
Un gib ess op main glik.

The scene evolves to a May Day celebration in the ghetto. Red paper flowers, red flags and posters decorate the stage. EVERYONE *wears red neckerchiefs or scarves. As the music ends,* KRUK *speaks.*

KRUK: After the events in Oschmany, the atmosphere in the ghetto was never the same. The people grew restless, irritable. Normally, ghetto inhabitants sleepwalk through life. They live like flies—from day to day. Things calmed down so they calmed down. What choice did they have? But there is a faction that refuses to be calm. At this moment Zalman Tektin lies in the prison hospital in critical condition. Yesterday he was shot during an attempt to rob a German munitions depot. He's eighteen. (HE *pulls a manuscript from his pocket*) This song was written by a comrade of Zalman's, if he were here he'd want us to do it for him. Let's sing it! (HE *hands it to* CHAJA) Can you do it? Or do you only know tangos?

CHAJA *steps on stage and takes the music and sings "Zog Nit Keinmol" (Never Say You Can't Go On).*

GHETTO

CHAJA *(Singing)*: Never say you can't go on, your day is done.
   Yes, a thick and smoky mist enshrouds the sun;
   But the sound of marching feet is drawing near
   And they're beating out the message: We are here!

   From the land of waving palms and drifting snow,
   We are coming braced by pain and steeled by woe.
   And where torrents of our blood have
   Stained the earth,
   There our strength and dedication find rebirth.

Gradually, the ENSEMBLE *joins in, a militant energy driving them.*

   Some day soon the sun will bless us with its light
   And our foes will be devoured by the night
   But until the sun can burn away the mist
   Then this song shall be our theme as we persist.

   Not a song the robin sings throughout the land
   But a song a people sings grenade in hand!
   It was written not with ink but with our blood
   Mid collapsing walls and storms of flying mud!

   So
   Never say you can't go on, your day is done,
   While a thick and smoky mist enshrouds the sun;
   For the sound of marching feet is drawing near
   And they're beating out the message:
      We are here!
   Yes, the sound of marching feet is drawing near
   And they're beating out the message:
      We are here!

GENS *bursts on stage.* EVERYONE *turns to him.*

GENS: What the hell is this? What are you thinking? A song like that—it
   could sink the whole ghetto. Do you know what would happen if
   the Germans even heard about this?
SRULIK: Mr. Gens . . .
GENS: I'm talking!
SRULIK: But Mr. Gens . . . you're the one who ordered us to create a
   theatre.
GENS: Not this kind of theatre! Not a song that incites riots! We've just
   calmed the place down for God's sake.
DUMMY: Like a graveyard.
GENS: People, please, there's nothing to fear now. The ghetto is finally
   secure.

DUMMY: Well . . . compared to Ponar . . .

GENS: This is no time to provoke audiences. Theatre, yes—but entertainment. Something to take people out of themselves. We need to show the world we're industrious, hardworking people, not maniacs.

DUMMY: Present company excepted.

GENS: You want to make fun of something, fine, make fun of your own: take a crack at people who won't look for work, at parasites.

DUMMY (*Pointing at* SRULIK): Here's one. He won't even help our German friends pick out their favorite Jews.

GENS: Look, I've got nothing against satire, but watch who you aim it at.

DUMMY: Whoever passes by. Parasites, traitors.

GENS: Who's a traitor? Me? The Jewish police? Just what the hell are you trying to say? The Jewish police will lead this place to freedom! Not you! It's a delicate balance we've achieved here. Upset that balance, and *you'll* be the traitors.

KRUK: That's what you call solidarity Mr. Gens? . . . One people.

GENS: Don't you preach morality to me! If there's a Jewish patriot here, it's me! I'm going to bring Hebrew into the ghetto starting right now! Tomorrow morning we begin Hebrew lessons in the schools. Required. No more Yiddish bibles. Hebrew bibles. Hebrew in elementary schools from day one. In kindergarten. And I'm also introducing Palistinography to the schools. Any objections? Me. I object. I object to the utter lack of Jewish national conscience in Wilna. I object! And in the theatre! A gala performance in Hebrew, how about that for an idea! Hebrew lectures, readings, a blue and white evening dedicated to reading the poetry of Bialik! Anyone not in agreement with the new policy of nationalism is hereby barred from all key positions. Alright now. Does anyone object?! I thought not.

KRUK: I'm sorry Dr. Paul isn't here. He was right. The Germans have been more successful than they could have dreamed.

GENS: What was that?!

KRUK: Nationalism breeds nationalism.

GENS: I beg your pardon. Are you saying the Germans have done this to me?

KRUK: Take it however you like.

GENS: This rehearsal is hereby dissolved. Everybody go home. Now!

The GROUP *disperses singing "Zog Nit Keinnmol." Only the* DUMMY *and* SRULIK *remain.*

DUMMY: Go home! Get out! Study Hebrew!

SRULIK: Please, not now. I can't take it anymore.

DUMMY: Pay attention! A historic moment. You'll want to tell your grandchildren you were there for the Hebrewization of the ghetto. At this moment in history, what could be more important than Hebrew. To say nothing of Palistinography. You don't know what Palistinography is, do you?

SRULIK: Yes I do. You stick your head into Palestine three times and you take it out twice.

DUMMY: But let's get down to brass tacks. How do you tell Chaja you want to sleep with her in Hebrew?

SRULIK: How did I get myself into this mess?

DUMMY: "*Ani chafetz bach*," I think. Or maybe "*Yesh li chefetz bach*"! What do you think? Which one? Could be important. Could be the difference between a "yes" and a "no."

SRULIK: Don't make me *meshugge!*

THEY *start to leave, the* DUMMY *still chattering.*

DUMMY: Chajale! Chajale! *Ani chafetz bach!* It's love! It's love! What do you say, Chajale? You wanna . . . *chafetz bach?* You think so?

THEY'*re offstage now, the* DUMMY'*s voice fading.*

My, my, my. The Hebrewization of the ghetto of all things. What next . . .

The scene shifts to the library. CHAJA *is looking for a book.* SHE *has changed. Her dress is simple, almost masculine. Her hair is pulled back.* KRUK *approaches and looks at her carefully.*

KRUK: May I help you?

CHAJA: No thanks. Just looking . . .

KRUK: Excuse me, but you come here every day and search for hours. Surely I could help you . . . you must be looking for something.

CHAJA (*A little defensive, protecting something*): I like to browse.

KRUK: I thought you were wonderful in the revue—"Pesche from Resche."

CHAJA: Wonderful?

KRUK: There's no need to be ashamed. It's a fine thing to be an actress.

CHAJA: Is it? I don't think so.

KRUK: No?

CHAJA: What good is theatre in our situation? It's trivial . . . even insulting.

KRUK: I thought that way once. I was against the theatre company from the beginning.

CHAJA: I know. You were right. You are right.

KRUK *(Shakes his head)*: No. Every form of cultural activity is essential here in the ghetto. It's the battle plan in our fight to remain human beings. The fascists can kill us at will—it's not even a challenge for them. But they can't achieve their real aim: They can't obliterate our humanity—not as long as we cling to a spiritual life, not as long as we reach for the good and the beautiful. They forbid flowers in the ghetto, we give one another leaves. And suddenly, leaves are the most beautiful flowers in the world. Theatre is essential.

Silence.

You must be looking for a book on theatre. Come.

CHAJA: I don't want a book on theatre. I want a book . . . on explosives.

KRUK *(Smiling)*: Why didn't you say so? I could have saved you precious time.

HE *climbs a ladder and takes a thin book from the top of the shelf.* HE *climbs back down and hands her the book.* SHE *looks through it quickly.*

CHAJA: Is this Russian?

KRUK: It's a Soviet army manual. I stole it from the university. It's the only book I've ever stolen.

CHAJA: But I don't know the language.

KRUK: You must have friends. Show it to your friends. Unless I'm mistaken, one of your friends will know Russian.

CHAJA: Thank you. I'll bring it back.

KRUK: Please, I don't even know you took it. A thief who steals from a thief is no thief.

CHAJA: Thank you. (SHE *heads for the door)*

KRUK *(When* SHE *is almost there)*: Wait.

From a tin box HE *takes a leafy stem and hands it to her.* SHE *takes it, and begins to sing "Dremlen Feigl," (Drowsing Birds) to him. As* SHE *sings the scene shifts.*

CHAJA *(Singing)*:
Baby birds in summer branches
Drowse in a downy nest
Down below a baby nurses
Softly on a stranger's breast
Lullaby, lullaby, croons the stranger
Rest, sweet little one, rest
Lulu lulu lu

There's a story I must tell you
Though you're much too small
Baby dear, your mama's gone
She won't be coming back at all
And when your daddy tried to save her
These eyes saw him fall
Lulu lulu lu

If you get a little older
This sad story you will know
Carry it with you like a blessing
Everywhere you go
Lullaby, lullaby, klaine schaine
Orphan child, I love you so.
Lulu lulu lu.

As SHE *sings and strolls, lost to this world, a strong flashlight beam catches her.* SHE *freezes, startled. It's* KITTEL.

KITTEL: Where have you been? Rehearsal?
CHAJA: Yes. Working on a new piece.

HE *reaches for her book.*

KITTEL: You sang very well at the party. Is this your new play? (HE *looks it over*) In Russian?
CHAJA: That's right. Do you . . . know Russian?
KITTEL: Sorry.
CHAJA: Pity. It's a good play.
KITTEL: What's it called?
CHAJA: *Beneath the Bridge.*
KITTEL: And you're performing it in Russian?
CHAJA: No, no. We'll adapt and improve it.

SHE *reaches for the book.* KITTEL *holds on to it.*

KITTEL: You dance and sing your way through the war, eh?
CHAJA: When I'm happy I laugh. When I'm sad I sing.
KITTEL (*Laughs*): Very good. (HE *hands her the book*) Perhaps—I hope—you'll wipe out your debt to me with this one.
CHAJA: I'll try.

SHE *runs off suddenly.* KITTEL *looks after her.*

KITTEL: What an exotic group of people. My God, they're strange.

HE *puts on his black, horn-rimmed glasses and becomes* DR. PAUL. HE
enters the library. KRUK *appears from behind a bookshelf.* DR. PAUL *waves
a manuscript* HE *has in his hand.*

DR. PAUL: I've read your study on the Karaites in Lithuania. Brilliant
work.

KRUK: Thank you.

DR. PAUL: You reach the conclusion that there's no connection whatever
between the Karaites and the Jews.

KRUK: That's what the research shows.

DR. PAUL: You argue the case so convincingly that I almost believed you
were telling the truth.

KRUK: I was.

DR. PAUL *(Chuckling)*: Mr. Kruk, there's no doubt whatever that the
Karaites are Jews. You know it and I know it. You've constructed
a monumental superstructure of falsehoods, half-truths and supposi-
tions, so skillfully built that it looks like "proof." And for no other
reason than to save the Karaites from annihilation. The Karaites—a
race that despises your own people. Why?

KRUK: You commissioned the study, Dr. Paul.

DR. PAUL: I didn't commission you reach this conclusion.

KRUK: My conscience is clear.

DR. PAUL: Scientific conscience? Or human conscience?

KRUK: Is there a difference?

DR. PAUL: And the truth? What about the truth?

KRUK: All my research rests on a single truth.

DR. PAUL: When you say "truth" you mean "lie," and vice versa. True?

KRUK: False.

DR. PAUL: Talking with you is a sublime experience, Mr. Kruk. A great
intellectual pleasure. I think you'll agree that the two of us—just
by talking, yes?—the two of us have managed to wipe out the distinction between what is true and what is false. Do you think?

KRUK: I don't think you came here for a symposium on truth and
falsehood, Dr. Paul.

DR. PAUL: Look, you had an opportunity here. All you had to do was
write the truth, and you would have had instant revenge on a sect
of collaborators who have been betraying you since the war began.
But no. You decide to protect them, and why? Don't you have *any*
aggressive urge, you people?

A moment of silence.

KRUK: You promised to send my report to Berlin.

DR. PAUL: You know what your friend Freud has written about the origin
of aggression?

KRUK: That it derives from an basic impulse toward death.

DR. PAUL: The death instinct, yes. So. German aggressiveness proves there's a death instinct in our souls, yes?

KRUK: You'd know more about that than I would.

DR. PAUL: While the Jews show no aggression at all, which means they have no death instinct, right?

KRUK: Could be.

DR. PAUL: You don't seem very engaged by this theory. As a Bundist—and an anti-Zionist—I would have thought you'd be very interested.

KRUK: I don't think I see the connection.

DR. PAUL: I think I can clarify it for you. The Zionist Jews in Palestine are completely different from you. They're an effective military organization, and they don't necessarily wait to be attacked. When I was in Palestine, I watched them make pre-emptive strikes on villages before the enemy had a chance to get organized. They're not like you, Kruk, they're no strangers to aggression. Is that the death instinct that you lack coming out in them, Kruk? Have we succeeded in transplanting it from the German soul into the soul of the new Jew?

KRUK: What are you talking about? Zionism existed long before you came to power.

DR. PAUL: I'm not just talking about Germany—I'm talking about two thousand years of anti-Semitism—persecution, pogroms. Please understand, Mr. Kruk: nothing in the world is more irritating than your endless capacity for suffering. It drives us wild. When we see the utter lack of killer instinct in you, we taste blood in our mouths—murder errupts in our souls. That's just the way it is—I sometimes think it's a chemical reaction. *(Pause)* The Jew only wants to survive, yes? He swallows degradation, humiliation, inhuman suffering—all just for the privilege of staying alive under appalling conditions. We rip the basic necessities of human survival out from under you and what do you do? Build a theatre. Sing and dance. All right, perhaps the German killer instinct is strong—but we're only carrying out the wishes of every nation in Europe. No other country would dare, that's all.

KRUK: No theory will justify your crimes.

DR. PAUL: You think not? Then why don't the Allies destroy the death camps? They're fair game, but no one touches them.

KRUK *stares at him, unable to summon a response.*

Well, never mind, time is short and I have another assignment for you. You'll survey all the monastaries in the district and catalog all the books in monastary libraries.

KRUK: I'll what? What's the point of that?

DR. PAUL: Point? No point. Beyond the fact that it'll keep you alive. If you work for me, you're safe.

KRUK *(Trying to get the real answer)*: I don't much care whether I live or die, under the circumstances . . .

DR. PAUL: How can you say that? The Eastern Front is collapsing, the Russians will invade Lithuania any day now . . .

KRUK *(Still prying)*: It's an attractive vision of events, Dr. Paul. I'm afraid I don't buy it.

DR. PAUL: It's true, believe me. They're sending untrained officers to the Eastern Front—men with no combat experience whatever.

A light begins to dawn for KRUK.

Everyone is needed to stop the Russians.

KRUK *(Filling in the pieces)*: Then why should I detain you here? You must be itching to join your brothers on the Front.

DR. PAUL: We're both intelligent men, Kruk. I'd like an inventory of the monastery libraries. Is that clear?

KRUK: Absolutely clear.

DR. PAUL: Very good. Goodbye, Mr. Kruk. (HE *departs*)

KRUK *(Dictates)*: A strange symbiosis is developing between this German and myself. I don't want to die in Ponar, he doesn't want to die on the Front. So, he's attached himself to me; I carry out a series of pointless tasks under his direction, and both of us remain alive. I spend my days traipsing from monastery to monastery in Wilna, places I'd never set foot in before. As long as it keeps me alive . . . why not?

GENS *and* WEISKOPF *enter.*

GENS: Well, this is the spot. Three thousand square feet of warehouse space. And a sewing machine takes what—six square feet?

WEISKOPF: That's not the issue here. What do I—

GENS: You could put five hundred machines here.

WEISKOPF: What do I need with five hundred machines? I'm trying to tell you—I don't need the machines, I don't need the workers. I can do perfectly well with—

GENS: They're dumping four hundred carloads of uniforms on you. You know how much work that is? The Germans'll give us another factory, no questions asked. It's a golden opportunity.

WEISKOPF: I already got a factory!

GENS: What?

WEISKOPF: Look, I need, at the most, fifty more operators. They can fit in the old place. With those fifty I can handle the German order, no problem.

GENS: No you can't.

WEISKOPF: Are you telling me my business? Do you doubt Weiskopf? Look, I worked it out exactly—I know my business. (HE *pulls a large spreadsheet from his pocket and unfolds it*)

GENS: What the hell is that?

GENS: The numbers. You can graph it right on a graph. Production rates per worker per hour, number of workers. I add fifty workers, I put them on split shifts, two hours additional per worker and the job gets done. It's in black and white.

GENS: Let's see.

WEISKOPF: Be my guest.

HE *gives* GENS *the spreadsheet.* GENS *looks it over.*

GENS: You're a thorough man, Weiskopf. You don't miss a trick.

WEISKOPF: Naturally. I know my business.

GENS *tears up the spreadsheet.*

What the hell are you doing? My numbers! I spent all morning—

GENS: Piss on your numbers!

WEISKOPF: Don't you speak to me that way!

GENS: Your numbers! You think I give a shit about saving money for the German army? Are you crazy? Five hundred more workers means five hundred more families saved. Does that make sense to you?

WEISKOPF: What am I, a welfare fund now? I run a factory, it's a business. I pay a decent living wage to my employees, and what little is left over I live on.

GENS: "What little is left over . . ."? The ghetto's newest millionaire! Believe me I don't care—you earned it, I'm no socialist. But even greed has its limits. Now listen to me Weiskopf: You'll build a second factory on this site, and employ five hundred workers supplied by the Ghetto Work Authority.

WEISKOPF: The Ghetto Work Authority! Cripples I'll get!

GENS: What are you running now, the Olympics?! You run a lousy factory stitching together lousy uniforms for the goddamn *enemy.* And Jewish cripples are very good at that, if it saves their lives.

WEISKOPF: It is not a "lousy" factory. It's a successful business enterprise. I built it with my own hands from nothing. The factory is my life—I *am* the factory. I'm not about to let you blow it to bits with your lousy philanthropy!

GENS: Tomorrow you start organizing a new factory!

WEISKOPF: No, no, no, no, *NO*! Understood?

GENS: Let me put it another way. It's an order!

WEISKOPF: An order? You think I take orders from you? Fuck your order. You're not the ultimate authority around here.

GENS: Oh really? So who is? Not you, by any chance?

WEISKOPF: Kittel.

A pause.

GENS: So help me, Weiskopf, if you speak to Kittel about this I'll—

WEISKOPF: You'll what?

GENS: Weiskopf.

WEISKOPF *stares at* GENS *defiantly.*

You will not speak to Kittel about this . . .

KITTEL *peers out from the bundle of clothing and climbs out, standing directly between the two.* HE *seems surprised to find the two men here.*

KITTEL: My goodness, Gens . . . what are you doing here? I've looked everywhere. You planning your next show?

GENS: No show. This is now the site of Weiskopf's new factory.

KITTEL: Well, that shows admirable initiative. What's wrong with the old factory?

GENS: We've outgrown it. The five hundred sewing machines won't fit.

KITTEL: Five hundred sewing machines . . . my, my. Growing by leaps and bounds. You planning to drape Europe in newly-minted shrouds?

GENS: It's the uniforms. Four hundred carloads . . . we have a contract to fulfill.

KITTEL *(Turning to* WEISKOPF*)*: A contract, yes. You need five hundred workers for this . . . contract?

WEISKOPF: Well, maybe not five hundred . . . I mean, perhaps we could . . . uh . . . make some adjustments . . .

GENS: Don't make promises you can't keep, Mr. Weiskopf.

KITTEL: You seem to have a slight disagreement here.

WEISKOPF: Yes, well, there are always different estimates in any situation. That is . . . *(HE begins to cough uncontrollably)*

KITTEL: Weiskopf! Are you hiding something?

WEISKOPF: Me? Why would I hide?

KITTEL: That's good.

WEISKOPF: Except—

KITTEL: Except what?

Silence.

Is there a disagreement here or not? Answer me!

GENS: No!

WEISKOPF *(Simultaneously)*: Yes!

KITTEL: Well, we cleared that up. *(Turning serious)* Now I want the truth. Disagreement? Weiskopf, you're a reliable businessman. How many more workers do you need? The truth, now.

WEISKOPF: I need about—

KITTEL: Precisely.

WEISKOPF: Fifty.

KITTEL: Fifty. So why this place? Gens, are you hiding something?

GENS: Nothing. He needs five hundred workers, not fifty.

KITTEL *(To WEISKOPF)*: Where are the figures you showed me? Your graphs?

WEISKOPF: I gave them to him.

KITTEL *(Turning to GENS)*: May I see them please?

GENS: I tore them up.

KITTEL: You what?

GENS: The figures were a joke. Mr. Kittel, the man is deluded, believe me.

KITTEL: Is that so, Weiskopf? Did you waste half my morning on a joke?

WEISKOPF: Mr. Kittel, if you give me an extra two hours per day per man and if you let me hand-pick fifty choice workers, if I don't have to hire cripples and half-wits, and if—

KITTEL: If, if, if . . .

WEISKOPF: If no one interferes with my work schedules—

KITTEL: Your next if, Weiskopf, is your last.

WEISKOPF: Mr. Kittel, I'm only trying to help save you money. I'm sure that if I were to speak to Göring about this—

KITTEL: That's enough! Talk about "chutzpah"! You're worse than the dummy at your theatre—at least he made me laugh.

WEISKOPF: You promised me a meeting with Göring!

KITTEL: Jesus, Weiskopf, can't you take a joke? I mean, people who can't take a joke get on my nerves.

WEISKOPF: I swear on my wife's head! Give me fifty workers and I'll finish the job. Believe me—

KITTEL: Weiskopf, you're hysterical!

WEISKOPF *(Trying to calm himself)*: Please. Let me explain it once more. With fifty workers . . .

KITTEL: Gens says you're deluded. He says it's impossible.

WEISKOPF: Well, Gens *is* the head of the ghetto . . .

KITTEL: You don't say.

WEISKOPF: I'm only trying to point out . . . he could have his own agenda, his own motives . . .

KITTEL: Are you sweating?

WEISKOPF: Not at all, I—

LEWAS *breaks in, carrying a bottle of cognac and a salami.*

LEWAS: You okay chief?

GENS: Not now!

LEWAS: But chief, you told me—

GENS: Piss off!

KITTEL: What is that, Lewas?

LEWAS: We searched his house. Weiskopf's.

KITTEL: My, my. In Weiskopf's house. (HE *takes the bottle and looks at the label*) Contraband cognac. And Hungarian salami. Weiskopf!

LEWAS: There's more. Rice. Olive oil, half a sack of sugar . . .

WEISKOPF: It was left over from the party. I—

KITTEL: Weiskopf, really. Nothing warms my heart like the sound of a man apologizing.

WEISKOPF: All right then. I'll tell you why he wants five hundred extra workers. I'll tell you the real reason. I'll tell. The real reason—

KITTEL: Gens? Free me from this leech.

GENS: Lewas! Take care of him.

LEWAS *turns to* WEISKOPF *and slaps him hard.* WEISKOPF *reaches up to protect his face and* LEWAS *lunges at him, pulling the buttons off his pants. His pants drop to the floor.* WEISKOPF, *more embarrassed than hurt, bends down and quickly retrieves his trousers. But* LEWAS *has taken the opportunity to get some brass knuckles on, and when* WEISKOPF *strightens up, holding his pants with both hands,* LEWAS *lets him have it again, this time tearing into his face.* WEISKOPF *topples to the floor with a scream. When* LEWAS *picks him up there is blood dripping from his face.* LEWAS *delivers one more battering punch to the face, and* WEISKOPF *goes down for good.*

Lock him up.

LEWAS *drags out* WEISKOPF. KITTEL, *who has been watching impassively, opens the cognac and takes a slug.*

KITTEL: Nicely done, Gens. (HE *gives* GENS *the bottle*) You learn quickly, you people. Call in your gorilla.

GENS: Lewas!

LEWAS *who has deposited the insensible* WEISKOPF *to the back of the stage and left him there, returns.*

LEWAS: Yes, chief.
KITTEL: Bring me the theatre troupe. All of them. Now.
LEWAS: Yes, sir!

LEWAS *goes back to* WEISKOPF, *drags him off stage.*

KITTEL: Now let's get down to business. I've been getting reports. People are escaping from the ghetto.
GENS: But that's impossible.
KITTEL: Horseshit, Gens. It's a fact and you know it. Since the day the bomb exploded beneath the bridge—the big fire—you remember?
GENS: Beneath the bridge, yes . . .
KITTEL: Since that day, thirty people have disappeared from the work crews.
GENS: What's the connection?
KITTEL: You tell me.
GENS: I don't get it. The Jews don't figure in it—the bridge was in a Lithuanian village. I thought . . .
KITTEL: You could blame the Lithuanians. Well, it played out that way, didn't it? Forty Lithuanians were shot for that firebomb; let's not mourn them, Gens. Let's just hope they were innocent creatures whose souls are in heaven—a place where they'll be safe from the likes of you and me, right Gens? (HE *laughs, then turns serious*) Tell me Gens, what do the words "mutual responsibility" mean to you?
GENS: It's a Jewish principle.
KITTEL: Right. What does it say in the Old Testament? "One hand washes the other"? Something like that.
GENS: All Jews answer for one another . . .
KITTEL: Right, close enough. Well, this beautiful Jewish adage is now the law of the ghetto, Gens. If anyone disappears, his family will be shot. If a family disappears, everyone who shared a room with them will be shot. If a roomful of people disappear, everyone who lives in the same house with them will be shot. All workers will be divided into groups of ten. One runs, the other nine die. Is that clear to you, Gens?
GENS: Clear. Yes.
KITTEL: Oh, and as for Weiskopf's factory . . . no expansion. No new work. Any questions?

GENS *remains silent.*

The weasel was right, of course. His calculations were accurate down to the minute. He explained it to me clearly this morning. What are you going to do about it?

GENS: Get him back?

KITTEL: What?

GENS: Weiskopf. Reappoint him, give him back his factory.

KITTEL: Jesus Gens! You people are really baffling. My whole life all I hear is how smart the Jews are, how resourceful. . . . Don't you know anything about the way the world works? There's no second chance in this world, Gens. A man collapses, you bury him. You don't prop him up with a stick. You think I care about who was right and who was wrong in your pitiful squabble with the weasel? Gens, really. Learn a little German philosophy: Among reasonable people the only conversation worth having is the one about *how* to achieve a goal. Who cares about the wisdom of the goals themselves? Who's got time? There are no just goals. *I* justify a goal. My will. When you and Weiskopf square off, the only thing that interests me is: Whose will prevails? Who is stronger? Not even really a challenge for you, was he? He caved in the minute you poked him, like a house of cards. I mean, it wasn't even any fun. He'll be in Ponar by the weekend. You're too damn good at what you do, Gens. Now, let's see the theatre troupe.

A series of massive, discordant notes from the BAND. *From out of the clothing pile there is a sudden, eerie explosion of clothes.* GARMENTS *wave about on the pile and cry in agony.*

SRULIK'S VOICE: Welcome to the last performance!

The "Finale" begins.

COSTUMES:
We have been living in hell!
We have been living in hell!

THEY *rise off the pile and begin to dance—stylized versions of the theatre troupe. The stage is eerily vacant of human form, but is filled with the swirling, dancing costumes.*

(Singing)
Scalding steam!
Choking fumes!

Thrashed with sticks in the
Laundry rooms!

Boiled in suds!
Soaked in lye!
Jabbed with naptha until we die!
Ai! Ai! Ai!

Stitched—and stretched!
Wrung out—and hung out!
And always that smell!
That disinfectant smell
That nothing can dispell!
We have been living in hell!

But when at last
We are free
Our threads will tremble
With ecstasy.
Ai! Ai! Ai! Ai!
Coats and pants
Will find a reason
To sing and dance.

Ai! Ai! Ai! Ai! *(Etcetera)*

SRULIK *(Over the music, to the* DUMMY*)*: What the hell's going on? You promised me these clothes would be neatly folded, sorted and stacked. Now they're all over the place. Can't you control them?

The DUMMY *beats the clothes. As* HE *sings and attacks them,* THEY *quietly go back to the pile and curl up, defeated.*

DUMMY *(Singing))*:
    Ai! Ai!
    You must be steamed and soaked with lye.
    Ai! Ai!
    You know that's your fate so don't fight it.
SRULIK: Shut up and lie down.
ALL: No!
SRULIK: No? No? Where else do you think you can go?
ALL:
    We will find a wardrobe,
    An armoire.
    Quality clothes need room to breathe.
    Quality clothes, that's what we are
    And quality clothes should have their own armoire.

The HASID's *head and upper torso burst out of the pile.*

HASID: Your Honor! Mr. Police Commisioner, sir. *(HE sings)*
    I read sleeves,
    I'll tell your future!
    Blessed is he who believes!
    Chet conquers Gimmel!
    Three becomes eight!
    The change in your future
    Will be great!
    Could be three days . . .
    Could be three weeks . . .
    Could be three months . . .
    Something in threes . . .
    Three million marks, if you please!

The CLOTHES *begin to agitate again.* THEY *make the pile swarm with life, holding out their palms to be read.*

COSTUMES *(Chanting)*:
    OUR FUTURE!
    OUR FUTURE! OUR FUTURE!
SRULIK: Their future?! Jesus, Ignatz, can't these people take a joke? I thought I could depend on you. Well, learn a little German philosophy. If you want a job done well . . .

HE *begins to unpack his saxophone case as the clothes continue to climb back off the pile.* SRULIK *pulls the saxophone from the case and begins to gun down the* COSTUMES *with it. A series of rim-shots from the pit and the* COSTUMES *all lie quietly in and around the pile. There is dead quiet for a moment. An oversize costume of* CHAJA *appears.*

CHAJA'S COSTUME: That's enough! That's enough! *(Sings)*
    We're done with suds! We're done with lye!
    We're done with naptha, you and I!
    We're going home . . . it can't be far . . .
    Home to our cozy old armoire!
COSTUMES *(Singing)*:
    We'll flee this damp and soapy spot
    Where some are spared and some are not.
    From fumes and steam we seek release
    So we can go and live in peace.
ALL *(Singing)*:
    La la la la la la la la *(Etcetera)*

DUMMY *(Singing)*:
    You're only rags, no more than rags!
    How dare you dream of being free!
    You're only rags, how stupid can you be?
ONE COSTUME: Look!
ANOTHER COSTUME: A wardrobe!
CHAJA: An armoire! (SHE *sings*)
    We're going home
    To our armoire . . .
    The finest clothes
    Is what we are . . .

ALL *(Singing)*:
    We're going home . . .
    It can't be far . . .
    Home to our cozy
    Old armoire!

    We're going home
    To our armoire!
    The finest clothes
    Is what we are!
    We'll have a home . . .
    A gracious home . . .
    A spacious home . . .
    We're going home!

    We'll have a home . . .
    A gracious home . . .
    A spacious home . . .
    We're going home!

CHAJA *(Singing)*:
    Ick benk a heym.
ALL *(Singing)*:
    We're going home!
    We're going home!
    We're going home!
KITTEL *(Applauds)*: Bravo! Bravo!

HE *whispers something to* GENS. GENS *exits.*

All right, everybody out. I said out!

Silence, the armoire stays shut.

ROUSE!

The armoire opens and one by one the PIECES OF CLOTHING *emerge.*

Line up!

The CLOTHES *form a line in front of* KITTEL.

Very good work. A great satire. I'd like to see the actors.
DUMMY: What actors? We're only clothing.
KITTEL: I said I'd like to see the actors. Now!

The faces of the ACTORS *slowly emerge from the clothing. One by one* THEY *become visible. But* ONE DRESS *remains empty.* KITTEL *is drawn to it.*

You too, my chanteuse. I want to see your face.

Silence. It grows uncomfortable. KITTEL *looks down the neck of the woman's costume.* HE *looks up, stunned.*

It's empty. Unbelievable! I said I want to see the entire troupe! All right, you've put on a great show. Full of Jewish wit and . . . what do you call it . . . *chutzpah?* Okay. The performance ends, I applaud loudly, and what has happened? An actress—an actress already in debt to me for two-and-a-half ounces of beans—is missing. Vanished from under your nose.

Silence.

You know what this means, according to the new rules of the ghetto? Mr. Gens can tell you about "mutual responsibility," an old Jewish concept, recently adopted.

Silence.

So. A Jewish satire. Very funny. *(Suddenly, the nightclub compere)* And now! A German satire: *Up Against the Wall!!*

EVERYONE *turns in terror and faces the back wall.*

Machine-gunner, front and center!

A blood-curdling screech, and GENS *enters, pushing a wheelbarrow. On it is a huge jam-pot labeled "JAM." Next to the pot is a basket loaded with sliced challah.*

Machine gun here! Load! Release safeties! (HE *releases the safety of his own gun*) Actors! About face!

The ACTORS *turn, their faces frozen death-masks of terror. It takes them a moment to even see the jam pot.* THEY *stare, bewildered.* KITTEL *roars with laughter.*

What, you thought I'd have you shot? After that fantastic number? German satire, I said. Look in these hard times, with the Russians threatening to march in here any day, you've given me a moment of transcendant joy that is solely the province of the arts. Your virtuosity has saved your lives, and here is my thanks. Break bread with me: Fresh-baked bread and red current jam. Please. Help yourself. Here's to your next performance! (KITTEL *takes a slice of bread, dips it in the jam and eats, bliss crossing his face*) If there's one thing I'm a sucker for it's red current jam. Mmm-mmm. Come on, try some. Please . . . join me?

The ACTORS *move hesitantly to the pot, their minds a scramble. But little by little,* THEY *join in, first slowly, then ravenously.* THEY *pack in close to the pot, jockeying for position. As* THEY *eat, the* DUMMY *sings.*

DUMMY *(Singing)*:
Gobble it up! Gobble it up!
Quickly! Quickly!
Today—you're here.
Tomorrow you'll all disappear!
Sooo . . .
Quickly! Quickly! Quickly!
Gobble it up!

As the DUMMY *sings and the* ACTORS *eat,* KITTEL *steps back. In a burst of energy* HE *swings round, raises his gun and fires hundreds of rounds into the crowd. Pandemonium. The* TROUPE *goes down in a hail of bullets and* ALL *fall forward with their heads in the jam pot. Only* SRULIK *and the* DUMMY *survive.* THEY *stagger back away from the pot.* SRULIK *is still in his Kittel costume. As* KITTEL *turns to* SRULIK, HE *confronts a grotesque mirror image of himself.*

DUMMY *(Singing impudently to* KITTEL*)*:
Finish it up! Finish it up!
Quickly! Quickly!
The master race?
You poor deluded man!

Go ahead! Brag!
Tomorrow you know what you'll be?

KITTEL *shoots the* PUPPET. *Blood runs from his mouth. As* HE *falls,* SRULIK's *Kittel costume falls away with him. Underneath,* SRULIK *wears a bathrobe, as at the opening. One of his arms falls away with the Kittel costume.*

SRULIK: A rag!
Finish it up!
Finish it . . .

HE *stares at the audience, an old, one-armed man. The clarinet is heard again, coming closer. As the music finally drifts away . . .*

Darkness.

END OF PLAY

The Songs

Shtiler, Shtiler (Be Still)   Lyrics by Schmerke Kaczerginski; music by Alec Volkoviski; English lyrics adapted by Jim Friedman.

Hot Zich Mir Di Shich Zerissn (Dance, Dance, Dance)   Anonymous; English lyrics adapted by Jim Friedman.

Ich Benk A Heym (I Long for Home)   by Lev Rosenthal; English lyrics adapted by Sheldon Harnick.

Wei Zu Di Teg (Crazy Times)   Lyrics by Katrielke Broide; music by Misha Veksler; English lyrics adapted by Sheldon Harnick.

Isrulik (They Call Me Izzy)   Lyrics by Lev Rosenthal; music by Misha Veksler; English lyrics adapted by Sheldon Harnick.

Friling (Springtime)   by Schmerke Kaczerginski; English lyrics adapted by Jim Friedman; music adapted by Gary William Friedman.

Zog Nit Keinmol (Never Say You Can't Go On)   by Hirsh Glick; English lyrics adapted by Sheldon Harnick.

Dremlen Feigl (Drowsing Birds)   by Leah Rudwitzky; English lyrics adapted by Jim Friedman.

Finale (Dance of the Clothes)   Lyrics by Sheldon Harnick; music by Gary William Friedman.

Postscript

A Theatre in the Wilna Ghetto

by Joshua Sobol

In 1942-43, with the horrors of the Holocaust well under way, a theatre was involved in putting on plays in the Wilna ghetto. It had its debut on June 18, 1942, about four months after the Jews of Wilna were deported to the ghetto, and a mere two months after the mass extermination in which over fifty thousand of the seventy thousand Jews were massacred.

The decision to found a theatre at such an agonizing time met with a stormy response in the ghetto. In his diary on January 17, 1942, the ghetto librarian and record-keeper Hermann Kruk, a Bundist, wrote: "In a cemetery there can be no theatre." When the slogan also appeared in the alleyways of the ghetto on the following day the head of the Jewish police, Jakob Gens, warned Kruk: if any such slogans appeared again, the librarian and his cohorts would be sent to Ponar.

Whose decision was it to found a theatre in those excruciating days? At a party marking six months since the theatre was established, its director Israel Segal noted that Gens himself had been behind it. Gens, head of the Jewish police at the time, was to become sole ruler of the ghetto as of July 1942; it was his brainchild, the ghetto theatre.

Despite the strong protest of political circles and intellectuals within the ghetto, the first performance was held as scheduled on January 18, 1942. The evening's artistic success was reflected in the ticket sales as well. Kruk himself noted in his diary that the proceeds were as high as four thousand rubles, all earmarked for charity, in keeping with the slogan: "Let no man go hungry in the ghetto." As news of the opening night success spread through the ghetto, it became clear that the theatre was there to stay. Fear of offending the public in a time of anguish and grief proved to be unfounded. "People cried and laughed—and their spirits were lifted."

Driven by his conviction that normalization and productivization of the ghetto were the key to saving as many people as possible, Gens regarded the theatre not only as a source of livelihood and employment for the actors but also as an invaluable emotional outlet which would boost morale and help to normalize ghetto life. This accounts for his insistence on cultivating the theatre and turning it into a permanent feature of ghetto life. A week after opening night, there was a repeat performance. Thanks to the warm reception the theatre had had at its debut, public objections subsided—despite the presence of German and Lithuanian officers in the audience. Among these, according to Kruk, were the Nazi officer Herring and the commander of the Lithuanian militias charged with the mass exterminations at Ponar. Kruk notes that the two of them left during the intermission.

In its first year, the theatre put on no fewer than 111 performances, selling a total of 34,804 tickets. The hall was usually packed and the shows were often sold out weeks in advance. By the time the ghetto was liquidated on September 20, 1943 the number of performances had doubled. A population of twenty thousand people had bought seventy thousand (!) tickets.

The performances included both light and serious theatre. In its two-year history, the theatre put on four variety revues based on original material written in the ghetto, mainly by Katriel Broide and Leib Rosenthal, whose poems and songs were especially popular.

The revues included programs like *Karena Yahren Un Wie Zu Die Tag* (July 1942), *Men Kann Garnicht Wissn* (October 1942), *Peshe von Reshe* (June 1943), and *Moshe Halt Sich* (August 1943). The latter was staged just when deportations to Estonia were at their worst, and continued until the liquidation of the ghetto on September 20, when the songs of the revue accompanied the last of the Wilna Jews being taken to the camps.

The repertoire also included the following five plays: *Grineh Felder* by Peretz Hirschbein, first performed in August 1942; *Der Mentsh Untern Brik* by the Hungarian playwright Otto Hindig, November 1942; *Der Otzar* by David Pinski, March 1943; *Havehudi Hanizchi* by David Pinski, first performed (in Hebrew) in June 1943; *Der Mabul* by Swedish playwright Henning Berger (August 1943), performed in the final weeks of the ghetto.

Rehearsals of *Tevya the Milkman* were well under way when the ghetto was liquidated. On its first anniversary, the theatre held a "Theatre Week in the Ghetto" at its home at 6 Rodnitzki Street. This was a full-fledged festival, including a revival of the first concert in the ghetto, two perfor-

POSTSCRIPT

mances of *Grineh Felder* and one of the *Men Kann Garnicht Wissn* revue, the Yiddish choir, recitals, light music concerts and a jam session of the jazz ensemble, as well as one symphony concert and a performance of the Hebrew choir. In its January 24th write-up on Theatre Week, the "Ghetto News" (printed under the auspices of the Judenrat) proudly noted that its pace of activity would do credit to a cultural center in any European metropolis.

Cultural activity in the Wilna ghetto was not confined to the theatre. Two days after the Wilna Jews were forced into the ghetto, a library was opened at 6 Strashon Street by Hermann Kruk, one of the cultural leaders of the Bund party, who had established hundreds of libraries and cultural centers in the Jewish communities of pre-war Poland. By September 19, with the extermination *Aktion* fully under way, 1,485 readers had registered at the library. Books were being borrowed at a rate of four hundred a day. Even during October 1941 with the *Aktionen* being implemented more intensely than ever, the library continued to supply its readers with books. On Yom Kippur (October 1, 1941) three thousand Jews were deported to Ponar. On the following day, 390 books were borrowed from the library. This continued at a rate of three hundred books a day, so that within a little over a year after it opened on December 13, 1942, the library proudly celebrated the borrowing of the 100,000th book. The readership had reached 4,700 by then, out of a total population of 17,000 in the ghetto.

The thriving cultural activity was apparent in other areas as well. There were competitions in music, the plastic arts, poetry and playwriting. The theatre foyer featured an exhibition of works by painters and sculptors in the ghetto, among them the nine-year-old Shmuel Back, whom Kruk mentions as being unusually gifted. Meanwhile, plans were under way to open a ghetto museum and Gens was working on a blueprint for a printing press and a publishing house which would go on operating after the war as well. This was in the early summer of 1943, only weeks before the liquidation of the ghetto. . . .

This vitality, so intensely reflected in the different areas of creative and intellectual activity, was channeled into other areas as well, such as the health-care system, schools and institutions for delinquents. There were dozens of lectures and symposia and morning assemblies for the workers. In addition to this cultural plethora, there was a strange vitality on the economic and commercial planes as well. In his diary, Kruk recorded the proliferation of cafe-theatres with every easing of pressure, along with an amazing rise and fall of the "King of the Ghetto" or the "Caliph of the Ghetto," Weiskopf, head of the clothing-repair shop.

Reading through the chronicles of the ghetto and the diaries of inmates—survivors as well as those who perished—and delving into the day-to-day affairs of the Wilna ghetto, one is overawed by the burst of vitality. Without it, there is no accounting for the ability of the defenseless survivors to cling dauntlessly to life, to retain their joy of life in the face of armed tormentors and murderers.

It is to the mystery of this vitality that I owe the play.

(Translated by Ami Weinberg)

Cathedral
of Ice

James Schevill

Characters

NARRATOR/ADOLF HITLER

MARILYN MONROE

KING OF THE MOUNTAIN

EVA BRAUN

NAPOLEON

HITLER'S FATHER

HITLER'S MOTHER

NEUMANN/HASIDIC MASTERS

THREE JEWISH WHORES

SCHRECK

HERMANN GÖRING

THE ARCHITECT

JOSEPH GÖBBELS

ERNST RÖHM

HEINRICH HIMMLER

RUDOLF HESS

JULIUS STREICHER

ULRICH GRAF

KARL MAY/HINDENBURG

HINDENBURG'S SON

RICHARD WAGNER

TRISTAN

ISOLDE

YOUNG MALE SINGER

YOUNG FEMALE SINGER

BORMANN

GELI RAUBAL

MALE PARTY OFFICIAL

WOMAN PARTY OFFICIAL

NIGHT

FOG

SS OFFICER

DR. FELIX KERSTEN

DR. MENGELE

VARIOUS VOICES, SS GUARDS, SS DOCTORS, DISCIPLES, PRISONERS, MEN AND WOMEN.

Time

Eternal present.

Cathedral of Ice was premiered at the Trinity Repertory Company in Providence, Rhode Island in 1975 under the direction of Adrian Hall. The set design was by Eugene Lee and the music by Richard Cumming. The production was assisted by a grant from the Rhode Island Committee for the Humanities. Simultaneously with the production, the play was published by Peter Kaplan and his Pourboire Press.

The Play

Cathedral
of Ice

Scene 1

As the audience enters the theatre they see the Dream Machine creating eerie comic and serious dream images. These dream images are taken from key scenes in the play such as the car sequence, the Old Shatterhand sequence, the songs, etc. Or the actors can improvise on images from their own dreams that fit into contemporary themes of power. The Dream Machine has a certain futuristic look, but it is also strangely archaic in appearance with obsolete, mythological panels and compartments pertinent to themes in the play.

NARRATOR *(Played by the actor who will play* HITLER*)*:
Ladies and gentlemen, welcome to the Dreams of Power.
Enjoy yourselves. Dream! This is your hour.
Do you fancy Love, Fame, Wealth?
(HE *motions to the three sections in which the audience are seated)*
In dream the choice is ours—let's choose our health.

Here, if HE *so desires and the opportunity seems right, the actor can improvise on his most recent night or daydream. When finished with these few lines* HE *points to the Dream Machine.*

Today, for our pleasure, we live by Dream Machines.
(HE *moves closer to inspect it)*
I love a good machine that slaves, washes, cleans;
(Patting the Dream Machine)

A scientific gadget that produces any dream I wish:
(TWO ACTORS *as a* CAR *appear from the Dream Machine*)
My dream car fast and sleek . . . (HE *drives his* CAR)
My favorite dish . . . (HE's *served with an all-American ice cream cone out of the machine*)

Talk shows and pro football on TV
And movies like they used to make for me,
The kind where every man dream of fun and sex.
(*Winking*) Glamour girls bursting in their upper decks . . .

Out of the Dream Machine bursts an actress dressed as MARILYN MONROE *speaking, dancing and singing in what Norman Mailer calls her "sweet little rinky-dink of a voice with all the cleanliness of all the clean American backyards."*

MARILYN MONROE: Cameras laugh as my breasts
Fly out of my dress.
Who sleeps when fame strips you naked?
You reach for sleeping pills
When Old Man Insomnia kills . . .

Singing refrain as the NARRATOR *joins her in a dream-like dance and song-duet.*

Fame will go by . . .
And, so long,
I've had you, Fame . . .

Mr. Boss shouts at me *Finished! Always late!*
Mr. Coroner numbers me *eighty-one, one, two, eight*—
Fame's number in a numbered time.
A sex symbol becomes a thing
And a thing cannot sing . . .

Refrain with NARRATOR.

Fame will go by . . .
And, so long,
I've had you, Fame . . .
MARILYN MONROE: Alone in my room I say
"Make it dark and give me air."
You've got to open the dark to dream,
But the lonely are always late,
The lonely have another date . . .

CATHEDRAL OF ICE

Refrain with NARRATOR.

Fame will go by . . .
And, so long,
I've had you, Fame . . .

After a turn with the NARRATOR, SHE *exits with her wriggling dance,*
singing her refrain and waving, as the NARRATOR *waves goodbye.*

NARRATOR (*Stepping towards her, holding out his hand to his dream of Marilyn*):
Dead . . . In the dark love flows away
And we learn to live another day . . .
If we can't have love, we call for Wealth, Fame . . .
On top of the heap we look out far
For the King of the Mountain, an American star . . .
High up there he glares, an eagle in flight,
Ends hunched over his tapes lost in the night,
Alone in his house where the frontier ends,
Writing his memoirs as the dark descends . . .

The KING OF THE MOUNTAIN *wears a Nixon mask. As* HE *sits listening*
to his tape recorder HE *hears his voice echoing eerily on tape. Sometimes*
HE *repeats part of the taped phrases in a strange counterpoint.*

KING OF THE MOUNTAIN: All I wanted was the lift of a driving dream . . .

The tape echoes "lift of a driving dream . . . lift of a dri—ving dream . . ."

Bee-trayed . . . Snake tapes . . . Those kids betrayed me . . . They
threw mudballs at the White House at every opportunity . . . They
wanted a red America . . . Never! . . .

The tape echoes "A red America—Never!" . . . HE *mouths the word*
"Never," looks angrily at the tape recorder, pokes it.

Snake tapes . . . Who would have thought the old tapes would pro-
liferate? . . . Why didn't I burn the tapes?

The tape echoes, "Why didn't I burn the tapes?"

How can you burn History when you've created it? . . . For the first
time in man's history I had it in my hands—to record power ac-
curately . . . Catch every little detail of power for the first time . . .

The tape echoes, "Every little detail for the first time . . ."

King of the Mountain, that's what they called me!

James Schevill

The tape echoes "King of the Mountain . . . King of the Mountain*"
as* HE *mouths the words.*

Bee—trayed! . . . Do they want to pick my carcass? . . . I'm not a skeleton yet . . . My writing will vindicate me . . .

*(*HE *pats the manuscript near him) Vin—di—cate* me! . . . *(Looking up)* Sky . . . Space . . . Moon . . . Beau—ti—ful . . . My name . . . American names on the moon . . . *Moooon* . . . In *my* time . . .

The tape echoes "Mooon . . . *In my* time . . ."

I did my best . . . *My* best . . . My *best* . . . In the best interests of the nation . . . Naaa—tion . . . Some mistakes . . . *Miss—takes* . . . Errors of judgment . . .

The tape echoes "Miss—takes . . . *Errors of judgment . . .*"

Those bastards . . . My advisers . . . I thought they'd throw themselves on a damn sword for me . . .

The tape echoes "Throw themselves on a damn sword for me . . . "

Those idiots with their domestic capers . . . Writing their spy stories . . . Their thrillers . . . They want to put my head in a cage . . . They want to put me on display in the papers . . . X-ray me on television . . . Media disease . . . *Me—di—a dis—ease* . . .

The tape echoes "Media disease . . . Me—di—a   dis—ease . . ."

Cri—sis . . . That's greatness . . . Hang in there . . . Throw the long bomb if necessary . . . No one else could decide . . . So many votes I got . . . They all loved me . . . My great game plan . . . I can still hear them applauding . . . I raise my arms . . . *(*HE *raises his arms in his victory stance)*

VOICES *(Echoing on tape as* HE *mouths the words)*:
   When the going gets tough, the tough get going . . .
     When the tough get going, the going gets tough . . .
       When the going gets going, the going gets tough . . .
         When the going gets tough, the going gets going . . .
           When the tough get going, the tough get going . . .
             When the going gets tough, the tough get going . . .
KING OF THE MOUNTAIN: *Beeee—traaaayed* . . . You bastard kids . . . We never conceived you . . . All you kids can do is say your filthy words in public . . . At least I had the decency to say them on secret tapes . . . How would you bastard children understand the mystery of hidden swearwords? . . . You kids shit on language, that's all you

do . . . All your goddamn demonstrations lost in time . . . You don't have me to kick around anymore . . .

The tape echoes "lost in time . . . You don't have me to kick around anymore . . ."

In time it will all come clear . . . My real game plan . . . To turn the earth into a game for all mankind . . . A peace game . . . A generation of peace . . .

The tape echoes ". . . a game for all mankind . . . A peace game . . . A generation of peace . . ."

Jeee—sus . . . No escape . . . Beee—trayed . . . Hidden tape recorders . . . My players couldn't even follow the script . . .

(Shouting at the tape recorder) Go on, pick my carcass . . . I was King of the Mountain . . . Your voices will die in time . . . I have my pardon . . . Publishers will pay me millions for my story . . . I'll write my story . . . Millions will read it . . . Translated all over the world . . . I'll be redeemed . . . *Re—deemed . . .*

The tape echoes ". . . redeemed . . . Re—deemed . . ."

Defiance then . . . Farewell to false voices . . . (HE *turns off the tape recorder) De—fi—ance . . . King of the Mountain . . .* My old stance . . . Against the world . . .

Slowly HE *fades back into the Dream Machine as the* NARRATOR *steps forward again.*

NARRATOR *(Staring at the machine):*
Be careful with this machine . . . Sometimes it speaks
Its own mind, wanders, races, leaks
What it pleases as is the way of dreams
When fact and fancy flow together in their streams . . .

(Looking at the machine a little apprehensively)
Tonight we hope it's programmed properly
To enter the dream-world where we learn to see
(The Dream Machine begins to work mysteriously)
With our machine's modern computer device
We conjure up a vast Cathedral of Ice . . .
(Light changes to indicate the Cathedral of Ice)

We'll search with you how dreams of power
Linger on today to haunt each waking hour . . .
(More lighting changes to intensify the effect of the Cathedral of Ice)

Now for our play excuse me, please.
Like all of us, my dreams must change
As I become Dream-Führer, power to arrange . . .

(HE *puts on a mustache, brushes his hair over his forehead, and becomes* HITLER)

As the NARRATOR *transforms himself into* HITLER, *the Dream Machine lights up with appropriate illumination.*

HITLER *(Exuberantly)*: I'm your Dream-Führer. Laugh, cry with me, ladies and gentlemen. Here in my Cathedral of Ice the dreams of power never die. What you hate by day you love at night. Against your enemies your Dream-Führer is a rainbow of hope. (HE *gestures and a large photographic image of* HITLER *as a knight in armor is projected on a screen above the Machine)* Laugh, ladies and gentlemen, laugh at your Dream-Führer. Laugh at the Dream-Führer's wife . . .

EVA BRAUN *makes her dream-like appearance out of the Dream Machine singing "Tea for Two" as* SHE *sang it in the bunker the night before* SHE *died.* HITLER *cuts her off after a time.*

That's enough Eva. You sang that song just before we died. You sing it too much.

EVA *(Stopping obediently)*: Yes, Adolf.

HITLER *(Continuing, to the audience)*: Through laughter, through song, we begin to feel the power of the will, how Dream-Führers conquer even in defeat. You think my toothbrush mustache an accident? My dangling forelock happened by chance? Pure dream images. Napoleon was almost midget-short, so small that he created a dream-stance of power for eternity . . .

HITLER *motions and in a niche, as if out of the Dream Machine, the figure of* NAPOLEON *appears.* HE *is seated on the imperial throne as if in Ingres's famous "Portrait of Napoleon I on His Imperial Throne" (1806). In addition to his imperial robe and crown,* HE *holds the Hand of Justice and wears the sword of Charlemagne.*

EVA *(Gaping, impressed)*: Look, Adolf, you've brought back Napoleon.

HITLER: On his throne when he become Emperor Napoleon the First. You see his sword and the Hand of Justice he holds? They belonged to Charlemagne.

EVA: Really? Charlemagne?

HITLER: Yes, Napoleon was the imperial successor to the Holy Roman Empire, the first leader before me to unify Europe. I'll tell you a secret, Eva. I always wanted to die on May 5, the same day Napoleon died . . .

NAPOLEON (*Sharply*): You died on April 30, six days before my death.

HITLER: The German people betrayed me. They couldn't hold Berlin.

NAPOLEON: You should never have invaded Russia.

HITLER (*Sarcastically*): You're an authority, of course . . . What happened to your artillery in the snow?

NAPOLEON: The winter was abnormally severe. You should have known your heavy tanks would get stuck in the ice. Anyway I reached Moscow. You never reached Moscow.

HITLER: I conquered the Ukraine. If Göring hadn't ruined the Luftwaffe I would have triumphed before winter set in. Next time we should strike the Ukraine again.

NAPOLEON: Nonsense, you went too far south. Next time we must have a frontal attack on Moscow the way I planned.

HITLER (*Shouting at* NAPOLEON): History has taught you nothing. I'll show you. I'll prove to the world man becomes great through dream-conquests. Struggle is the father of all things. Virtue lies in blood. Leadership is primary and decisive . . .

EVA (*Tugging at his sleeve*): That's one of your old speeches, Adolf . . .

HITLER (*As* NAPOLEON *fades away*): Napoleon will have to learn if he's going to remain a real Dream-Führer . . .

Actors as STALIN, ROOSEVELT, CHURCHILL, *perhaps in masks, are seen in an eerie, dream-like "Yalta Dance," perhaps around a round table, as* THEY *shake hands formally, push* ROOSEVELT *around in his wheel chair, etc.*

EVA (*Gaping again*): Look . . . Your enemies . . .

HITLER: Don't worry . . . Only fading dream-figures . . . Stalin, Roosevelt, Churchill, in their Yalta dance . . .

EVA (*Smiling*): Their Yalta dance?

HITLER: Yes, those dreamers thought they could divide Europe. Stalin tricked them. I'll defeat them all in time. They won't get into my Cathedral of Ice . . .

The dream-figures of STALIN, ROOSEVELT *and* CHURCHILL *fade away.*

EVA (*Excitedly*): They're gone? Adolf, you *are* Dream-Führer . . .

HITLER (*Complacently*): Out of my Dream-Apparatus I continue to create my Third Reich. In our dreams we begin to discover ourselves, escape from our parents . . .

Something explodes in the Dream Machine and two performers dressed like Hitler's MOTHER *and* FATHER *appear.*

EVA (*Nudging* HITLER *as his back is turned*): Adolf, I don't think you've escaped . . .

Hitler's FATHER *speaks his customs official title twice, sharply, as if correcting his wife and son, reminding them of his position, then bows stiffly.*

EVA: Is that your father?

HITLER: Don't worry about him. He's just a ghost. He was a man who wanted only to be respectable.

MOTHER (*Impatiently to* FATHER): Uncle Alois, Uncle Alois . . .

EVA: What's she saying?

HITLER: My mother always called my father, "Uncle Alois."

EVA *breaks into laughter.*

Even in the bedroom she called him "Uncle Alois."

FATHER (*Calling sharply*): You never respected my uniform.

HITLER: Your uniform never meant anything. The uniform of a minor Austrian customs official, that's all.

MOTHER (*Protesting*): You should respect your father, Adolf.

HITLER: Poor little tyrant. What does that ghost know about real power? His uniform only obscured the dreams of authority that he tried to enforce on me.

FATHER *calls out his title again sharply and dogmatically.*

MOTHER (*Alarmed as* THEY *begin to fade away in the Apparatus for Dreams*): Uncle Alois, Uncle Alois . . . He's the Führer!

HITLER (*Impatiently as* THEY *disappear into the Dream Machine*): No one thinks of my parents anymore. Lost in their bourgeois roles, they left me to become the real dreamer. They sentenced me to school where more bourgeois authorities tried to confine me . . .

An old, grim-looking provincial Austrian SCHOOLTEACHER *appears dimly, in dim light as if struggling vainly to become a real dream.* HE *is waving a pointer menacingly at* HITLER.

All those provincial Austrian schoolteachers could do was induce boredom as they waved their pointers at me over some bit of nonsense. My first report card was so bad I got drunk, tore it up and used it for toilet paper . . .

EVA (*Laughing*): You didn't!

The DREAM-TEACHER *holds up a torn report card and waves the pointer menacingly at* HITLER *who smiles and waves him back into the Apparatus for Dreams.*

HITLER: Goodbye to school. Lessons of power are learned in the streets. Today every new Dream Machine adds to the power of the Dream-Führer. *(Gesturing at the Apparatus)* Look carefully, ladies and gentlemen, out of my Dream Machine I continue to shape my Cathedral of Ice for the future . . .

The unpredictable Dream Machine explodes again and NEUMANN *steps out of it with the Jewish coat.*

NEUMANN: And the past, Führer. Don't forget the past.

HITLER: Neumann . . . You don't belong here.

NEUMANN: You can't eliminate every little man so easily.

HITLER: Get out of my dreams.

NEUMANN *(Smiling)*: I wish I could. I brought your Jewish coat. You'll need it to keep warm in the Cathedral of Ice.

EVA *(Nudging HITLER)*: Who is that old man? What's he mean by Jewish coat?

HITLER *(Ignoring her; to NEUMANN)*: I don't need your filthy old coat anymore. It was long ago in Vienna, when I was a poor student, I bought it from you. You tried to swindle me, you Jewish peddler.

NEUMANN: I gave it to you. I did your business. We lived in the same poorhouse.

HITLER: You never gave away anything. I'll build my Cathedral without Rome, without Jews.

NEUMANN: I sold your painted postcards, gave you money to live on. You'll need your coat . . .

HITLER: All you sell is filth. I cleaned up Vienna. I got rid of you, Neumann. You're dead, you and all your disgraceful Jewish whores spreading their syphilis . . .

Mockingly, NEUMANN *begins to sell* HITLER'*s postcards while* THREE WHORES OF VIENNA *like satirical, antagonistic ghosts sing "The Ballad of the Jewish Whores of Vienna."*

THE JEWISH WHORES *(Singing)*:
That's what we do
From dusk until dawn—
We infect with disgrace
All the Aryan race—
We're the Great Jewish Whores of Vienna . . .

HITLER *(Shouting at them)*: Out of my Cathedral of Ice! Out! You attack everyone with syphilis . . .

EVA *(Plucking at his sleeve)*: Syphilis, Adolf, syphilis . . .

THE JEWISH WHORES *(Singing)*:
    That's what we do
    From dusk until dawn—
    We attack, we attack
    Though flat on our back—
    We're the Great Jewish Whores of Vienna . . .
HITLER *(Raving at them)*: You're dead, you Jewish whores. Only one thing
    triumphs, terror and force . . .
THE JEWISH WHORES *(Singing)*:   That's what we do
    From dusk until dawn—
    We use terror and force
    And show no remorse—
    We're the Great Jewish Whores of Vienna . . .

Laughing THEY *drop their roles as* WHORES *and return to their positions
as observers in the Cathedral of Ice.* NEUMANN *continues to sell* HITLER'*s
painted postcards.*

NEUMANN: Postcards for sale . . . Little painted postcards by Adolf
    Hitler . . . Rare reproductions . . . Pictures of famous Viennese
    monuments . . . All by Adolf Hitler . . . Reduced prices . . .
EVA: You shouldn't let him sell your work so cheaply, Adolf . . .
HITLER: Stop selling my work cheaply, Neumann. It's worth much more
    today.
NEUMANN *(Continuing his pitch to the audience)*: Come buy, ladies and
    gentlemen . . . Remember the Inflation . . . Get your little painted
    postcards . . . The little painted postcards of Adolf Hitler . . .
HITLER *(Proudly)*: They're worth a fortune now, my postcards . . . I'm
    a better painter than Winston Churchill . . . Come here, Neumann.
NEUMANN *(Approaching mockingly)*: Yes, Führer . . . What is your wish?
HITLER: Take back your Jewish coat.
NEUMANN: It's cold in the Cathedral of Ice . . . My coat will help.
HITLER: It's got lice in it.
NEUMANN: What do you expect from a Vienna poorhouse?
HITLER: You know how I hated that poorhouse, but I always kept my
    clothes clean. You gave me a dirty coat.
NEUMANN: You were glad enough to wear it . . .
HITLER: I never wanted your Jewish coat . . . That miserable city of lotus-
    eaters was five years of shame for me . . .
NEUMANN *(Smiling)*: We Jews lotus-eaters? If there were any food to in-
    duce forgetfulness we'd eat it . . .
HITLER: You tried to be a good Jew and seduce me with your coat. But
    you hid your money like the rest of them.

NEUMANN *(Shrugging)*: What money? If you find yourself tied to a Hitler who needs money?

EVA: Get him to sell something else. That's all he's good for.

HITLER *(Producing a box of campaign ribbons out of the Dream Machine)*: Why don't you sell my campaign ribbons? . . . It's time to remember my great victories . . .

As NEUMANN *only smiles,* HITLER *starts hawking the ribbons and medals.*

Poland, 1939 . . . France, 1940, my greatest triumph . . . Belgium, Holland . . . Norway, Finland, Denmark, the Scandinavian countries . . . An endless list . . . All of Europe . . . North Africa . . . Greece, Yugoslavia . . . Come, ladies and gentlemen, help me build my Cathedral of Ice . . . What will you give me for my great Russian Campaign Medal? *(HE starts to shiver as the Apparatus begins to ice over with a chill)* Turn up the heat . . . It's cold in here . . .

NEUMANN *helps him put on the coat.*

That damn Russian winter killed my troops . . . Why don't you sell some real souvenirs? . . . *(With increasing frenzy)* Sell them my new weapons . . . The military powers need my buzz-bombs, my rockets, my new jet planes, my tanks . . . If you want a real souvenir, sell them my Mercedes touring car . . .

SCHRECK *(Shooting angrily out of the Dream Machine)*: You can't sell the Mercedes . . . It was my car too . . . I drove it, I polished it, I cared for it until you spoiled everything . . .

EVA *(Delighted to see* SCHRECK, *although* HE *ignores her)*: Adolf, it's Schreck, your chauffeur. He's come to drive us to Berchtesgaden. We'll have some fun . . .

HITLER: Schreck, we had good times together. How can you say I spoiled everything?

SCHRECK *(Doggedly like a child)*: You forbade me to drive fast anymore . . .

HITLER: We couldn't run down every peasant who came out to cheer me.

GÖRING *(Appearing in the Dream Machine, waving a cigar)*: Forget him, Führer. He's only a chauffeur. We don't need him in the Cathedral of Ice.

HITLER *(Raging)*: You don't know who we need. I decide who lives here.

GÖRING: I committed suicide for you at Nürnberg.

HITLER *(Gesturing with contempt at* GÖRING's *cigar)*: You know I hate smoking . . . How many times do I have to tell you you can't be represented in a historical monument smoking a cigar . . .

GÖRING *shrugs, continues to smoke his cigar, watching.*

HITLER *(Crying out, summoning the* ARCHITECT*)*: Where's my Architect? . . .

The ARCHITECT *appears and walks to* HITLER.

This Architect is mine. He draws the plans for my new world. Every drawing is corrected by my pen . . . (HE *tugs at his coat. To the* ARCHITECT*)* You want my Jewish coat from Vienna? I can't . . . can't get it off . . .

The ARCHITECT *moves to help him and* HITLER *thrusts the* ARCHITECT *away.*

Get away . . . You're useless. If you're my Architect why can't you design me a real home?

ARCHITECT: Yes, Führer, what style would you like?

HITLER: Like my old home at Obersalzberg, the only place where I could relax . . . That's what they want to see in the Cathedral of Ice . . .

EVA: Let's go to Obersalzberg . . . We had the most fun there . . .

ARCHITECT: Yes, Führer . . . *(Calling)* The procession to the Teahouse at Berchtesgaden . . .

The ARCHITECT *signals and a procession forms on the ramp that represents the curving mountain walk to the Teahouse at Obersalzberg.*

HITLER: That's right . . . For once you've got the right idea . . . The walk to the Teahouse is my favorite walk . . .

On the ramp two SECURITY MEN *lead the procession. Everyone in this scene is dressed in civilian clothes so at first the gaiety of the walk dominates. After the initial humorous confusion, the rigidity of the nightmare-like, ritualistic walk becomes apparent.*

ARCHITECT *(Near the foot of the ramp)*: If anyone is Hitler's friend, I am his friend . . . So I always have to accompany him . . . The path up the mountain to the Teahouse is narrow . . . Room for only two abreast . . . Two security men lead the procession . . .

Mechanically the SECURITY MEN *start up the path.*

Then comes Hitler talking to his immediate favorite . . .

HITLER *starts up the path talking genially to one* MAN. *Two* OTHER MEMBERS *of the walking group appear. The rear of the procession is brought up by a female* SECRETARY *and* EVA BRAUN.

CATHEDRAL OF ICE

At the procession's end march his secretary and his mistress Eva Braun . . .

EVA *(Correcting him)*: I'm his wife now . . .

ARCHITECT *(Continuing as a dog barks)*: His police dog darts about . . .

HITLER *(Calls sharply; shurgs when the dog fails to appear)*: Here, Blondi . . . Here Blondi . . . Blondi . . .

HE *turns, summons another favorite, which causes a frantic, abrupt adjustment in the order of the procession.*

No, no, you've got it all wrong . . . Can't you remember the way it went?

ARCHITECT *(At the rear of the procession now)*: Every German wonder that I learned as a boy hangs in the air over this walk . . . If only the Führer will summon me again to be a great architect . . . For the commission to design an important building I'll sell my soul . . .

The ritualistic walk begins again revealing its increasingly mechanical, servile nature. Suddenly HITLER *turns, beckons impatiently to the* ARCHITECT, *who jumps to the* FÜHRER's *side. The* ARCHITECT *assumes the favored position beside* HITLER *and behind the security men in the procession.*

HITLER: How do you like the Obersalzberg?

ARCHITECT: Magnificent . . .

HITLER: Here I spend the finest hours of my life . . . *(HE calls to his dog again)* Blondi! *(Then affectionately)* That dog never minds me . . . *(Sharply)* He's the only one . . .

ARCHITECT: It is a beautiful view.

HITLER *(Musing)*: All my great projects are conceived and ripened in these mountains . . . *(HE points)* You see the Untersberg?

ARCHITECT *(Staring)*: Lovely.

HITLER *(Sharply)*: The Empereror Charlemagne sleeps there. *(Reverently emphasizing the legend to the* ARCHITECT*)* You remember the legend, "When he arises, the past glory of the German Empire will be restored." . . . Hear me Emperor Charlemagne . . . In your tomb do you hear me? . . .

The CAST *echoes the sound of "Charlemagne."*

Germany is finished with playacting. No longer will Germany be betrayed by Jews and bourgeois democrats. Hear me, Charlemagne!

The CAST *echoes "Charlemagne" again.*

James Schevill

I pledge you a new German empire. My troops will march again
through the streets of Europe. Rise from your tomb . . . Hand in
hand we'll walk across the map of Europe . . . Charlemagne! We'll
rule together in the Cathedral of Ice!

The entire CAST *sings the "Ballad of the Cathedral of Ice."*

HITLER: Charlemagne!
　　Rise from your tomb.
　　Dreams have no price.
　　Power lives on
　　In my Cathedral of Ice . . .
CAST: Charlemagne!
　　Come buy your joy or sorrow.
　　In the Cathedral of Ice
　　We freeze you for tomorrow.
HITLER: Charlemagne!
　　I pledge you a new Empire,
　　A new Aryan race
　　Out of blood, war, fire!
CAST: Charlemagne!
　　Come buy your joy or sorrow.
　　In the Cathdral of Ice
　　We freeze you for tomorrow.
HITLER: Charlemagne!
　　Into history, into time,
　　Our troops march on
　　Forever into dream.
CAST: Charlemagne!
　　Come buy your joy or sorrow.
　　In the Cathedral of Ice
　　We freeze you for tomorrow . . .

*Slowly, costumed like a kind of 19th century Wagnerian reincarnation of
medieval power, the dream-figure of* CHARLEMAGNE *rises from his tomb
in the Dream Machine and dances a little jig of power with* HITLER *as
the* CAST *sings the final refrain.*

CATHEDRAL OF ICE

Scene 2
Hitler's Children

After CHARLEMAGNE *disappears back into his tomb,* HITLER *signals in frenzied exultation and a large Nazi flag drops down.*

HITLER: At last our Dream Machine is working perfectly. Here, with my favorite Architect (*A gesture to the* ARCHITECT) we create for eternity our famous German ruins. We freeze all traitors, Jews, into the ice-walls of our national fortress. (*To the* ARCHITECT) Invite them to meet my children.

ARCHITECT (*To audience*): Ladies and gentlemen, we invite you to meet Hitler's children . . .

A corner of the flag is drawn up and we see the beginning of the line of CHILDREN *wavering uncertainly in time.*

HITLER (*Interrupting*): No, let me speak first . . . I'll put my children in the right perspective . . .

As HITLER *steps up on a platform to start the introduction of his "children," the flag is raised higher and the full line of* CHILDREN *is revealed.*

How petty are the thoughts of small men. I always aim at something a thousand times higher. I want to become the destroyer of Marxism. I am still going to achieve this task. I will destroy communism throughout the world! When I stood for the first time at the grave of Richard Wagner, my heart overflowed with pride in his genius. He had forbidden the usual sort of flowery inscription such as *Here Lies His Excellency, Baron Richard Von Wagner.* He gave himself to the world without any titles of vanity. I am proud to follow in his footsteps. The man who is born to be a dictator is not forced into it. His will triumphs. There is nothing immodest about this. Is it immodest for a worker to drive himself to heavy labor? Is it presumptuous for a thinker to ponder through the nights until he gives the world a great invention? The man who is called upon to govern has no right to say, "If you summon me I will cooperate." No, it is his duty to step forward even through death.

HITLER *steps forward. His* CHILDREN *cry "Sieg Heil!" three times.*

HITLER (*Smiling to the* ARCHITECT *with satisfaction*): Come forward my children . . . Behave yourselves . . .

At the head of the line GÖBBELS *steps forward to celebrate* HITLER. *While* GÖBBELS *speaks* HITLER *listens, nodding with satisfaction, occasionally slapping the short whip that* HE *carries against his coat.*

GÖBBELS: Like a rising star before our wondering eyes you appear . . . You perform miracles to clear our minds . . . You speak the greatest words Germany has heard since Bismarck . . . You unify the Great German Reich, purify it for eternity . . . You name the need of a new generation . . . We thank you . . . Europe and the world will thank you . . .

HITLER *(To* GÖBBELS*)*: A good speaker . . . That's why you're my propaganda minister . . . You're faithful. But I had to teach you a lesson. In power, you can't trust anyone. Remember what you called me once at an early Party meeting?

GÖBBELS *(Forced to recall a nightmare)*: *I demand that the petty bourgeois, Adolf Hitler, be expelled from the Nazi Party for accepting favors and privileges from the wealthy!* *(Hysterically)* Can't you ever forget?

HITLER: A dictator never forgets his bastard children. You went to college too much. Eight universities, wasn't it?

GÖBBELS: Yes.

HITLER: You confused your mind with too many subjects—history, philosophy, literature, art, Latin, Greek . . . You wrote bad plays, a poor autobiographical novel . . .

GÖBBELS *(Agreeing reluctantly)*: It was a terrible novel . . . *(Under his breath)* You weren't a good painter either.

HITLER *(Shouting)*: What's that? . . .

GÖBBELS *mutters, "Nothing."*

The important thing is I taught you how to use the arts for political power.

GÖBBELS: You taught me everything.

HITLER: Not quite. Your crippled foot . . . You still want to climb into bed with every little actress you can find just to assert your masculinity . . .

GÖBBELS *(Spitting out venomously)*: My limp kept me chained to a desk, walking lopsided, a dwarf of history . . .

HITLER *(Gesturing with his whip)*: Without your limp you're nothing. It gives you the instinct of hatred . . .

GÖBBELS: Yes . . .

HITLER *(Tapping his leg with his whip)*: A touch of hatred gives a man a mysterious quality . . .

GÖBBELS: You've always been the mysterious Führer to me.

CATHEDRAL OF ICE

HITLER (*Smiling a little, now that* HE*'s humiliated* GÖBBELS): My problem is still to give my *Hakenkreuz*, my swastika, a new dramatic mystery. I want it to strike the eye of even the most simpleminded person.

GÖBBELS: Your design remains an inspiration to us all . . .

HITLER (*Pointing to the flag*): In red I see my war against communism. In white the cause of nationalism. And in the swastika the final victory of Aryan man. Stand aside, Joseph . . . Let's see the rest of my children.

> HITLER *pokes up the corner of the flag a little with his whip and looks down the line of "*CHILDREN*" as if to make sure of their appearance and obedience in the Cathedral of Ice.*

What simple creatures. You'll never sell me out to the peacemongers, eh? A strong party needs men like you . . .

GÖBBELS (*Wide-eyed with reverence*): Only such men can conquer the bourgeoisie . . .

HITLER (*Nodding assent*): If a bourgeois gives me a hundred marks he thinks he's given me all of Bavaria. But these men, what sacrifices they're willing to make . . . All day at their jobs . . . All night off on a mission for the Party.

> THEY *nod assent in their distinctively crude ways.*

Especially I look for men a little rough in appearance. When they walk into a hall, people sit up. A bourgeois in a stiff collar ruins everything.

GÖBBELS (*Eagerly*): As a favor may I introduce them, Führer?

HITLER (*As if granting a favor to a child*): If you wish. Let's have Schreck first. I'm going to need him again.

GÖBBELS (*Announcing*): Julius Schreck, private chauffeur and bodyguard to the Führer . . .

As THEY *pretend to drive through history with* SCHRECK *at the wheel, the* CAST *joins in "The Ballad of the German Motorists."*

CAST (*Singing*): We're motorists of Germany.
Inventors of the People's Car,
So small and cheap that anyone
Can buy a bug to ride in fun.

SCHRECK (*Speaking*): Have you bought your People's Car?

CAST (*Singing*): Volkswagen, Volkswagen . . .
We'll drive from Berlin to Cannes
On the Autobahn, Autobahn . . .

We're the motorists of Germany,
Creators of the fast sports car,
Building free the Autobahn
To speed forever on and on . . .

SCHRECK *(Speaking)*: Have you bought your fast sports car?

CAST *(Singing)*: Porsche, Porsche . . .
We'll drive from Berlin to Cannes
On the Autobahn, Autobahn . . .

We're motorists of Germany,
Designers of the new sedan—
We seat your family on a throne
Of power where you rule alone . . .

SCHRECK *(Speaking)*: Come buy your family a sedan!

CAST *(Singing refrain)*: Mercedes, Mercedes . . .
We'll drive from Berlin to Cannes
On the Autobahn, Autobahn!

SCHRECK *(With sudden bitterness, pleading to* HITLER*)*: Can I drive fast again?

HITLER *(Impatiently)*: Soon, soon . . .

SCHRECK *(Possessed,* HE *won't be put off)*: I'm a great driver. I could have been Germany's number one race driver. In our supercharged Mercedes we used to pass all the American cars. We'd force them to the side of the road . . .

HITLER *(Remembering pleasantly)*: American cars were nothing compared to a Mercedes. Their motors would overheat. They'd pull over with steam pouring out of their radiators. What fun . . .

SCHRECK *(Shouting)*: Then you ordered me not to drive over fifty. Me, a great driver!

HITLER *(Annoyed)*: Poor simple Schreck . . . You won't learn . . . You have the vision of a great driver, but no sense of public destiny. I created Volkswagen, Porsche and Mercedes . . . They owe everything to me . . .

Impatiently HE *waves* SCHRECK *off with his whip and motions* GÖB-BELS *to continue with the introductions.*

GÖBBELS *(Announcing with glee)*: Heinrich Hoffman, your official photographer . . .

EVA BRAUN, *disguised as Hoffman, steps forward and snaps pictures of* HITLER *as* HE *poses smiling in his new role of power.*

HITLER *(As* HE *poses)*: Heinrich, you're a man who knows the camera's power. As a photographer you're always in the background at the

right time. You can still help me along with the right photographs . . .
And you introduced me to Eva Braun when she worked for you,
eh, Heinrich?

EVA *(Taking off her hat and grinning at* HITLER*)*: Yes, Adolf.

HITLER *(Laughing with delight)*: Eva, you rascal. You always play games
on me. Go on now . . . You're holding up my children.

SHE *laughs, snaps another photo, and runs off. A weird figure emerges
grimly from the line of* CHILDREN. HE *struggles futilely to speak through
time. It is* ERNEST RÖHM *trying to redeem his place in history.* HE *struggles furiously to push his way forward as the* BULLY-BOYS *try to keep him
back in line.*

RÖHM: I demand to be heard . . . I'm your old comrade . . . My only
wish is to be a soldier for the Third Reich . . .

HITLER *(Hysterically)*: How did he get into my Cathedral of Ice? *(To* GÖB-
BELS*)* I don't permit traitors here. *(Turning on* RÖHM*)* Ernst Röhm,
traitor, that's your name. I had you shot . . .

GÖBBELS *(Groveling)*: He won't die . . .

RÖHM *(Struggling with the* BULLY-BOYS*)*: There is some error, Adolf.
If you want to kill me why don't you do it yourself?

HITLER *(Screaming)*: Don't call me Adolf. No one calls me by my first name.
I am the Führer . . .

GÖBBELS *(Trying desperately to placate* HITLER*)*: Touch him with your whip,
Führer. Make him disappear in time.

HITLER *(Lashing out with his whip)*: Back to your death, Röhm. Tell your
story to the grave . . . No one listens to your lies. The Führer stands
alone in history . . . *(*HE *takes a defiant stance of loneliness beneath the
swastika)*

The BULLY-BOYS *subdue* RÖHM.

GÖBBELS *(Cautiously)*: Shall I go on, Führer . . .

HITLER *(Shaking suspiciously again)*: Is Röhm silent? . . .

GÖBBELS *(Soothingly)*: Yes, I'm sure he won't be any more trouble . . . The
next is Rudolf Hess, your loyal secretary . . .

HESS *steps forward, pleased, slightly bewildered, mad in time.* HE *recites
like a schoolboy from his prizewinning essay at the University of Munich,
"What Will the Man Be Like Who Will Lead Germany Back to Her
Old Grandeur?"*

HESS *(Reciting)*: Where all authority has vanished, only a man of the people
can restore authority. The deeper the dictator is rooted in the masses,
the better he understands them psychologically . . .

HITLER (*As if nodding encouragement to a child*): Very good, Rudolf. You're better as a student . . .

HESS (*Continuing with new confidence*): Like every great man the dictator is all personality. When necessity commands he does not shrink from bloodshed. Great questions are always decided by blood and iron. In order to reach his goal he is prepared to trample on his closest friends . . .

HITLER (*Impatiently*): That's a lie. Too bad you lost your mind . . . Your crazy flight to England . . . You should have crashed in the English channel.

With his whip HE *motions* HESS *back into line.*

GÖBBELS (*Maliciously, enjoying the next encounter*): Hermann Göring, fat man, drug addict . . .

GÖRING (HE *is clad in elements of a once-glorious hunting costume, hat, shorts, colorful high stockings, leather vest, dagger at his waist. Immediately* HE *attacks* GÖBBELS): Shut up you crippled dwarf . . . I answer only to the Führer . . .

GÖBBELS (*Taunting him*): Is that why you're so far back in line? . . .

HITLER (*In a tirade to* GÖRING): We don't need your ridiculous hunting costume here. Killing animals, if one must eat meat, is the butcher's business. To dress up in ridiculous costumes might be all right if you used a bow and arrow, but all you use is a fat belly and a gun . . .

GÖRING (*Unhearing, enthusiastic, remembering as if in a dream*): I bagged a buck . . . He was drinking at a stream when we spotted him from the ridge above . . . Then he caught wind of us and bolted halfway up the mountain . . .

HITLER (*Annoyed*): I don't want to hear about your hunting. We have important business.

GÖRING: Is anything wrong?

HITLER: I want you to spend less time on hunting and devote yourself more to our transit problems.

GÖRING (*Slowly*): Cars and highways? But the Luftwaffe . . .

HITLER: I want Autobahns everywhere. Everyone should have his Volkswagen.

GÖBBELS (*Jumping in smoothly*): We can make the newspapers print special sections on the pleasures of traveling by car.

HITLER: Excellent . . . That's the kind of action I want. (*To* GÖRING) What do you think?

GÖRING (*Carefully*): We must consider carefully. The Air Force must be our first effort . . .

HITLER *(Raging)*: You're ruining the Luftwaffe . . . You're a drug addict . . . Hard drugs . . . Heroin . . . I won't have it.

GÖRING *shrugs and turns back into line.*

GÖBBELS *(Enjoying* GÖRING*'s put-down)*: Heinrich Himmler, head of the SS and the Gestapo . . .

HIMMLER *(Stepping forward, tight-lipped)*: Führer, everything we discussed about the camps was strictly in privacy.

HITLER: You can't keep your mouth shut . . . A small poultry farmer, that's all you are, Heinrich . . . You have the simple mind of a clerk. Somehow you became the most feared man in the world. By hating you they love me. That's why I keep you around . . .

HIMMLER *(Saluting)*: Ja, mein Führer . . . *(*HE *steps back into line)*

GÖBBELS *(Pointing to the line)*: Should we bother with the bully-boys?

HITLER: One or two if you wish . . .

GÖBBELS: They go quickly . . . Julius Streicher, Party leader of Franconia, newspaper editor . . .

STREICHER *steps out warily.*

HITLER *(Angrily)*: Julius Pornographer . . . We don't want him . . . *(To* STREICHER*)* You keep a camera in the ceiling over your bed to record your sexual escapades . . .

STREICHER *(Protesting)*: I'm your strongest supporter . . . I call you by your first name, Adolf . . .

HITLER: A privilege you never deserved . . . You should use your whip like a lion tamer. You only use it for your private sadism . . .

HE *lashes* STREICHER *back into line.*

GÖBBELS *(Continuing hastily to appease* HITLER*'s wrath)*: Ulrich Graf, your bodyguard . . . Butcher's apprentice, amateur wrestler . . .

HITLER *(With satisfaction, inspecting* GRAF*'s muscles)*: A good bodyguard. You like to fight. Great physical strength . . . At Party meetings you can be useful in throwing out troublemakers.

HE *pats* GRAF*'s arm, patting him back into line.*

That's enough children, Joseph . . .

GÖBBELS: Yes, my Führer . . .

HITLER: Let them entertain me.

GÖBBELS *and the* CHILDREN *sing "The Big Lie."* HITLER *stands with the* ARCHITECT *beneath the swastika, beating time with his whip. The*

James Schevill

archaic, dignified figure of KARL MAY, *dressed in formal civilian clothes
of around 1900, appears upstage behind the* CHILDREN *during the song,
waiting impatiently to address* HITLER.

CHILDREN *(Singing "Song of the Big Lie")*:
　　Tell the Big Lie—
　　It's the Truth,
　　It's the Truth
　　　if it's told
　　　　long enough . . .
GÖBBELS *(Singing the refrain)*:
　　Big Lies will bring you triumph sweet
　　If you repeat, repeat, repeat . . .
ALL *(Echoing)*: Repeat, repeat, repeat, repeat . . .
GÖBBELS: Make the stars revolve around the earth . . .
HESS: Tell a man his race is damned from birth . . .
GÖBBELS: Teach the public eye that Rome is Greece . . .
HESS: Pound the message home that war means peace . . .
ALL *(Singing)*: Tell the Big Lie—
　　It's the Truth,
　　It's the Truth
　　　if it's told
　　　　long enough . . .
GÖBBELS: Big Lies will bring you triumph sweet
　　If you repeat, repeat, repeat . . .
ALL *(Echoing)*: Repeat, repeat, repeat, repeat . . .
STREICHER: Sell cheap things in a fancy box . . .
GRAF: It won't smell like skunk if you call it fox . . .
RÖHM: Repetition is the road to wealth . . .
HESS: If it makes you sick, pretend it's health! . . .
ALL *(Singing)*: Tell the Big Lie—
　　It's the Truth,
　　It's the Truth
　　　if it's told
　　　　long enough . . .
GÖBBELS: Big Lies will bring you triumph sweet
　　If you repeat, repeat, repeat . . .
ALL *(Echoing)*: Repeat, repeat, repeat, repeat . . .
GÖRING *and* GRAF: Hire muscle-men to protect the State . . .
HESS *and* HIMMLER: Teach the small to venerate the Great . . .
RÖHM *and* STREICHER: Big Lies will bring you triumph sweet . . .
ALL: If you repeat, repeat, repeat!

　　Tell the Big Lie—
　　It's the Truth,

It's the Truth
  if it's told
    long enough . . .

THEY *exit in an eerie, grotesque version of a vaudeville line.*

GÖBBELS *(Whispering at the head of line):*
  Big Lies will bring you triumph sweet—
  If you repeat, repeat, repeat . . .
ALL *(As THEY go out—very softly):* Repeat, repeat, repeat, repeat . . .

Scene 3
Old Shatterhand to Power

KARL MAY *(Impatiently steps forward to address HITLER):* Repeat, repeat, that's all you still do. I won't permit you to be alone in history . . . *(Pointing indignantly at the swastika flag)* You never got your swastika right. The Indian swastika runs the other way to keep the luck in. Your swastika is turned around the wrong way with the luck running out!

HITLER *(Soothingly, turning on his charm as if back in a dream childhood):* Come here, old man . . . *(Aside)* These dreamers must learn about dreams. *(HE puts his arm around MAY and sits down with him)* You know when I was a boy the first thing I read of your kind of western story was *The Last of the Mohicans* . . . But a friend told me, "Fenimore Cooper is nothing. You must read Karl May."

MAY: That's right. Fenimore Cooper is nothing. I, Karl May, am the most popular writer in the world of western stories.

HITLER: Yes, I devoured all of your books, Karl May. I fell in love with your hero, Old Shatterhand . . .

MAY *(Dreamily):* Old Shatterhand . . .

HITLER: He used to cry, "I am great! I am marvelous!" after each victory.

MAY *(Grudgingly):* But you should have gotten the swastika right.

HITLER: Never mind about the swastika. In Germany we need room to live in . . . You were my geographer . . . You showed me how to create a new West, new frontiers of our own with their raw, heroic virtues . . .

MAY: The West was open, free . . . That's what I tried to show in my books, the space, the freedom . . .

HITLER: Freedom, yes, for the strong . . . Freedom is always for the strong.

MAY *(Sharply):* Old Shatterhand knew what to do . . .

HITLER *(Dreaming):* Old Shatterhand . . . He isn't afraid to act. He kills the thieving Indians. He shows how the strongest race conquers.

MAY: The strongest race, yes. But don't forget my great Apache leader, Winnetou.

HITLER (*Laughing*): How can I forget Winnetou? I love him . . . Why not? Everyone in Germany had his favorite Jew, just like your West where everyone had his favorite Indian. But the Indians had to die like the Jews . . .

MAY (*Indignantly*): Winnetou will never die!

HITLER: Old Shatterhand is destiny. He has to triumph. (*Smiling*) You know I'm Old Shatterhand . . .

MAY (*Haughtily*): Never. You can't even turn the swastika the right way.

HITLER (*Laughing, patting* MAY's *shoulder*): Forget the swastika. You still don't understand. You were dead when I defeated senile old Hindenburg, when I became Chancellor . . .

MAY (*Drawing away*): You're not Old Shatterhand . . .

HITLER (*Smiling*): I became Old Shatterhand . . . Don't you see? Hindenburg was like a senile western sheriff who permits the outlaw Indians to flourish . . .

MAY (*Indignantly*): No, Hindenburg was Germany's greatest war hero. Millions of Germans donated one mark to the Red Cross. They won the right to pound a nail into the giant, wooden statue of Hindenburg that stood in Berlin outside of the Reichstag building. I'll show you . . .

MAY *transforms himself into the tall figure of* HINDENBURG *hunched in aged, somber senility. An* ACTOR *steps forward to play* HINDENBURG's SON, *a colonel in army uniform who wipes his father's forehead, listens to his mutterings, dusts the hunting trophies and the picture of the Virgin Mary above* HINDENBURG.

HITLER (*Gleefully*): Hindenburg was only our hitching post. As we Nazis rode through the city we hitched our horses to him.

MAY (*Transforming himself as* HINDENBURG): He was our great Field Marshall. Six feet five inches tall, more than two hundred pounds. How his blue eyes glittered above his flowing mustache that cut the air like a sabre . . .

HITLER: He lived on too long. When I rode in to meet him he lived in a tomb of war relics, battle flags, hunting trophies, and an enormous collection of pictures of the Virgin Mary. His son, a Colonel, had to wipe his nose. When the army begged Hindenburg to run for President he was already a muttering seventy-seven years old . . .

HINDENBURG/MAY (*Muttering to his son*): I want my peace . . . I want my peace . . . (MAY *emphasizes*) *Peace*, that's what he wanted . . .

HITLER (*Mimicking* HINDENBURG): *I want my peace* . . . How can such an idiot keep order in the wilderness that Germany has become? We

need Old Shatterhand to keep order. With the help of our bully-
boys I made Göring Chairman of the Parliament, the Reichstag . . .
(Calling) Hermann, come here!

GÖRING *(Entering, cautiously)*: You forgive me, Führer?

HITLER *(With a gracious gesture)*: For the moment. Climb into your seat,
Hermann. Show how it went in our frontier days . . .

Gleefully, GÖRING *climbs into the Chairman's seat and bangs his gavel.*
HINDENBURG/MAY *stares, dazed, as if caught in a nightmare.*

GÖRING: Order! Order in the Reichstag! Order!

HINDENBURG/MAY *totters down on his* SON*'s arm and prepares painfully to read his acceptance speech.*

HITLER *(With a malicious smile)*: When Hindenburg was elected President
he had to read his acceptance speech from a paper on which the
letters were printed so large you could read them from the visitor's
gallery through a pair of opera glasses.

Satirically HITLER *looks through a pair of opera glasses at the scene.*
HINDENBURG/MAY *reads his acceptance speech painfully and laboriously
from an enormous sheet of paper that his* SON *hands him.*

HINDENBURG/MAY *(We hear only a mumble and a few distinct words)*: . . . the
German Republic . . . *Republic* . . . maintain constitutional integrity . . . *Vigilance* . . . Vigilance of the *law* . . .

HITLER *(Sneering)*: Vigilance of the law . . . You never knew what that
meant. Old Shatterhand was waiting with his troopers ready. Then
we were betrayed. Our own S.A. men turned into renegade Indians . . .

RÖHM *stalks on stage as if fighting against his confinement in a historical
dream.* HE *is wearing an Indian headdress and a painted face over his
S.A. uniform.*

HINDENBURG/MAY: Who is that?

HITLER: One of your traitorous redskins, Ernst Röhm. Old Shatterhand
must punish him . . .

RÖHM *(Doggedly)*: Some mistake has occurred. I, Ernst Röhm, was never
an Indian . . . I don't accept my fate . . . From my childhood I had
only one thought, one wish—to be a soldier . . .

GÖRING *(Banging on his gavel)*: Out of order! The Führer banishes you.
You're an outlaw . . .

HITLER *(Screaming)*: Röhm, you redskin traitor . . .

RÖHM *(Doggedly)*: There has been some mistake . . . *(Feeling the paint on his face)* My face . . .

HITLER *(Accusing RÖHM)*: With your insane militaristic dream you tried to take over the army and state . . .

RÖHM *(Addressing HINDENBURG/MAY)*: As leader of our Nazi street army, the S.A., I demand, President Hindenburg, that our defense organization be represented in the Reichstag.

GÖRING *(Banging his gavel)*: Impossible. We don't accept Jewish Indians in the Reichstag.

HINDENBURG/MAY *(To his SON)*: We must save the country from these gunmen.

RÖHM *(Blindly, doggedly)*: The National Socialist movement is a fighting movement of the people, not the aristocrats . . .

GÖRING *(Banging his gavel and roaring)*: Silence! We'll fix you if you don't shut up . . .

HITLER *(Screaming)*: Indian renegade . . . Treason . . . You traitor . . .

HINDENBURG/MAY *(Muttering to his SON)*: We must stop these outlaws . . . Restore frontier justice . . . That Austrian corporal, Hitler . . . He thinks he's Old Shatterhand . . . He's only a corporal, a lowly corporal . . . We must have the King back . . . The Kaiser . . .

HINDENBURG'S SON *(Wiping his father's face)*: Yes, Father. Don't agitate yourself. The army will take care of these redskins.

HITLER *(Shrieking)*: Treason . . . Get rid of Röhm . . . He betrayed us to the redskins . . .

RÖHM: It's not true . . . Why can't I get rid of this paint? . . . If Adolf wants to kill me he'll have to do it himself . . . We call each other by our first names . . . I'm Ernst . . . He's Adolf . . .

HITLER: No one calls me Adolf anymore. I'm the Führer. I'm Old Shatterhand.

GÖRING *(Banging his gavel gleefully)*: My orders! I give our SS troops full legal powers to curb the S.A.

HITLER: Shut up. In Bavaria I assumed personal charge of suppressing the revolt . . .

As Old Shatterhand HE accepts a western Stetson hat from the ARCHITECT.

A disgusting scene of savage vice, redskin bestiality . . .

With the ARCHITECT and several other ACTORS, HE pretends to ride a posse of horses against the S.A.

From the Munich airport we sped to the hotel on the Tegernsee where Röhm and his S.A. savages were sleeping after their debauchery . . .

CATHEDRAL OF ICE

THEY *rein in the horses as* THEY *dismount in front of the hotel.*

SS GUARD *(After storming into the hotel* HE *stops short, peering)*: Führer, look! It's Edmund Heines, the S.A. Obergruppenführer of Silesia. He's in bed with a boy.

HITLER: Shoot him! *(Turning)* Where's that traitor, Röhm?

SS GUARD *brings* RÖHM *forward.*

HITLER: Strip him . . .

The SS GUARD *strips* RÖHM *to the waist.*

RÖHM *(Protesting)*: Adolf, I fought with you in the streets. We're old comrades . . .

HITLER *(Ranting at him)*: I'm your Führer. After all these years how can you betray me? . . . All you want is military power. You think you can become chief of staff . . .

RÖHM *(Still in his stubborn trance of time)*: From my childhood I've had only one thought—to be a soldier . . .

HITLER: Germany is more than an army . . . Germany is racial destiny . . .

RÖHM: The S.A. remains Germany's destiny

HITLER *(Enraged)*: How many times do you and your degenerate redskins have to learn the price of treachery? *(To the* SS GUARD*)* Give him a pistol.

The SS GUARD *puts a pistol beside* RÖHM.

RÖHM *(Looking slowly at the pistol)*: What's this?

As the SS GUARD *turns away* RÖHM *tosses him the gun.*

If you want to kill me do it yourself, *Adolf* . . .

HITLER *(Furiously)*: Shoot the redskin swine.

HINDENBURG/MAY *(Suddenly jolted into speaking)*: No, shoot him yourself, Old Shatterhand.

HITLER *(Ignoring* HINDENBURG/MAY*)*: Kill him.

As RÖHM *stands at military attention the* SS GUARD *shoots him down.*

GÖRING *(Pounding his gavel with glee)*: All over Berlin we killed the corrupt redskins.

HITLER *(Crying out eerily and waving his Stetson)*: I am great . . . I am marvelous . . .

James Schevill

HINDENBURG/MAY *(Recoiling)*: Old Shatterhand's cry . . . *(Protesting)* No, you're not Old Shatterhand . . .

HITLER *(Crying again, mockingly)*: I am great . . . I am marvelous . . .

HINDENBURG/MAY *(Muttering and shaking)*: That Austrian corporal . . . Shooting everybody like a Wild West show . . .

HITLER *(Shouting)*: You'll never forgive me, Hindenburg, because I was only a corporal. You insulted Old Shatterhand. At our first meeting you received me standing up. You wouldn't let Old Shatterhand sit down. You, the president of a collapsing redskin-infested government, tried to humiliate me by forcing me to stand . . .

HINDENBURG/MAY *rises icily to portray the meeting.*

HINDENBURG/MAY: Herr Hitler, because of the dangerous situation I cannot transfer the power of government to your new, untried party. Your National Socialist party does not even command a majority. It is intolerant of other groups, noisy, undisciplined . . . *(Getting more. and more agitated)* Your stormtroopers have clashed with the police . . . You have committed excessive violence against the Jews . . . All of these incidents have convinced me that certain unruly elements in your party are beyond your control.

HITLER *(Aside to GÖRING)*: Will the old fool never stop talking?

HINDENBURG/MAY *(With increasing agitation)*: You must give up your one-sided idea of complete power . . . Cooperate with the parties of the right and center . . . Only then can you eliminate the widespread fear that a National Socialist government will misuse its power. However, if you can secure a workable majority in the Reichstag for a *positive* program—mind you I say a *definite, positive* program . . .

HITLER: Old Shatterhand has such a positive program in mind . . .

HINDENBURG/MAY *(Persisting)*: If you can present this workable majority and the positive program, I will give you the chancellorship.

HITLER *(Immediately)*: I accept.

HINDENBURG/MAY *(Quavering on)*: Otherwise I offer you the vice chancellorship under Von Papen. Von Papen will rule as president by emergency decree . . .

HITLER *(In a furious outburst)*: Von Papen! That unknown rabbit! Only I am great . . . Shoot them all!

Sounds of street fighting, shouts of "Down with the Republic," "Hitler for Chancellor," "Old Shatterhand to the Rescue," etc.

I am great . . . I am marvelous . . .

CATHEDRAL OF ICE

GÖRING (*Banging his gavel triumphantly as shots and machine gun bursts are heard*): Burn the Reichstag! Old Shatterhand knows how to burn redskin villages . . . Burn the Reichstag . . . Blame the fire on the redskins . . . Burn the Reichstag.

A glow of fire is seen.

HITLER (*Stepping up to* HINDENBURG/MAY *with a decree*): In view of the savage disorders created by the burning of the Reichstag, you must sign this emergency decree. (HE *presents the decree*)

HINDENBURG/MAY (*Glaring at him*): Emergency decree?

HITLER: To protect the people and the state against communistic violence. Sign this defensive measure. (HE *holds the decree close to* HINDENBURG/MAY*'s weak eyes*)

HINDENBURG/MAY (*Reading with mumbling comprehension*): Restrictions on . . . personal . . . lib—er—ty . . .

CAST (*Erupts into an Indian ragtime choral reaction, "The Chorale of Censorship," singing to* HITLER): I am great . . . I am marvelous . . .
Re—strict—shuns . . . on per—son—al . . . lib—er—ty . . .

HINDENBURG/MAY (*Speaking, mumbling*): Restrictions . . . on the rights of assembly . . . and association . . .

CAST (*Singing*): I am great . . . I am marvelous . . .
Re—strict—shuns . . . on the rights . . . of as—sem—bly . . .
and of . . . as—so—ci—a—*shun* . . .

HINDENBURG/MAY (*Mumbling*): Violations . . . of the privacy . . . of postal, telegraphic . . . and telephonic communications . . . CAST (*Singing*): I am great . . . I am marvelous . . .
Vio—la—*shuns* . . . of the privacy . . .
of pos—tal . . . tele—graph—sick . . .
tele—phoney. . . . commun—ic—a—*shuns* . . .

HINDENBURG/MAY (*Mumbling*): Warrants for house searches . . . Confiscations of property . . . Emergency situation . . .

CAST (*Singing*): I am great . . . I am marvelous . . .
War—rents . . . for house sear—ches . . .
Con—fis—ca—shuns . . . of pro—per—tyy . . .
E—mer—gen—cyyy . . . E—mer—gen—cyyy . . .

HITLER (*Joining in exultantly, singing eerily*):
Sign here without fear . . .
E—mer—gen—cyy . . . E—mer—gen—cyyy . . .
I am marvelous to see
In an e—mer—gen—cyy . . .

CAST *(Singing)*: I am great . . . I am marvelous . . .

HINDENBURG/MAY *(Crying out at end of final chorus)*: No, you're not Old Shatterhand!

HITLER *(With new, brisk authority)*: Farewell, Hindenburg. I sentence you to live forever in the pantheon of German history. Play the role of noble Winnetou, the honorable Apache warrior who sacrifices himself for his lost people.

Mockingly GÖRING *puts an Indian headdress on* HINDENBURG/MAY.

HINDENBURG/MAY *(Crying out)*: No, Winnetou is *my* glorious warrior!

Members of the CAST *begin to sing a jagged version of the "Horst Wessel" song.*

HITLER: Bury Hindenburg! Let the dying old Field Marshall serve as a warrior-symbol of our national power. Die with honor, noble Winnetou!

HINDENBURG/MAY *(Another agonized protest)*: No, Winnetou lives forever!

HITLER *(Riding over the protest)*: Today and forever here in the Cathedral of Ice a magnificent ceremony of solemn dedication is unveiled to the German people and to the world.

An SS GUARD *has been helping* HITLER *to put on a long, formal, cutaway coat.*

In this cathedral lie buried the sacred bones of Frederick the Great . . . Here the Hohenzollern kings are worshipped. Here I convene the Reichstag to inaugurate my new Empire . . .

As if hypnotized in time by the transformation of the old church at Potsdam into the Cathedral of Ice, HINDENBURG/MAY *begins to totter down the aisle in his Indian headdress. The* CAST *cheers him on mockingly.*

HITLER: Now President Hindenburg pauses before the empty seat of honor reserved in the imperial gallery in memory of Kaiser Wilhelm the Second.

The empty seat of honor lights up in an intense white glare. In a daze HINDENBURG/MAY *salutes the ghost of Kaiser Wilhelm.*

Heil Winnetou! Heil Kaiser Wilhelm!

CAST: Heil Hitler! . . . Heil Hitler! . . . Heil Hitler!

Mockingly HITLER *raises his hand to acknowledge the applause as* HE *becomes chancellor again in memory. Slowly several* SS MEN *emerge to central positions as* HITLER *begins to speak in acceptance of the chancellorship. The rhythm of the play changes abruptly from the mockery of the ghost-like historical ceremony at Potsdam to the sense of cold, impersonal, secret police power.*

HITLER *(Bowing to* HINDENBURG/MAY*)*: Thanks to you, Herr Generalfeldmarschall, we celebrate in this historic place the union between our ancient Prussian greatness and our new international strength. We pay you homage, Winnetou. Here in this immortal cathedral of power Providence reveals itself. A divine spirit protects the new forces of our great destiny.

With a "show of deep humility," as Shirer describes it, HITLER *bows low to* HINDENBURG/MAY *and grips the aged President's hand firmly. Slowly* HITLER*'s handshake turns into a macabre death-grip. The* SS TROOPERS *move together singing the "Horst Wessel" song: "Raise high the flags! Stand rank on rank together. Storm troopers march with steady, quiet tread, etc."*

HINDENBURG/MAY *(Crying out)*: Wait . . . *Please* . . . Bury Winnetou with honor . . .

HITLER *releases his grip on the dead* HINDENBURG/MAY, *and signals to the* SS TROOPERS, *who stop singing abruptly and stand frozen in time.*

HITLER: Old Shatterhand has conquered. *(Suddenly* HE *lets out his uncontrollable whoop of triumph, throwing away his Stetson hat)* I am great! . . . I am marvelous! *(Then with proper historical humility again)* Bury him with honor. Bury Winnetou's ghost.

Hand over his heart, HE *stands at attention as banners of black crepe fall down and* HIMMLER *moves his* SS TROOPERS *around coldly, gesturing with his riding crop.*

KARL MAY *(Jolted out of his* HINDENBURG *death-trance, accusing* HITLER*)*: No, Winnetou is not dead. You're *not* Old Shatterhand. My west is not like this. My west is open, adventurous, free . . .

HITLER *(Ignoring him, extending his arm)*: Heil Hitler! We're in power forever. Sing!

The "Horst Wessel" song starts again.

Vanish in history, Winnetou. Heil Old Shatterhand!

CAST *(Echoing)*: Heil Old Shatterhand! . . . Heil Hitler!

HINDENBURG/MAY *(As HE collapses, shouting desperately)*: You're not Old Shatterhand . . . You're not my hero . . . Old Shatterhand is a legend, an immortal myth!

As HITLER stands at attention, his arm extended, ignoring HINDENBURG/MAY's dying protests, HIMMLER supervises the SS MEN. THEY lift up HINDENBURG/MAY's body as if carrying it in a funeral procession. Singing the "Horst Wessel" song THEY carry out HINDENBURG/MAY's body.

Scene 4
Wagner And Hitler At Bayreuth

Abruptly the "Horst Wessel" song dissolves into a rapt chorus singing the "Awake" chorus from WAGNER's Die Meistersinger. *Cheers as HITLER and the ARCHITECT enter the Dictator's box at the Bayreuth Festspielhaus. HITLER waves and graciously acknowledges the applause. HE points out the details of the auditorium to the ARCHITECT as if to show his affinity with Bayreuth.*

ARCHITECT *(Extremely impressed)*: Marvelous, Führer. What a privilege to visit Bayreuth with you again, to hear *Tristan and Isolde*.

HITLER *(With anticipation)*: Wait till you see who's conducting.

ARCHITECT: Have you summoned back Furtwängler?

HITLER: That Jew-lover? An impossible snob . . .

ARCHITECT *(His attention riveted suddenly on the conductor who enters)*: Look! . . . It can't be . . .

HITLER *(With childish delight)*: Of course it is.

ARCHITECT *(Entranced by the romance of it all)*: Führer, I don't believe it . . . It's *Wagner.*

HITLER: If King Ludwig could have his private performance of Wagner why can't I?

ARCHITECT *(Hastily)*: Who can deny you?

WAGNER *(Rapping with his baton for attention)*: Please pay attention, Führer. The key to an understanding of destiny is *Liebestod*.

HITLER: The "Love-Death" . . . I'm ready, Herr Wagner.

WAGNER: Fame, honor . . . Nothing of that kind can refresh me. My only need is love.

HITLER *(Nostalgically)*: We all need to make people love us.

WAGNER *(Sharply)*: You fail to understand that true love requires sacrifice—*Liebestod*.

HITLER: I understand, Maestro, love as death. *(To the* ARCHITECT*)* Wagner likes to lecture me.

WAGNER *(Waving his baton)*: Tristan and Isolde, the greatest love ever portrayed . . .

HE *begins to conduct the "Love-Death" sequence from* Tristan and Isolde. TWO ACTORS *appear miming the roles as the music is heard on tape.*

HITLER *(Sinking moodily into the music)*: Yours is the greatest German music ever written, Herr Wagner.

As WAGNER *conducts and speaks, the music is heard softly in the background.*

WAGNER: Do you hear the bliss of quitting life? Can you feel the glory of dying to find redemption? Entering that world of wonder that is forbidden if we try to enter by force. Dare we call it *Death?* Or is it the wonderful world of night? The night when an ivy and a vine spring up in locked embrace over Tristan and Isolde's marriage-grave . . .

HITLER *(Brooding)*: Marriage-grave . . . The wonderful world of night . . .

WAGNER *(Conducting with an exuberant burst)*: Night is the time for love. The time when love frees us from nightmares and becomes our salvation. *(Conducting sensuously)* Listen to the ecstasy of Tristan embracing Isolde. For the first time I portray the climax of physical love in music . . .

HITLER: Superb. How fascinating. *(To the* ARCHITECT*)* The singers are fully clothed too. That permits the imagination to work.

WAGNER *(Conducting vigorously)*: Love's dreams endure beyond mere sexual acts . . . Love triumphs over every obstacle . . .

ISOLDE *(Stopping the music abruptly,* SHE *turns, speaks to* WAGNER*)*: Maestro! Maestro! I can't hear myself. Can you please have the orchestra play a little softer?

WAGNER *(Bristling)*: Impossible. Here the orchestra carries the passion. You must sing louder, clearer . . . Try just speaking the words for Herr Hitler . . .

WAGNER *resumes conducting as the music starts again.*

ISOLDE *(Reciting passionately)*:
". . . To drown in the infinity
Of the World Spirit
To sink into

The Void of Thought
Is the highest bliss!"

WAGNER *(Transformed as* ISOLDE *dies over* TRISTAN's *body)*: The Void of Thought . . . There's poetry for you. They die and live forever. Resurrection—the immortality of love . . .

HITLER *(Transfigured, meditating)*: If only the whole world could die this way. *(To* WAGNER*)* Maestro, what a privilege it would be to die your heroic "Love-Death."

WAGNER *(Haughtily)*: The world can be transformed only by art.

HITLER: Or by politics.

WAGNER: No, the politician rules briefly. The great artist endures until the end of time.

HITLER *(To the* ARCHITECT*)*: You see what I mean by ego? This Bayreuth theatre of Wagner's is nothing compared to what we'll build.

WAGNER *(Suspiciously)*: Did you criticize my theatre?

HITLER *(Hastily)*: No, Maestro, Please continue. *(Petulantly to the* ARCHITECT*)* Wagner has no appreciation of my ability as an architect.

WAGNER *(Turning, calling to* TRISTAN *and* ISOLDE *who are still lying immortally dead on stage)*: Rise now. We'll return to the "Love-Death."

TRISTAN *(Staggering up in dazed humility)*: Maestro, every time I sing your immortal work I find it more difficult to return to this mundane world.

WAGNER *(Snapping)*: Of course. You're finally learning the work.

HITLER *(To the* ARCHITECT, *echoing* WAGNER's *criticism of the tenor)*: Mundane world. What does that tenor know of the world?

TRISTAN *(Protesting to* WAGNER*)*: Maestro, it's a long, difficult part.

WAGNER: Do you think love and death are short, simple?

TRISTAN *(Abjectly)*: No, Maestro, I didn't mean . . .

WAGNER *(Furiously)*: You still don't understand the depth of character in Tristan. Only the future will understand Tristan.

HITLER *(Leaning forward intently)*: That's right, Maestro. I will show the world the meaning of Tristan.

WAGNER *(Rapping with his baton for attention)*: Again, the *Liebestod* . . . *(Warning* TRISTAN*)* Remember, Tristan, you must really wish to die for love.

HITLER *(To the* ARCHITECT*)*: Now we'll hear something great.

The music from the famous Act II, Scene 2 sequence is heard on tape. WAGNER *conducts triumphantly with increasing passion. As the voices soar out* HITLER *translates rapturously, as if transformed by the meaning of the words.*

"Eternal night,
Sweetest night . . .

CATHEDRAL OF ICE

Loftiest night of Love!
Those whom you seize,
Those whom you trance,
How can they ever wish
To wake from your sleep?
Fear is now banished . . .
Gracious Death,
We yearn for your mercy,
Your Love-In-Death . . ."

Transported, poking the ARCHITECT, HITLER *shouts at* WAGNER.

Give them no mercy, Death!
WAGNER *(Ecstatically as* HE *conducts)*: Death, you must die! Tristan and
Isolde's love is too strong for you . . .

TRISTAN *and* ISOLDE *continue their duet.*

HITLER: "Within your arms
We find your peace, Death . . .
Your ancient, holy warmth
Freed from Life's awakening . . ."

The peace of Death . . .
WAGNER *(Conducting radiantly)*: Redemption! Freedom from death.
My "Love-Death!"

The CAST *picks this up mockingly around the theatre in a sound poem
based on the syllables "Love-Death." This sound poem and the music,
with* WAGNER *conducting fervently, continue under* HITLER'*s final speech
to the end of the scene.*

CAST: (SOUND POEM ON "LOVE-DEATH"):
Looooh . . .
Loooov—aaalll . . .
Looooov—*debt* . . .
Loooov—debt . . .
Loooov—deaaarth . . .
Loooov—deaaaaarth . . .
Loooov—Eaaaarth . . .
Loooooov—Breaaaaath . . .
Looooooov—Breaaaaaaath . . .
Loooooov—Deaaaaaaaath . . .

Love-Death . . .
Love-*Death* . . .
Love-Death! . . .

HITLER (*Entranced, magnetized,* HE *speaks so forcefully that the* ARCHITECT *shrinks back in fear*): Our "Love-Death!" Eternally our "Love-Death" in the Cathedral of Ice. Maestro, you have found the cure for the world's problems. However weak a man may be, when he acts as Providence directs he becomes immeasurably strong. Anyone who interferes with his divine mission becomes an enemy of the people. Maestro, I give you my sacred word. As Führer I will turn the world into the greatest "Love-Death" it has ever seen!

Scene 5
Sentimental Interlude

Creating an immediate, strange, sentimental contrast to Tristan and Isolde, *a banal 1930s musical comedy "Love-Death" song is heard, "The Ballad of German Love." It is sung by two nervous, popular, young film stars whom* EVA BRAUN *and* HITLER *have invited to their sanctuary. The scene is another reflection of* HITLER's *desire to recreate his dream memories of Berchtesgaden.* HITLER *is going over some of his favorite architectural projects with the* ARCHITECT. GÖRING *and* GÖBBELS, *forced to be present for another long evening, already show their impatience to escape. During this scene, until the end of Scene 6,* HITLER *does not wear the Jewish coat.*

The TWO YOUNG SINGERS *are singing "The Ballad of German Love."*

MALE SINGER: Love is a tree of many leaves
FEMALE SINGER: Love is the sentiment that always grieves . . .
TOGETHER: Love is a spiderweb of doubt,
    Love is a mystery within, without!
MALE SINGER: Who will find love must look within . . .
FEMALE SINGER: Our German love is immortal sin . . .
TOGETHER: Who will find love must look without
    For love must always smile, never doubt.

    Love is a tree of many leaves,
    Love is the sentiment that always grieves.
    Our German love will conquer the sun
    When we two become eternally one!

EVA (*Entranced*): Aren't they marvelous singers, Adolf? Let's watch their new film. I can hardly wait . . .
HITLER (*Waving her off*): In a moment, Eva. I'm discussing a proper memorial with my architect.

EVA *(Dejected)*: Yes, Adolf.

GÖRING *(Fidgeting uneasily, determined to steal away)*: If you don't mind, Führer, please excuse me. I have an important appointment. *(HE gets up to leave)*

HITLER *(Aside, maliciously)*: He's off to steal another picture or lounge around in one of his fancy costumes.

GÖRING *(Aside)*: I can't stand another boring evening. *(To HITLER)* Good night, Führer. I hope you enjoy your film. *(HE exits)*

GÖBBELS *(Hesitantly)*: Führer, I too must leave. I'm sure you'll enjoy their new musical film, *Love in the Alps.*

HITLER *(Suspiciously)*: Is it about skiing? I hate skiing.

GÖBBELS: There's hardly any skiing. It's based on a Lehar operetta.

HITLER: Good, I love operettas.

GÖBBELS: Please excuse me, Führer. *(HE goes)*

HITLER *(Maliciously)*: Göbbels is off to climb into bed with another of his film girls. If I were his wife . . . *(Calling)* Bormann!

BORMANN *(Appearing)*: Yes, Führer.

HITLER: Let's have the film.

BORMANN *(Aside to the fidgeting SINGERS)*: Don't be so nervous. *(HE pinches the WOMAN SINGER)*

HITLER *(Aside to the ARCHITECT)*: Who wouldn't be nervous with Bormann around? He puts his nose into everything . . . This place is beginning to look like the cheap interior decorations on an ocean liner.

ARCHITECT *(Unrolling plans)*: I think you'll find these plans exciting.

HITLER *(To the SINGERS)*: I've heard a great deal about your popularity with young people.

MALE SINGER *(Stiff with fear HE salutes)*: Führer, it is a privilege to be here.

EVA *(Excitedly)*: Oh, Adolf, I heard them in Munich in *Fledermaus.* They were so good . . . *(To the SINGERS)* Your new song is all the rage.

HITLER *(To the ARCHITECT)*: Yes, their song was quite good, don't you think?

ARCHITECT *(A little grimly)*: Excellent.

HITLER *(To EVA and the SINGERS)*: We'll be with you in a moment.

MALE SINGER: Certainly Führer.

FEMALE SINGER: We are overjoyed to be here.

As the SINGERS converse nervously with EVA, HITLER talks to the ARCHITECT about the plans.

ARCHITECT *(Pointing at the plans)*: There's one difficulty here. To achieve the right space, we must move the Nürnberg Zoo.

HITLER: Why not? We'll give them a new, more beautiful zoo. *(Pointing)* This is the marching area for our troops?

ARCHITECT: Yes.

HITLER: Is that large enough?

ARCHITECT: Larger than the palace areas of Kings Darius and Xerxes at the height of their power in fifth century Persepolis . . .

HITLER *(Pointing)*: What about the stands here?

ARCHITECT: Seats for 160,000 spectators. And this central viewing platform for important guests is crowned by a large sculpture of a woman.

HITLER: Is it larger than the Statue of Liberty?

ARCHITECT: Ours will be forty-six feet higher.

HITLER: Excellent. Everything must be simple, in good taste.

ARCHITECT: The problem of the stadium is difficult.

HITLER: I want the stadium to hold 400,000 people.

ARCHITECT *(Hastily)*: As you can see it's designed to be larger than the Circus Maximus in Rome which held almost 200,000 people. Our stadium will have a volume three times that of the Pyramid of Cheops . . .

HITLER: Good. You wonder why I want to build the biggest monuments in history?

ARCHITECT: I understand.

HITLER: Each German must have his self-respect restored. To every German I want to say, "We are not inferior." We are equal to and superior to every other nation.

ARCHITECT: It is a great cause. However, my staff has estimated the costs and . . .

HITLER *(Gesturing impatiently)*: Bormann will take care of the costs. That's the only reason I keep him around—to raise money.

ARCHITECT *(Pointing to some figures)*: The cost may be as much as a billion marks.

HITLER *(Waving this aside)*: That's less than two battleships of the *Bismarck* class. These monuments will stand forever. When the Finance Minister asks their cost don't answer him. Let him stew . . . Come, let's watch the film. I'm very pleased with your plans.

HE *crosses to congratulate the* SINGERS *who relax visibly.* HITLER *converses with them, asking "Would you like a cup of tea or a glass of wine?" etc.*

EVA *(Talking to the* ARCHITECT*)*: Bormann is after that secretary again. That man is disgusting. I don't see how his wife stands him.

ARCHITECT *(Shrugging)*: Perhaps because they have six children.

EVA: He's sickening. Whenever the Führer is near Bormann moons over his wife and children as if they were his only treasure. He calls her sweetheart mine, dearest heart, even beloved mummy-girl.

ARCHITECT: Beloved mummy-girl?

EVA *(Indignantly)*: Can you believe it? Then he runs off to chase another secretary.

CATHEDRAL OF ICE

ARCHITECT (*As* HITLER *returns*): Shh . . .
HITLER: We're ready. Start the film, please.

> HITLER *and* EVA *sit in adjacent chairs. Deliberately the* ARCHITECT *sits as far behind them as possible, since* HE *too is bored with these occasions but can't escape. The film is shown flickering offstage, invisible to the audience.* HITLER *and* EVA *begin to gossip.*

EVA: You'll like this actress. She's very entertaining.
HITLER: She has excellent posture.
EVA: They sing so well together.
HITLER: She has attractive legs too.
EVA (*Pouting*): Don't you like my legs?
HITLER: You're wearing high heels again. You know I don't like high heels.
EVA (*Defiantly*): They're quite flat.
HITLER (*Pointing to her shoes*): Look at them. It's bad for your health to wear such high heels.
EVA (*Gesturing at the film*): You don't mind that actress wearing high heels.
HITLER (*Protesting*): It's only a musical comedy. You must look after yourself.
EVA (*Pouting, concentrating on the film*): She's really excellent in *her high heels.* She reminds me a little of Jenny Jugo.
HITLER: Not at all. She's more like Henny Porten. Her smile.
EVA: She seems so happy.
HITLER: That's what a film should be.
EVA: Why can't we have more entertaining films like this?
HITLER: Göbbels doesn't value entertainment enough. That's what comes from being an intellectual. We must have films that appeal to the masses. Any true leader knows the masses are essentially feminine.
EVA: Feminine?
HITLER (*Smiling*): You don't convince audiences. You conquer them.
EVA: Even in a musical?
HITLER: In any kind of performance.
EVA (*Coquettishly*): What if I tried to conquer you?
HITLER: Women captivate, they don't conquer.
EVA (*Smiling*): Some day I'll test your theory. (*Pointing at his tie*) You know, Adolf, you're wearing your old tie again.
HITLER: I can't walk down the street blazing like a furnace.
EVA: Your ties are too drab. Every time I give you a bright new tie you go back to the old ones.
HITLER: You know how I feel about loud colors.
EVA (*Teasingly*): I'm going to test you. (SHE *rises*) I'll be right back.
HITLER: Where are you going?

EVA: You'll see. (SHE *laughs and rushes out*)

HITLER (*Calling after her*): What are you up to now, Eva? (*Turning to the* ARCHITECT) Women—you never know what she'll do next.

ARCHITECT (*Rousing himself hastily;* HE's *been falling asleep like other members of* HITLER's *entourage*): She's charming, Führer.

HITLER: It's good to relax. All day long I hear nothing but heavy, noisy, masculine voices.

ARCHITECT (*A little taken aback*): You're lucky to have Fräulein Braun.

HITLER: An attractive young thing—and she's loyal. Of course I had her investigated. Bormann took care of that. I couldn't have a mistress tainted with Jewish blood.

ARCHITECT: She's so fine looking.

HITLER: You can never tell where it's hiding. Did you know her sister worked for a Jewish doctor?

ARCHITECT: Really?

HITLER: I put a stop to that. (*Complaining*) The problem always is Eva wants to marry me. What would I do with a wife?

ARCHITECT: It would be a burden, Führer.

HITLER: Impossible for a man in my position. Heads of state should never marry. For you it's different . . . You can have a private life.

ARCHITECT (*Through the vision of his un-private life*): Yes, Führer.

HITLER: You have your privacy, your family security, your wife and children.

ARCHITECT (*Unable to resist*): When I'm able to see them, Führer.

HITLER: Why don't you invite your wife here? Come and live with me. I'll build you a house. (*Then, reflecting*) You know the real reason why I can never marry?

ARCHITECT: Why, Führer?

HITLER: Think of the danger if I had children.

ARCHITECT: I don't understand.

HITLER: Great men always have sick children. Napoleon's son . . . Goethe's son who was a cretin. How could I ever take such a risk?

ARCHITECT: I'm sure Fräulein Braun would never . . . She's so healthy.

HITLER (*Moodily*): I could never take the risk.

Suddenly the film stops. EVA *has had it stopped.* SHE *enters in blackface as Al Jolson singing "Sonny Boy."* HITLER *is stunned. The* ARCHITECT *is frightened, afraid that* EVA's *masquerade will bring on one of* HITLER's *tantrums. The* OTHERS *are tense, waiting to see what will happen.*

EVA (*After finishing her song and dance act* SHE *laughs and approaches* HITLER): How do you like it, Adolf? I've been practicing for you.

HITLER (*Slowly changing his mood*): It's *you*, Eva.

EVA *does a final, gay turn around him.*

HITLER *(Dissolves into laughter and everyone relaxes)*: Eva, Eva, you funny girl . . . You are so funny . . .

EVA: I knew you'd like it.

HITLER *(Recovering himself)*: You are naughty. This American, Al Jolson, is a Jewish entertainer.

EVA *(Laughing and patting him)*: It's only a game. No one will ever tell.

HITLER *(Looking around at the subdued audience)*: That is true. *(Then laughing again as* HE *pats* EVA*)* You are a little performer, Eva. Perhaps I should let you go on stage instead of keeping you to myself.

EVA: I'm quite happy, Adolf, as long as you let me perform for you. *(Then pouting)* But you keep me away so much. Can't we at least live together all the time?

HITLER: We'll see. If I can arrange it without any gossip.

EVA *(With delight)*: Oh, you promised. You promised.

HITLER: Come, let's go upstairs. If you don't take off that blackface you'll be stuck with it.

EVA *(Laughing)*: That's an old witch's tale.

HITLER: Women are witches.

As THEY *approach the staircase the ghostly figure of* GELI RAUBAL, HITLER'*s niece with whom* HE *lived before* SHE *committed suicide, appears on the staircase.*

HITLER: I'm getting chilly. That damnable wind . . . *(*HE *puts his hand up against the wind)*

EVA: Is something wrong? There's no south wind here.

HITLER *(Agitated)*: It's blowing right through that window. Can't you feel how depressed it makes me? *(Staring at* GELI*)* She hated that wind even more than I.

EVA *(Puzzled)*: She?

HITLER *(Staring)*: Don't you see her there? Geli . . . My niece, my love, Geli Raubal . . .

EVA: Don't keep tormenting yourself. Geli is dead. She killed herself.

GELI *(Mockingly to* HITLER*)*: I died for you. I shot myself with *your* pistol.

HITLER *(With immediate self-pity)*: Yes, you died for me. I'll never forgive myself.

EVA *(Jealously)*: You must forget her . . . She's dead.

HITLER: Why did she do it? *(To* GELI*)* I would have given you anything.

EVA: It wasn't your fault.

GELI: I want to go to Vienna to live my own life. I want to sing.

HITLER *(Angrily)*: You want to make a whore of yourself. I couldn't let you leave me for that city of Jewish whores.

GELI: You keep me hidden away. You keep me a prisoner.

HITLER *(Hysterically)*: I give you everything you want.

GELI: You won't marry me. You would never marry me.

HITLER: How can I? You're my niece . . . It would ruin me politically.

GELI: All you care about is politics.

HITLER *(Turning on* EVA *suddenly)*: Get her away. She doesn't belong here. Why do you women keep threatening me with suicide?

EVA: That's not fair.

HITLER *(Hysterically)*: You're all the same. Selfish witches if you don't get your way. *(To* EVA*)* Promise me you'll never try to commit suicide again.

EVA *(Confessing)*: I was lonely. I didn't mean to kill myself.

HITLER: You were jealous of Geli, weren't you?

EVA: You stayed away from me for weeks at a time. When I found I was only wounded I called the doctor myself. I didn't want to die.

GELI *(Laughing)*: I wanted to die, but I can't die . . .

HITLER: How can I trust you women? The nation demands my sacrifice. I give myself to it completely. Promise me you'll never do such a silly thing again.

EVA: I promise. You know how much I love you.

GELI *(Mockingly)*: I promise. You know how much I love you.

HITLER *(Like a child to* EVA*)*: Forgive me, I need you. It's terrible how much I must demand of you . . . It takes great sacrifice to serve a man in my position . . . For the time being Germany must be my wife, do you understand?

EVA *(Soothingly)*: I understand.

GELI *(Echoing* EVA *mockingly)*: I understand.

HITLER *(Brightening)*: After my task is accomplished I promise you I'll retire with pleasure. I'll devote myself to artistic tasks. We'll live in these mountains, free from all the parasites that surround us. We'll be able to live together, travel wherever we wish. I'll have time to paint again, work on my architectural plans.

EVA: Don't worry, Adolf. I'll always do what you want. You know you can do anything you want with me.

GELI *(Echoing her mockingly)*: You know you can do anything you want with me.

THEY *draw him away as the scene ends.*

CATHEDRAL OF ICE

Scene 6
The Führer Rituals

EVA *appears, wiping away her blackface. Moodily* HITLER *strides up on a platform, brooding on his private balcony, staring into the night and stars. High up we see one star twinkling.*

EVA: As mistress of Hitler's home I practice invisibility. When the Führer holds meetings or receives foreign diplomats I'm forced to disappear. A housekeeper takes care of everything. I made her my ally so Bormann couldn't operate behind my back. A cook mixes all of the vegetarian foods that the Chief requires. *(Smiling)* I like to call him the Chief! Whenever I can, I smoke in secret. I fill the air with French perfume to cover the cigarette smell that the Chief hates. The Chief! (SHE *laughs, does a turn, and withdraws*)

HITLER *(Brooding, looking at the stars)*: The stars of heaven . . . What kind of worship is that? A Jew, Saul of Tarsus, created the Christian heaven . . . Look at the planets . . . Venus, Mars, Jupiter . . . They're not Christian . . . Man becomes great through struggle, not pity. States which offend this simple law fall into decay. Force is the first law. To transform the world the power of leadership must be recognized.

The distant star twinkles and transforms into a swastika as if in HITLER's *mind. After a moment* HITLER *steps down from the balcony as an* SS MAN *enters followed by two genial* NAZI PARTY OFFICIALS, *a man and a woman.*

HITLER: Have you carried out my orders about the new greeting?

MALE PARTY OFFICIAL *(Reading instructions)*: Yes, Führer. The greeting of "Heil Hitler" will become the official greeting. It is no longer necessary to say "Hello" or "*Gruss Gott*" to a friend. To celebrate the Führer say joyously, "Heil Hitler."

HITLER: Be sure to emphasize *joyously.* My government is supported by the entire people.

WOMAN PARTY OFFICIAL *(Continuing instructions)*: If people are members of the same social group it is customary to raise the right arm at an angle so the palm of the hand becomes visible. (SHE *demonstrates*) As you raise your arm *joyously* say "Heil Hitler," or at least "Heil."

HITLER: Make sure to include "Hitler" after "Heil."

WOMAN PARTY OFFICIAL *(Correcting hastily)*: The official greeting should include the complete, joyous name, "Heil Hitler."

MALE PARTY OFFICIAL *(Taking over from the distraught* WOMAN OFFICIAL*)*: If one sees an acquaintance in the distance (HE *imitates seeing a distant* *acquaintance)* merely raise the right hand in the manner described. (HE *demonstrates)*

HITLER *(Annoyed)*: Put it more positively. (HE *demonstrates)* The pride of a people's greeting.

MALE PARTY OFFICIAL *(Nervous now too)*: If one encounters a person socially inferior, then stretch the right arm fully out at eye level. (HE *demonstrates)* At the same time say warmly with pride, "Heil Hitler!"

HITLER: That's better.

MALE PARTY OFFICIAL *(Encouraged* HE *motions for the* WOMAN OFFICIAL *to take his right arm)*: If your right arm is engaged by a lady as you walk down the street, the greeting should always be carried out with the left arm. (HE *demonstrates with his left arm calling, "Heil Hitler!")*

HITLER *(Nodding and smiling)*: Always be courteous to women and children. The family is the germ-cell of the nation.

A banner falls reading "THE FAMILY IS THE GERM-CELL OF THE NATION."

WOMAN PARTY OFFICIAL: Absolute priority, Führer, must be given to a growing birthrate.

HITLER *(Reflecting)*: Yes, the German mother is sacred. The problem is how to promote babies without having one myself. What if we award special medals to mothers? What if we give them the privilege of saying, "I have donated a child to the Führer."

The PARTY OFFICIALS *indicate their enthusiasm. As if in a fantasy* TWO MOTHERS *enter and line before the* PARTY OFFICIALS. THEY *carry doll-babies to indicate their fertility. The "Song of the Procreators and the Baby-Making Machines" begins, interspersed through the next section.*

SS MEN *(Singing)*: We are the Procreators . . .

WOMEN: We the Baby-Making Machines . . .

TOGETHER: Our duty is to mate,
    For Germany create—
    Four, five, or ten . . .

SS MEN: A race of Supermen . . .

WOMEN: And Superwomen . . .

WOMAN PARTY OFFICIAL *(Proclaiming and giving medal)*: The Party is proud to affirm that the German mother occupies the same honored place in the community as the front-line soldier . . . To Frau Inge Dorfmann, the Silver Honor Cross of the German Mother for bearing more than six children . . .

FRAU DORFMANN *(As* SHE *accepts the medal)*: Heil Hitler!

CATHEDRAL OF ICE

WOMAN PARTY OFFICIAL: To Frau Ortrud Grossobst, the Gold Honor Cross of the German Mother for bearing more than eight children . . .

HITLER *(Musing to himself)*: Can you believe it? Eight children . . .

FRAU GROSSOBST *(Almost dropping some doll-babies—*SHE *has so many)*: Heil Hitler!

MALE PARTY OFFICIAL: In the future all members of the Party's organizations will be duty-bound to salute wearers of the Mother's Honor Cross. Thus our citizens will pay homage to our German mothers.

There is a temporary crisis as THEY *run out of candidates for German motherhood. The* WOMAN OFFICIAL *whispers frantically to* HITLER. *We hear her saying, "We do not have enough Mothers, etc."*

HITLER *(Calling impatiently)*: Himmler! Himmler!

HIMMLER *enters.*

We are running out of sacred German mothers. Impossible. We must increase our population by stronger measures.

HIMMLER: Führer, I'm pleased to report that our SS scientists have solved this problem. We have created the *Lebensborn*—the Spring of Life . . .

Another banner drops reading, "LEBENSBORN—THE SPRING OF LIFE."

HITLER: What is this Spring of Life?

HIMMLER: Our new SS Foundation for Unmarried Mothers. Their children are fathered by superior SS men and other racially valuable Germans.

HITLER *(Squirming a little)*: We must be careful of illegitimacy. My father suffered from this curse.

HIMMLER: We will wipe out the disgrace of illegitimacy, Führer. Every woman in our Lebensborn Foundation will consider it an honor to bear you a child. (HIMMLER *steps forward to address the* SS LEBENSBORN MEN) Comrades, only he who leaves a child behind can die peacefully in battle. Beyond the bonds of bourgeois law, German women, acting from a profound moral seriousness, have the sublime task of becoming mothers. You will be their temporary husbands. Destiny alone knows if you will return or die in battle for Germany. Your heritage of the strongest German stock must be passed on. *(Pointing)* The red dot in our banner symbolizes the triumphant German embryos of future children. Heil Hitler!

As the SS MEN *salute him in return,* HITLER *and* HIMMLER *exit.*

SS MEN *(Singing)*: We are the Procreators . . .
TWO WOMEN CANDIDATES *(Singing as if on their way to the* Lebensborn*)*: We
the Baby-Making Machines . . .
TOGETHER: We'll make our country purer
By mating for our Führer—
Four, five, or ten . . .
SS MEN: A race of Supermen . . .
TWO WOMEN CANDIDATES: And Superwomen . . .
FIRST WOMAN CANDIDATE: Where are you going?
SECOND WOMAN CANDIDATE: To the *Lebensborn.* I've been chosen to be im-
pregnated for the Führer.
FIRST WOMAN CANDIDATE: So have I.
SECOND WOMAN CANDIDATE: Isn't it a great honor?

Whispering and giggling anxiously THEY *sit on a bench across from the*
SS MEN.

FIRST SS MAN *(Rubbing his arm)*: They've taken enough blood out of us
to service a regiment.
SECOND SS MAN: Shhh, the doctor's coming.
SS DOCTOR *(Entering and addressing the* SS MEN*)*: Your blood tests show that
you belong to Group A—the pure Nordic group. After inquiries into
your background, you've both been certified to come from pure
Aryan stock. We've gone back as far as the 18th century to check
your ancestors.
FIRST SS MAN *(Awed)*: 18th century . . .
SS DOCTOR *(Continuing)*: We German scientists have proved that generations preserve outstanding racial aptitudes. Bach, Beethoven, Wagner
all belonged to a long line of superior musicians. The Krupp family has given Germany supreme inventors and military technicians.
(With a smile) In your SS training I'm sure you've always admired
thoroughbreds. Stud farms have proved that a fine mare mated with
a purebred stallion will produce a champion thoroughbred—nine
times out of ten.

The FIRST SS MAN *nudges his companion.*

Unfortunately modern science is still unable to cure all of the errors of heredity. In foreign countries an alcoholic may copulate with
a Jew or a syphilitic. Within a few generations you have an abnor-
mal population. Our race purification program is designed to pro-

duce that pure, regenerative blood which we need to carry out the Führer's will.

FIRST SS MAN: We'll do our best, Sir.

The SS DOCTOR exits. Sentimental, romantic operetta music is heard. The SS MEN approach the WOMEN CANDIDATES, who are sitting, waiting.

FIRST WOMAN CANDIDATE *(To her companion)*: I hope that dark one asks me. What's the matter with you?

SECOND WOMAN CANDIDATE: I'm sorry . . . I feel a little as though I'm selling myself.

FIRST WOMAN CANDIDATE: Don't be stupid . . . You're serving your country.

FIRST SS MAN *(To SECOND SS MAN)*: I want that blonde. I've been dreaming of breasts and hips like . . . *(HE demonstrates)*

SECOND SS MAN: Ask her to dance with you.

FIRST SS MAN: Just like that?

SECOND SS MAN: How else can you choose?

THEY greet the two WOMEN and begin to dance with them.

SECOND WOMAN CANDIDATE *(Summoning her courage and smiling at the SECOND SS MAN)*: So you're supposed to be a *procreator* . . .

SECOND SS MAN *(Laughing)*: That's a fancy name . . . Call me Franz.

SECOND WOMAN CANDIDATE *(Hesitating)*: Did you choose me becuase there wasn't anyone else available?

SECOND SS MAN: Don't be silly . . . What's your name?

SECOND WOMAN CANDIDATE: Bertha.

THEY continue dancing.

FIRST WOMAN CANDIDATE *(Mockingly to FIRST SS MAN)*: I'm ready, Herr Procreator.

FIRST SS MAN: Come off it. I've had my eye on you.

FIRST WOMAN CANDIDATE: Tell me, I'll bet you're engaged to another girl.

FIRST SS MAN *(Taken aback a little)*: Not really.

FIRST WOMAN CANDIDATE *(Laughing ironically)*: Not really? What does that mean? Still, what difference does it make? *(Defiantly)* Here I am—your official, state baby-making machine.

FIRST SS MAN *(Shocked)*: You shouldn't speak like that. You're giving your body to Germany and the Führer.

SS MEN AND TWO WOMEN *(Singing)*:
We are the Procreators . . .
We the Baby-Making Machines . . .

Our duty is to mate,
For Germany create—
Four, five, or ten . . .

A race of Supermen . . .
And Superwomen . . .

We are the Procreators . . .
We are the Baby-Making Machines . . .

We'll make our country purer
By mating for our Führer—
Four, five, or ten . . .
A race of Supermen . . .
And Superwomen . . .

Eagerly THEY *go off to their procreation tasks. The mood changes with Nazi martial music. Another banner falls reading: THE SECRET POLICE RITUALS. Projections of the Nazi invasions are shown.* HITLER, HIMMLER, GÖRING *and* GÖBBELS *enter as if for a secret conference.*

HITLER: France has fallen. Czechoslovakia, Hungary, Poland, Greece, Yugoslavia, belong to us. The Third Reich stretches from Norway to Africa. Are the Russian plans prepared?

GÖRING: The Luftwaffe is ready, Führer. The Russian air force has no possibility for serious combat. You can call me Meier if one Russian bomb ever falls on Berlin.

HITLER *(Snapping at* GÖRING*)*: Don't tempt me. *(*HE *turns to* GÖBBELS*)*

GÖBBELS: We've prepared the greatest propaganda force in the world, Führer. This will be the final assault against Jewish communism.

HITLER *(Turning to* HIMMLER*)*: What about the SS?

HIMMLER: Never before have our men been so well-trained.

HITLER *(Aside)*: That's the only thing Himmler is good for—training secret police. *(To* HIMMLER *abruptly)* Have you prepared the Final Solution?

HIMMLER *(Uneasily)*: That takes time, Führer.

HITLER *(Flaring up)*: Time? I promised the nation. If the international Jewish financiers plunge the world into another war, I promise it will be their end. The Jewish race must be annihilated.

HIMMLER: That is a giant task, Führer. There are millions of Jews in Russia alone, three million in the Ukraine. In Poland two and a quarter million. Three quarters of a million in France. A third of a million in England. As for America . . .

HITLER *(Raging)*: Don't tell me your numbers. I want a solution.

GÖBBELS: We must have foreign workers to man our factories.

GÖRING: Draft them, send them where needed.

HITLER: Force is not enough. We need Night and Fog.

HIMMLER: Night and Fog?

HITLER *(Sharply)*: Anyone who endangers our national security—Jew, communist, criminal—must be transformed into Night and Fog.

HIMMLER *(Misunderstanding)*: We in the SS are not yet experts on the weather.

HITLER *(Snapping)*: I'm not talking about weather. I'm talking about the function of the camps.

HIMMLER: We're doing our best. The new gas chambers at Auschwitz . . .

HITLER: It's not enough to kill. We need thousands of anonymous workers to produce more aircraft, tanks, artillery.

HIMMLER: We only send those prisoners unfit to work to the gas chambers. All others are segregated for forced labor.

HITLER: Work or die is not enough. You don't understand spiritual problems. We must eliminate all bourgeois ideas of personality that prevent our triumph. To achieve victory we must transform these criminal elements into Night and Fog.

An SS OFFICER in a death's-head uniform enters and salutes the Führer. As the music of "Night and Fog" is heard, two CAMP PRISONERS, a man and a woman, almost naked, are brought in. The SS OFFICER examines them briefly, poking at them with his whip.

SS OFFICER: Your names?

MALE PRISONER: Night . . . *(Then singing)*
In the Night
I lose my name.
I am the Night . . .

SS OFFICER *(To the FEMALE PRISONER)*: Yours?

FEMALE PRISONER: Fog . . . *(Then singing)*
In the Fog
I lose my name.
I am the Fog . . .

SS OFFICER: What do Night and Fog wear?

NIGHT: Burlap undershorts.

As the PRISONERS answer, the SS OFFICER hands them the burlap items of clothing.

FOG: Burlap shirt.

THEY *put on the shirts.*

NIGHT: Burlap jacket.

THEY *put on the jackets.*

FOG: Burlap overcoat.

THEY *put on the overcoats. Now* THEY *are almost identical looking— their identities vanished.*

SS OFFICER: What are the shoes of Night and Fog?
NIGHT: Wooden clogs.

The OFFICER *hands the* PRISONERS *the clogs.*

SS OFFICER: What food do Night and Fog eat?
NIGHT: Warm water with cabbage leaves.
FOG: Mice if we can catch them.
SS OFFICER: How does Night catch mice?
NIGHT: I make a burlap trap. There are lots of mice in our straw beds.
SS OFFICER: Do you cook the mice?
FOG: We find some wood near the factory. We make a little fire.
NIGHT: We cook the mice in an iron saucepan.
SS OFFICER: Do you skin the mice before eating them?
NIGHT: Night eats only the meat.
SS OFFICER: You have tools for skinning?
FOG (*Quickly*): Tools are forbidden.
NIGHT: Night and Fog use pieces of glass, bits of iron lying around the factory.
SS OFFICER: What is the schedule of Night and Fog?
FOG: Reveille going at 4:30 AM.

The gong and roll call is heard.

NIGHT: Night, here!
FOG: Fog, here!
SS OFFICER: How do Night and Fog march to work?
NIGHT: In ranks of five, flanked by guards and dogs, we march through the sleeping city . . .

The cadence of Links, Recht, Links, Recht, *etc. is heard offstage as the* PRISONER CHORUS *is heard singing their song.*

PRISONER CHORUS: In the Night
We lose our names,

    We lose the light,
    We are the Night . . .

SS OFFICER: No one sees you in the city?

FOG: No one sees Night and Fog.

SS OFFICER: Who knows the names, Night and Fog?

NIGHT: No one knows our names.

SS OFFICER: How long do Night and Fog work?

FOG: Twelve hours a day.

SS OFFICER: What happens to Night and Fog if they are ill?

NIGHT: They wake at dawn—in the gas chamber.

SS OFFICER: What is the religion of Night?

NIGHT: Darkness.

SS OFFICER: What is the religion of Fog?

FOG: To enter the darkness.

SS OFFICER: Night and Fog, *Achtung! Vorwaerts Marsch! Links, Recht, Links, Recht, Links, Recht.*

HE *marches them out as* THEY *sing. The* PRISONER CHORUS *is heard behind them.*

NIGHT *and* FOG: In the Night
    We lose our names
    I am the Night,
    I am the Fog . . .

PRISONER CHORUS:
    In the Night
    We lose our names,
    We lose the light,
    We are the Night . . .

HITLER *(To* HIMMLER*)*: Night and Fog disappear into the service of the state. No information will be given out about them. Records will contain only the initials of Night and Fog. Their graves will be unmarked. You are in sole charge of the Final Solution.

HIMMLER: As you command, Führer. It is a heavy task for my men.

HITLER: For strong nations history demands precedents. Only the weak permit their enemies to prosper.

HIMMLER: I understand, Führer.

HITLER: Report to me when your plans are ready.

HIMMLER *salutes and leaves with* GÖBBELS *and* GÖRING.

HITLER *(Brooding in the night)*: Night and Fog surround me . . . Cover the stars that my destiny may triumph . . . Mankind has grown powerful through eternal struggle . . . Strength lies in attack, not defense . . . The world will only perish through eternal peace.

Through the darkness NEUMANN *steps forward.* HE *is holding the old coat that* HITLER *wore in the opening scenes.*

NEUMANN (*Offering* HITLER *the coat*): Here is your coat, Führer.
HITLER (*Staring*): Neumann.

NEUMANN *helps him on with the coat.*

NEUMANN: Your old Jewish peddler friend.
HITLER: You're dead.
NEUMANN (*Smiling*): When you've known a Hitler it's hard to die. You can't keep me out of Night and Fog.
HITLER (*Raging*): You've never done anything for me, Neumann. There's no room for you in my Cathedral of Ice.
NEUMANN (*Shrugging*): I'll stand over the gate and hold your sign. (HE *puts on the coat and hat of a Hasidic master and moves to a top level holding the sign,* "Arbeit Macht Frei")
HITLER (*Raging*): You can't hold that sign. The world will thank us for ridding the earth of you parasites. (*Brooding,* HE *turns his back on* NEUMANN)

Scene 7
The Final Solution

Around the theatre a series of mysterious, contrapuntal events conflict in time—fantasies of the past that haunt the present. HITLER *struggles to create his version of history.* NEUMANN *mocks him by playing various Hasidic masters to show how faith survives even after the Holocaust.* NIGHT *and* FOG *portray their own struggle for survival. There is always a sharp counterpoint between* HITLER'S *shaking, paranoid struggle to create his Cathedral of Ice, the forces that serve his fantasies although shaken by their own fate in time (*HIMMLER, GÖRING, *the* ARCHITECT, *etc.), and the forces that resist his fantasies although still condemned to be part of them (*NEUMANN, NIGHT *and* FOG, *etc.). All of these events flow eerily together in a fantastic collage as if the entropy of history cannot be stopped. Hasidic music is heard as* NEUMANN *transforms into a Hasidic master on the upper level. A* DISCIPLE *is trying to dance on a ladder.*

NEUMANN/MASTER (*Mocking* HITLER, HE *plays the* HASIDIC MASTER *speaking to the dancing* DISCIPLE): Dance, you parasite. Dance.

DISCIPLE *(Clinging desperately, afraid to dance on the ladder)*: I'm afraid, Master, I'll fall. How can I dance on this ladder?

NEUMANN/MASTER: Would you prefer to dance on the head of a pin? Your feet must soar from the wood.

DISCIPLE *(Puzzled, still struggling to dance)*: How can I soar on a ladder?

NEUMANN/MASTER: Man is a ladder placed on earth. Only the top of the ladder touches heaven.

DISCIPLE *(Afraid, peering up)*: Master, I can't see the top. It's invisible. Smoke obscures the view.

NEUMANN/MASTER: Dance through the smoke. Let joy enter your feet.

Frantically the DISCIPLE *struggles to dance.* NEUMANN/MASTER *laughs.*

Your feet are not even rising one inch. What good is a level dance? Dance higher. When your feet soar, when your body lifts up, your soul too will ascend.

The DISCIPLE *continues his struggle to dance higher on the ladder.*

After escorting the prisoners, NIGHT *and* FOG, *beneath the sign, the* SS GUARD *stops before a stand with tattooing equipment.*

SS GUARD *(Ordering)*: Hold out your arm.

NIGHT *draws back.*

It's only a tattoo, a little number. It doesn't hurt.

NIGHT *and* FOG *hold out their arms and the* SS GUARD *tattoos numbers into their arms. Then the* SS GUARD *points up at the sign beside* NEUMANN.

See that sign. What's it say?

NEUMANN *(Reading it deliberately)*: Arbeit Macht Frei.

NIGHT: Work makes you free.

SS GUARD: That's our motto. *(Pointing)* If you can't work there's always the Perfume Factory.

FOG *clutches her stomach.*

What's the matter?

FOG *(Hastily)*: Nothing. That smell.

SS GUARD: What do you expect from a Perfume Factory? How do you feel?

FOG *(Straightening up)*: I feel fine.

SS GUARD *(To* NIGHT*)*: How about you? You sure your health is good?

NIGHT: Yes, I want to work.

SS GUARD: Good. (HE *writes on a form*) "Fit for work." (*Motioning*) You can start on the rock pile here.

NIGHT *and* FOG *start to work on the rock pile as the* SS GUARD *relaxes, watching them casually.*

NIGHT (*Struggling with a rock*): Why do they make roads out of such big rocks?

FOG: Don't be stupid. Maybe God wants the road to this camp made out of big rocks. (SHE *struggles to hoist a rock and fails*)

NIGHT: Why call me stupid? God wouldn't be caught dead with a rock like that.

FOG: You're right. Maybe He's just here as a witness.

NIGHT: Are you crazy? Would God want to be a witness in a place like this?

THEY *work in silence, eyeing the guard furtively.*

If God would give you one wish now—If God would give you anything you wanted—what would you choose?

FOG (*Reflecting*): Feh, what a question. I'd choose that God would come here.

NIGHT (*Mockingly*): When should He come? Should He come tomorrow?

FOG: Tomorrow is already too late. Yesterday God should come.

THEY *continue wearily to hoist and carry rocks. Reflecting their agony,* NEUMANN *begins to dance as if around a coffin, assuming the identity of the* RABBI OF BERDITCHEV.

NEUMANN/RABBI (*Chanting*): The dance of the rocks.

FIRST DISCIPLE (*Observing, troubled*): Look, the Rabbi of Berditchev is dancing.

SECOND DISCIPLE: It's a shame. His people are dying and he's dancing.

FIRST DISCIPLE (*Disturbed, approaches* NEUMANN/RABBI): Rabbi, please stop.

NEUMANN/RABBI (*Continuing to dance*): Let me alone. Can't you see I'm dancing?

SECOND DISCIPLE: Please, Rabbi, it doesn't seem right.

FIRST DISCIPLE: Should we join you or stop you?

SECOND DISCIPLE: Which is the right way, Rabbi, that of sorrow or joy?

NEUMANN/RABBI (*Dancing to illuminate his words*): The Divine Presence cannot dwell in a body of dejection. He who is truly joyful is like a man whose house has burned down. Deep in his soul he feels his need.

He dances. He builds again. As he carries stones to rebuild his house, his heart rejoices. He dances with joy.

Slowly the DISCIPLES *join in his dance and* HE *dances with them. Suddenly the* SS GUARD *moves toward* NIGHT *and* FOG.

SS GUARD *(To* NIGHT*)*: Lawyer, you're getting too weak to work. Maybe you need another job.

NIGHT: Yes, Sir.

SS GUARD *(Calling to* SECOND SS GUARD*)*: Hey, Fritz, come here. *(Motioning to* NIGHT*)* Look at his hands. He can't work anymore. He needs rest. Maybe it's time for him to become a paratrooper.

NIGHT *(Standing at attention)*: What's a paratrooper, sir?

SS GUARD *(Jovially to* SECOND GUARD*)*: He doesn't know what a paratrooper is.

SECOND SS GUARD: We walk you up the path there. You're on top of the rock quarry. You look around, see the beautiful view.

SS GUARD: Then you jump off into heaven.

TOGETHER: And that's how you learn to be a paratrooper.

The two GUARDS *laugh.*

SS GUARD: Listen, Jew, you're not a bad Jew. We'll give you one more chance before we turn you into a paratrooper.

NIGHT: Yes, sir.

SS GUARD *(Pointing to* SECOND SS GUARD*)*: You see Fritz there?

NIGHT: Yes, sir, Herr Fritz.

SS GUARD: I'll tell you a secret about him. Fritz has a glass eye. Isn't that true, Fritz?

SECOND SS GUARD *(Smiling)*: My glass eye is so perfect I can see Jews with it.

SS GUARD *(To* NIGHT*)*: If you can tell which one of Fritz's eyes is glass we'll keep you out of the paratroops.

NIGHT *(Hesitating)*: That's difficult, sir. His eyes are so clear and blue.

SS GUARD: Of course they're clear and blue. Like the sky.

NIGHT: May I move a little closer? *(HE edges his way a little closer and studies the eyes of the* SECOND SS GUARD*)*

SECOND SS GUARD: Not too close, Jew.

SS GUARD *(Impatiently)*: Well, which one is glass?

NIGHT *(Pointing suddenly)*: His right eye, sir.

SECOND SS GUARD *(Angrily)*: The bastard guessed right.

SS GUARD *(To* NIGHT*)*: You cheated. How did you find out?

NIGHT *(Tired, not caring anymore)*: You really want to know, sir? His glass eye stands out. It looks different. It has a kindly gleam.

The action freezes with the menacing sense that NIGHT *has gone too far.
Above,* NEUMANN *begins chanting and singing softly again. In his coat*
HITLER *steps forward shaking to accost* HIMMLER.

HITLER *(To* HIMMLER*)*: Did you ever ask yourself what is a Jew?
HIMMLER: Yes, Führer, I've conducted a great deal of research in that field.
HITLER *(Looking up at* NEUMANN*)*: In my Viennese years of poverty I en-
    countered many crazy Jews like that one. I went to synagogues, lis-
    tened to their whining services. I wandered down the streets where
    the poisonous Jewish whores of Vienna lived. I saw how they in-
    fected the city with venereal disease. How many great German
    geniuses died from syphilis . . .
NEUMANN *(Calling mockingly)*: Some Jews too.
HIMMLER: Too many, Führer. Nietzsche, Beethoven, Hugo Wolf . . .
HITLER *(Annoyed)*: I know who got syphilis.
HIMMLER *(Apologizing hastily)*: I'm sorry, Führer.
HITLER: I learned how Jews corrupted the newspapers, how they con-
    trolled the banks. There is only one way to stop the international
    Jewish conspiracy.
HIMMLER: What is that, Führer?
HITLER: God must cease to exist for the Jews.
HIMMLER *(Puzzled)*: We don't permit religious services for any of our
    Jewish prisoners.
HITLER *(Raging)*: I'm not talking about praying. The Jewish god must
    be destroyed.
HIMMLER *(Amazed)*: You think there is a Jewish god?
HITLER *(Annoyed)*: Not to us of course. But the Jews believe in the com-
    ing of a messiah. It gives them the strength to endure.
HIMMLER *(Suddenly beginning to understand)*: I see. You want their faith taken
    away from them.
HITLER: When they lose their faith—that is the Final Solution.

Reacting to this NEUMANN *becomes the* BAAL SHEM TOV. *A* DISCIPLE
approaches him.

FIRST DISCIPLE: Master, please tell me. How shall I make my living in
    the world?
NEUMANN/BAAL SHEM: You shall be a cantor.
FIRST DISCIPLE *(Astonished)*: A cantor? But Master, I can't even sing. I
    have a voice like a crow.
NEUMANN/BAAL SHEM: With your crow's voice you'll croak with lyrical
    fervor. I shall bind you to the world of music. Beyond your voice
    shall emerge the song. They shall call you the Cantor of the Baal
    Shem Tov.

Croaking at first, the FIRST DISCIPLE *begins to sing. As* HE *continues with lyrical fervor* HE *listens to himself with increasing joy. As the* FIRST DISCIPLE *continues singing* NEUMANN/BAAL SHEM *begins to dance. After a moment the two* DISCIPLES *join in the dance. Suddenly* NEUMANN/BAAL SHEM *seizes the sacred scroll of the Torah and begins to dance with it.*

NEUMANN/BAAL SHEM: Take up the Torah . . . Dance, sing with it . . .
FIRST DISCIPLE *(Shrinking back, afraid)*: Look, he's dancing with the Torah!
SECOND DISCIPLE: He's gone too far. The sacred book is *dancing*.

Abruptly, NEUMANN/BAAL SHEM *lays down the scroll.*

FIRST DISCIPLE *(Whispering fearfully)*: What's he doing now?
SECOND DISCIPLE: Has he lost his mind? Now he's abandoning the Torah.

NEUMANN/BAAL SHEM *begins to dance and sing again.*

FIRST DISCIPLE: Look, he hasn't forgotten the Torah. Do you see what's happening to his body?
SECOND DISCIPLE *(Staring)*: Grace is coming out of his flesh.
FIRST DISCIPLE *(Awed)*: Fire is coming out of his body.
SECOND DISCIPLE: He has laid aside the Torah, the visible teachings.
FIRST DISCIPLE: His body is dancing with the spiritual teachings.

Panting, disturbed by his visionary efforts, NEUMANN *pauses beside the sign. Below the* SECOND SS GUARD *ushers in a newly arrived prisoner, a dignified* OLD MAN. *Near a pile of clothes* NIGHT *and* FOG *are standing with the* FIRST SS GUARD.

SECOND SS GUARD *(Shoving the* OLD MAN *toward the pile of clothes)*: Go on, welcome our new arrival. Show him how my glass eye works.
FIRST SS GUARD *(To the* OLD MAN*)*: He means he wants you to select your uniform. *(Pointing to the pile of clothes)* You Jews like fine clothes.
SECOND SS GUARD: Even with my glass eye I can see the quality of those clothes. You're a lucky old man to select from such a pile.
OLD MAN *(Hesitating to approach the clothes,* HE *turns to* NIGHT *and* FOG*)*: What kind of clothes are these?
NIGHT *(Whispering)*: Dead men's clothes.
FOG *(Whispering, pointing furtively)*: Soon you will see the smoke. They are done for. You must wear their clothes.
OLD MAN *(Frightened)*: I can't wear their clothes.
FIRST SS GUARD: Hurry up, old man. Be careful to pick the right clothes, the best clothes for your new job.
OLD MAN *(Whispering)*: What is my new job?

FOG *(Whispering)*: I don't know.
SECOND SS GUARD *(Laughing)*: You'll need the best clothes you can find to cover up the smell of your new job.

The SS GUARDS *laugh and converse together.*

NIGHT *(Whispering to the* OLD MAN*)*: Go on. They'll beat you.
FOG: Pick out the best clothes.

Slowly, fearfully, the OLD MAN *picks out an elegant, black velvet vest and holds it up tentatively. Then as* NIGHT *and* FOG *gesture encouragement to him, the* OLD MAN *begins to comprehend and pulls out a handsome, old-fashioned spring coat with silk lining.*

FIRST SS GUARD *(Calling, laughing)*: A fine spring coat, old man.
SECOND SS GUARD *(Mockingly)*: He'll be a real cock of the walk.

The SS GUARDS *laugh. Helped by* NIGHT *and* FOG *the* OLD MAN *joyously selects an incredible top hat, a high hat with the rim cut off, and puts it on.*

FIRST SS GUARD *(Breaking up with laughter)*: That's a real topper.
SECOND SS GUARD: A Jewish dunce topper.

The OLD MAN*'s face lights up with a radiant smile.* HE *strikes a grand, formal pose in his ridiculous, brilliant costume.*

FIRST SS GUARD: Doesn't he look like a Berlin banker ready to swindle the public?
SECOND SS GUARD: Call your chauffeur, Mr. Banker.
FIRST SS GUARD: We're ready, Mr. Jew Banker. Shall we go to your bank?
SECOND SS GUARD *(Pushing the* OLD MAN *around and pointing)*: It's right there, Mr. Jew Banker. Can you smell it?
FIRST SS GUARD: Stand in front of the latrine. You're the new *Scheissmeister.*
SECOND SS GUARD: You see that everyone shits fast on time.
FIRST SS GUARD *(Reaching into the pile of clothes and pulling out an old gold watch)*: Here's an old gold watch, *Scheissmeister,* to help you keep time.
SECOND SS GUARD *(Picking out a silk scarf)*: Your silk scarf to keep the stink out of your banking nose.

With dignity the OLD MAN *endures the scarf being tied over his nose and mouth and the watch being put into his hand. The* SS GUARDS *face him toward the latrine.*

FIRST SS GUARD *(Blowing his whistle, shouting)*: Ready, *Scheissmeister.*

CATHEDRAL OF ICE

NEUMANN *begins to dance again, chanting softly. In an agony of stomach cramps* HIMMLER *falls before his doctor, the physical therapist,* DR. FELIX KERSTEN. *Shaking,* HITLER *watches this final series of fantasies from the side of the playing area.*

HITLER *(Raging)*: Himmler, all of this should be secret.

HIMMLER *(Clutching his stomach)*: Dr. Kersten, please help me . . . I cannot breathe.

KERSTEN: Where does it hurt, Herr Himmler?

HIMMLER *(Opening his shirt, pointing to his stomach)*: Here, here . . . always the same pain . . . (HE *lies down on a couch)*

KERSTEN *(Soothing as* HE *massages* HIMMLER*)*: One minute. I'll help you. You know what causes these pains.

HIMMLER: These cramps are unbearable.

KERSTEN *(Kneading him like a baby)*: Relax . . . You're tight as a drum.

HIMMLER: What would I do without you? With you I can talk in complete confidence.

KERSTEN: It is a heavy burden you carry.

HIMMLER: No one knows how heavy. The Final Solution is a purification the Führer is determined to carry out.

KERSTEN: The Final Solution?

HIMMLER: No one has seen the bodies. Do you know what it is to see a pile of five hundred, a thousand bodies?

KERSTEN: I'm a doctor. I see one dead person at a time.

HIMMLER: The extermination camp is an absolute necessity. As the Führer told me, we must be as strong as the Americans.

KERSTEN *(Puzzled)*: The Americans?

HIMMLER: Yes, the Americans were not afraid to exterminate the Indians to secure their land. We must be as strong.

KERSTEN *(Massaging him deeply)*: But many Americans protested. Isn't there a danger? Is that better?

HIMMLER *(With a deep sigh)*: For the first time today I can breathe without pain. No, Doctor, you forget. Only a few whites protested when Americans marched the Indians hundreds of miles to their reservations. Why should Europeans protest our difficult task with the Jews and the Russian communists?

KERSTEN *(Carefully)*: If you go on worrying like this you'll never get better. You know how badly things are going.

HIMMLER: What can I do?

KERSTEN: If you saved some of your prisoners you would be honored instead of hated. You are a powerful man. *(Flattering* HIMMLER*)* You could earn yourself a place in history like Henry I, the German emperor you admire.

HIMMLER: Henry I. *(Sitting up abruptly)* I forbid you to talk like that. It's treason. *(Pointing to his SS belt buckle)* You see my SS motto—*Honor is loyalty.*

KERSTEN *(Massaging him down on the couch again to stop his protests)*: There, there. The pain will return if you agitate yourself.

HIMMLER: Do you really think I could be like Henry I?

KERSTEN: Of course, Herr Reichsführer. Show the generosity of your soul.

HIMMLER *(Agitated)*: Soul? Have you ever seen the soul of a Jew fly off?

KERSTEN *(Uneasily)*: What do you mean?

HIMMLER: A Jew's soul is like a bat. It flaps through the sky.

KERSTEN: Really?

HIMMLER *(Rising up again in his agitation)*: The Jew's soul flaps through the sky like a giant bat. Have you ever smelled the smoke of a thousand bats burning?

KERSTEN *(Pushing him down soothingly)*: Lie down now. Your body is tense again.

HIMMLER: Kersten, your hands are the only things that help me. My stomach is burning.

KERSTEN: Rest. I'll take care of your stomach.

> *Shaking with paranoia* HITLER *holds up his arm and the masked figure of the* SS DOCTOR MENGELE *appears high up across from* NEUMANN. NEUMANN *reacts madly as* RABBI ZUSYA, *the Hasidic master of Hanipol.* HE *begins to scream and gesticulate with ecstasy.*

FIRST DISCIPLE *(Anxiously to* SECOND DISCIPLE *who is reading from scripture)*: What's the matter with Rabbi Zusya?

SECOND DISCIPLE: I don't know. *(HE tries to read from scripture)* "And God said . . ."

NEUMANN/ZUSYA *(Pounds on the wall ecstatically and chants repetitively)*: "And God said . . . And God said . . ."

FIRST DISCIPLE *(Staring)*: Zusya's lost his mind. Try to get him back to the scripture.

SECOND DISCIPLE *(Trying again)*: "And God said . . ."

> *As* HE *continues to read the scripture it is drowned out by* ZUSYA's *ecstatic, screaming chant of "And God said . . . And God said . . ." as* HE *dances and hammers on the wall.*

FIRST DISCIPLE *(Abruptly)*: Stop reading. Don't you understand?

SECOND DISCIPLE *(Looking up, bewildered)*: What?

FIRST DISCIPLE: Listen to Zusya. *(THEY listen)* One word is enough.

SECOND DISCIPLE: One word?

FIRST DISCIPLE: If a man speaks in the spirit of truth one word is enough.

SECOND DISCIPLE (*As* THEY *watch* NEUMANN/ZUSYA): With one word the world can be redeemed.

THEY *join* NEUMANN/ZUSYA *in his ecstatic, screaming chant and dance. Up a ramp several* CAMP PRISONERS, *including* NIGHT *and* FOG, *the* OLD MAN, *and a* FOURTH PRISONER, *move like spectres. At the top of the ramp,* DR. MENGELE, *with his riding crop, motions the* PRISONERS *to the left or the right, to life or death in the gas chamber.*

FIRST DISCIPLE: Rabbi Zusya, tell us who goes to hell, who to paradise?

NEUMANN/ZUSYA: The bold-faced go to hell, the shame-faced to paradise.

SECOND DISCIPLE: Zusya is being God's fool again.

NEUMANN/ZUSYA (*Praying, shouting ecstatically*): He who is shame-faced must beware of touching evil. He must walk the heights of paradise. He who lacks courage must cling to heaven. But he who is bold in holiness may descend to hell. In the alleys of shame he may live and not fear evil.

HE *motions to his* DISCIPLES *to follow him. Afraid,* THEY *hesitate.*

FIRST DISCIPLE: We are not bold-faced, Master.

SECOND DISCIPLE: How will we know which way to turn?

NEUMANN/ZUSYA *summons them and hesitantly* THEY *follow him, joining the line of* CAMP PRISONERS *beneath* DR. MENGELE. *In their old-fashioned Hasidic dress* THEY *make a strange contrast to the grotesque prison uniforms.*

NIGHT (*To* FOG, *gesturing furtively at* DR. MENGELE): That's Dr. Mengele. If he points to the left you die. If he points to the right you live.

FOG: How does he decide?

NIGHT: Who knows? He's a doctor. If he likes your looks.

OLD MAN: A doctor yet. He's a disgrace to his profession.

FOG: He should have had a Jewish mother.

NIGHT: What good would a Jewish mother do him?

FOG: She would have taught him not to point.

DR. MENGELE *signals the* PRISONERS *to approach for inspection.*

FOURTH PRISONER (*Holding back*): I can't. I don't want to die.

OLD MAN: Don't let him see you're afraid. Death isn't the worst thing.

NIGHT: He's right. We'll meet again in a better world.

FOG: What better world?

NIGHT *(Grinning)*: We'll meet in a shop window as soap.

> DR. MENGELE *motions him to the left and* FOG *to the right.*

(Calling to FOG*)* Don't worry about me. They'll make a sweet toilet soap from my fat.

> DR. MENGELE *waves the* OLD MAN *to the left and the* FOURTH PRISONER *to the right.* FOG *hesitates as if to join* NIGHT.

No, you live. Remember even soap does not forget.

> NIGHT *and the* OLD MAN *go off to the left,* FOG *and the* FOURTH PRISONER *to the right.* NEUMANN/ZUSYA *and his* DISCIPLES *approach* DR. MENGELE.

FIRST DISCIPLE *(Afraid)*: Master, we are at the crossroads.

SECOND DISCIPLE: God is not here. Which way do we go?

NEUMANN/ZUSYA *(Peering up and around, shaking his head)*: To the left is the fire. How crude is Zusya's body that it fears fire. To the right is the safety of earth. Earth, earth you are better than I. Yet I trample you with my feet. Soon I shall lie under you and be subject to you.

> ZUSYA *and his* DISCIPLES *begin chanting again as* THEY *await.* DR. MENGELE*'s motion to the left or right.*
>
> *As if dream-walking* GÖRING *shoulders past* HITLER *ignoring* HITLER*'s shaking protests.* GÖRING *is deep in the memory of his drug addiction. Abstractly* HE *gazes at the jewels on his fingers, at a painting he has stolen.* HE *is dressed in a luxurious emerald-velvet dressing gown with a giant ruby brooch pinned to the satin lapel. His face is covered with a thick layer of rouge, his fingernails lacquered a bright red. The* ARCHITECT *enters, trying to control himself, angry and upset, at this late night summons from* GÖRING.

ARCHITECT: You sent for me. *(Aside)* Look at him.

GÖRING *(Abstractly)*: Oh, it's you.

ARCHITECT *(Aside)*: He's on heroin again. *(To* GÖRING*)* Why did you call me here in the middle of the night?

GÖRING *(Vaguely)*: Yes, it came to me suddenly. *(*HE *extracts some diamonds and rubies from his pocket and rolls them in his hand)*

ARCHITECT *(Impatiently)*: What came to you?

GÖRING: The way we can conquer.

ARCHITECT *(Incredulously, looking back at* HITLER*)*: Win the war? At this point? Have you told the Führer about your discovery?

GÖRING: Don't be so nervous. We're the technicians, eh, Architect? We'll never be defeated. Some German will always invent a new technique to save us.

ARCHITECT: Herr Göring, I don't have much time. The situation is grave. There's a severe steel shortage.

GÖRING *(Reacting)*: Don't worry. I have the solution to our problems. At heart—even though he won't see me—the Führer knows he can trust me. *(Pointing to the picture)* How do you like my new Van Dyck?

ARCHITECT *(Trying to control himself)*: Very fine, but . . .

GÖRING: It belonged to a French Jew. He had one of the great collections. *(Pointing)* Remarkable hands, don't you think?

ARCHITECT *(Impatiently)*: What is your plan to win the war?

GÖRING: I haven't told the Führer yet. He's a little angry with me. Is it my fault our air force suffers from lack of production? Isn't it true that enemy bombers have smashed our factories, our trains?

ARCHITECT: Yes, there's a special problem with the shortage of locomotives.

GÖRING *(Lighting up with enthusiasm)*: That's what I mean. I have the solution to manufacturing locomotives. With new locomotives we'll haul supplies and build planes again. *(HE lapses into vacancy)* How do you like my jewels? If you like I'll have a brooch made for your wife.

ARCHITECT *(Trying to force him to the point)*: About the locomotives.

GÖRING: The locomotives—yes. Transportation has been the German genius. Planes, highways, buses, trains. The world has never seen such a transportation system.

HE *wanders again and contemplates his jewels.*

You're wondering where my jewels came from. No, not from France. You'll never guess.

ARCHITECT *(Sharply)*: What about the locomotives?

GÖRING *(Dreamily)*: Yes . . . Tell the Führer I've solved the steel shortage. I've discovered a new material with which to build our locomotives.

ARCHITECT: What material?

GÖRING: Concrete.

ARCHITECT *(Astonished)*: CONCRETE?

GÖRING *(Nervously rolling the jewels in his hand)*: Concrete doesn't have the strength of steel, but we can make up for this by building more locomotives. We have no shortage of concrete.

ARCHITECT *(Sarcastically)*: How would it hold together?

GÖRING *(Excitedly)*: A locomotive is crude compared with a plane. It doesn't need to hold together long. Just until we conquer.

ARCHITECT *(Carefully)*: I'm afraid the weight . . .

James Schevill

GÖRING: A minor problem. A concrete locomotive needn't be that heavy. You can camouflage it more easily. Don't worry, it'll work. *(Another abrupt change)* Would you like to see my new painting that I acquired in the eastern campaign? I found a beautiful Vermeer, very rare you know.

ARCHITECT *(Intent on escape)*: I'm afraid I must leave. The Führer is expecting me.

GÖRING: I'm glad you're going to the Führer. You can tell him my plan.

ARCHITECT *(Aside)*: The Führer won't believe me if I tell him Göring has painted his fingernails red.

GÖRING: Don't forget to tell the Führer. *(Calling louder as the ARCHITECT turns to flee)* Concrete locomotives, you understand, *concrete.* Use foreign slave labor to build concrete locomotives.

As the ARCHITECT flees to the angry HITLER, HITLER signals again to DR. MENGELE as NEUMANN/ZUSYA and his DISCIPLES face the final decision.

FIRST DISCIPLE *(Fearfully)*: Rabbi Zusya, which is the path to heaven?

NEUMANN/ZUSYA *(Trembling)*: The way to the fire is the path to heaven.

SECOND DISCIPLE *(Pointing to MENGELE)*: Is that the Devil?

NEUMANN/ZUSYA: Inside the uniform is a man.

FIRST DISCIPLE: I can see only the uniform.

NEUMANN/ZUSYA: I will show you the man. *(HE approaches DR. MENGELE)* Sir, you have light coming out of you.

DR. MENGELE: Back!

NEUMANN/ZUSYA *(Kneeling and stretching out his hand)*: Let me touch you.

DR. MENGELE *(Striking NEUMANN down with his whip)*: How dare you touch me, Jew.

NEUMANN/ZUSYA *(Rebounding radiantly)*: Sir, I envy you. When you turn to God each of your flames will become a ray of holy light. *(Screaming)* AND GOD SAID: A GREAT LIGHT WILL SHINE . . .

DISCIPLES *(THEY begin to scream with NEUMANN/ZUSYA)*: AND GOD SAID: A GREAT LIGHT WILL SHINE . . .

NEUMANN/ZUSYA *(Through the DISCIPLE's voices)*: Sir, I envy you your flood of holy radiance . . . "And God said . . . And God said . . ."

DISCIPLES *(Joining him)*: "And God said . . ."

As DR. MENGELE motions angrily the DISCIPLES continue with ZUSYA to repeat the words. The SS GUARDS lead NEUMANN/ZUSYA and his DISCIPLES off left to the gas chamber.

HITLER moves, shaking, toward EVA BRAUN. It is as if THEY are in their final nightmare in the Berlin bunker.

HITLER: That's the end of Neumann. I'll show him how to die. *(Bitterly to* EVA*)* The German people have betrayed me. I trained them to be strong. I trained them to be merciless. They've become weak. We must show the world how we died, how we live on.

EVA: What are you going to do?

HITLER: I'm going to marry you.

EVA: Another wedding. Oh, thank you, Adolf.

HITLER: And then we're going to kill ourselves.

EVA *(Entranced)*: Liebestod . . .

HITLER: Greater than *Liebestod* . . . Wagner is only a composer. I'm an architect of new societies. *(Motioning)* Take down my will. *(Hastily* SHE *gets a notebook)* Of my own free will I choose immortality.

EVA *(Looking up)*. What about me?

HITLER *(Impatiently motioning to her to continue)*: In the Cathedral of Ice I have decided to take as my wife the woman who, after many years of faithful friendship . . .

EVA *(Looking up)*: Of love, of love . . .

HITLER *(Ignoring this)*: . . . of faithful friendship, entered this place in order to share my fate. Our death will compensate us for the companionship we have lost through my work in the service of my people who have proved themselves unfit to achieve victory.

SHE *nods assent and* HE *launches into a more vehement attack.*

In the future I charge the world leaders to scrupulous observance of the laws of race. I demand their merciless opposition to the universal poisoner of all peoples—International Jewry. From our death will spring the renaissance of our National Socialist movement. We shall not fail to realize a true community of nations. Our spirit will endure forever . . .

EVA *(Beginning to understand)*: We will become immortal . . .

HITLER: Wherever men dream they will think of me. My Nazi Fantasies will triumph.

EVA *(Writing exultantly)*: "The Nazi Fantasies will triumph."

HITLER: Wherever men speak of politics, power, art, they will speak of me. *(*HE *shows her a poison capsule and a pistol)*

EVA: What are those?

HITLER: Here is your poison . . . The pistol is mine.

EVA *(Shrinking back a little)*: You promised to marry me. Don't forget to marry me first . . .

HITLER *(Exultantly)*: Marriage, why not? Love—Death . . . Immortality . . . My Nazi Fantasies triumph in the Cathedral of Ice . . .

HE *tears his coat off, throws it away, then signals and the Dream Machine erupts—with all of The Power Fantasies occurring simultaneously in the niches.*

In the first niche KARL MAY *dressed up as* OLD SHATTERHAND *repeats and elaborates on his cry,* "I am great . . . I am mar—vel—ous! . . .

In the second niche the ARCHITECT, *slowly, maniacally as if condemned in time, hammers at a model of one of* HITLER'S *monuments, crushing it into perfect ruins.*

In the third niche a dream version of Mephistopheles drops a variety of incredible paper superbombs on GÖRING/MEIER *who is forced to keep dodging as if pestered by eternal mosquitoes.*

In the fourth niche SCHRECK *the chauffeur, drives madly through time.*

In the fifth niche WAGNER *conducts grandly.*

In the sixth niche NAPOLEON *presides over a dance of power with* STALIN, ROOSEVELT *and* CHURCHILL.

In the seventh niche the KING OF THE MOUNTAIN *hunches over his tape recorder trying to penetrate the dream-sounds of the taped voices that echo forever in his mind.*

In the eighth niche NEUMANN, *as one of the Hasidic masters, looks down on* KERSTEN *massaging the pain-wracked stomach of* HIMMLER.

In the ninth niche GÖBBELS *and his* WIFE *stare at each other over the poisoned bodies of their children like a German Macbeth and Lady Macbeth.*

In the tenth niche CHARLEMAGNE *appears in an imperial dream-pose.*

At the climax of the simultaneous Fantasies of Power the entire CAST *sings "The Ballad of the Cathedral of Ice."*

HITLER *and* CAST: Charlemagne!
   Rise from your tomb.
   Dreams have no price.
   Power lives on
   In my Cathedral of Ice.
CAST: Charlemagne!
   Come buy your joy or sorrow.
   In the Cathedral of Ice
   We freeze you for tomorrow . . .

The ACTORS *freeze in their niches in dream-like attitudes of power as the actor who plays* HITLER *steps forward.* HE *takes off his mustache, brushes back his hair, and resumes his role as* NARRATOR *to say farewell to the audience.*

NARRATOR: Good night, ladies and gentlemen . . .
   Sweet dreams with your dreams of power . . .

CATHEDRAL OF ICE

The clocks begin to send us into space;
Our dreams still soar to rule each waking face . . .
Who we are, what we hope to be
We learn behind the masks of history—
We wish you well—and praise the stage
Where we meet to celebrate our joy, our rage . . .

After the initial applause the entire CAST *sings the final stanzas of "The Ballad of the Cathedral of Ice."*

NARRATOR *and* CAST: Charlemagne!
Into history, into time,
Our troops march on
Forever into dream.

Charlemagne!
Come buy your joy or sorrow.
In the Cathedral of Ice
We freeze you for tomorrow . . .

END OF PLAY

A Selected Bibliography
of Plays of the Holocaust

The following bibliography is not meant to be exhaustive. Included are dramas which are set during the Holocaust, deal with survivors of the Holocaust, depict non-Jews who were involved in the Holocaust, or use the image of the Holocaust as a significant dramatic mataphor. The annotations give brief plot synopses, but cannot wholly reveal each playwright's philosophical, political, economic and/or aesthetic approach to the Holocaust. Works are listed according to the authors' countries. The dates are either initial publication or performance dates. Most titles are translated into English.

Austria

Bernhard, Thomas. *Eve of Retirement.* (1979)* +
A family of contemporary Nazis, including a father who is a former SS officer and now a chief justice, celebrate Himmler's birthday and confront their beliefs in the Third Reich's ideals.

Ullman, Viktor. *The Emperor of Atlantis.* (n.d.)
This opera, written in Terezin by prisoners, is an allegorical representation of life in the concentration camp.

Zwillinger, Frank. *Between Life and Death.* (1967)* +
In a ghetto hospital in Lemberg, Poland, Jewish doctors decide to commit suicide so that their soon to be deported patients can escape. The play compares this act to the heroic suicide at Massada.

*published in original language
+translated into English

Appendix

France

Atlan, Liliane. *The Messiahs.* (1969)*+
   The play centers on eight *deus absconditus*; the Author and her Cortege; and
   the Dead People on the Raft (Jews refused safe harbor during World War
   II). It mixes medieval pageantry with modern technology—masks with
   radios, chasubles and prayer shawls with telescopes and mobile galaxies.

———. *An Opera for Terezin.* (1986)
   A four overture full-night multimedia opera about children from a world
   in which there is no emotion who relive the experiences of Terezin.

Billetdoux, François. *How Goes the World, Mossieu? It Turns, Mossieu!* (1964)*
   The journey of a Frenchman and an American who escape from a concentration camp.

Delbo, Charlotte. *Who Will Carry the Word?* (1974)*+
   The lives of female French concentration camp prisoners, expressionistical-
   ly recounted by two survivors.

Gatti, Armand. *Chronicles of a Provisional Planet.* (1962)*
   Astronauts discover a planet on which Jews are being murdered and which
   is governed by characters who parallel Hitler, Himmler, Eichmann, etc.

———. *The Infant Rat.* (1960)*
   Guilt for inhuman acts in the camp haunts survivors.

———. *The Second Existence of the Tatenberg Camp.* (1962)*
   The continued impact of the camps on the lives of a fairground troupe.

Grumberg, Jean-Claude. *The Workroom.* (1979)*+
   Four Jewish survivors and four French employers of a post-war French
   clothing workroom attempt to throw off the grip of the Holocaust and the
   second World War.

Kalisky, Rene. *Jim, the Temerarious.* (1972)*
   A survivor, who escaped deportation, exiles himself to his bed and creates
   a world populated by Hitler, Himmler, etc.

Mnouchkine, Ariane. *Mephisto.* (1979)
   An adaptation of the novel by Klaus Mann about the actor Gustav Grund-
   gens who collaborated during the Third Reich.

Sartre, Jean-Paul. *The Condemned of Altona.* (1959)*+
   A German family confronts its war guilt.

Germany

Borchert, Wolfgang. *The Outsider.* (1946)*+
   A homecoming play about a German soldier.

APPENDIX

Brecht, Bertolt. *The Private Life of the Master Race.* (1935-38)*+
Scenes depicting civilian life during the Third Reich.

———. *Roundheads and Peakheads.* (1934)*+
Brecht's adaptation of Shakespeare's *Measure for Measure* which presents Hitler's racial policy in Marxist terms.

Hochhuth, Rolf. *The Deputy.* (1963)*+
An historical play that depicts the attempt by a priest and rebellious SS officer to persuade the Pope to speak out against the extermination of the Jews.

Kipphardt, Heino. *Joel Brand.* (1964)*
Hungarian Jewish leader Joel Brand's attempt to buy the lives of one million Jews from the Germans with the help of the Allies.

Schneider, Rolf. *Prozess in Nürnberg.* (1968)*
East German documentary drama of the Nürnberg trials.

———. *The Story of Moischele.* (1965)
The play depicts, in twelve scenes, the life of a poor Polish villager from ghetto to concentration camp to post-war profiteering to a re-education camp in East Germany.

Speer, Martin. *Koralle Meier.* (1970)*
The depiction of the life of a "beloved whore" in a town bordering on a concentration camp.

———. *Tales from Landshut.* *
The competition for the contracts to build the Nazi concentration camps is contrasted to the competition for contracts to build internment centers for German prisoners of war.

Sylvanus, Erwin. *Dr. Korczak and the Children.* (1957)*+
A Pirandellian presentation of the life of the protector of the orphans in the Warsaw ghetto.

Walser, Martin. *Oak and Angora.* (1971)*+
Scenes from 1945 to the present detailing the absurd existence of the castrated German survivor Alois.

———. *The Black Swan.* (1964)*
A Hamlet-like tale in which a son discovers his father's SS past.

Weiss, Peter. *The Investigation.* (1965)*+
A documentary drama based on the Frankfurt Auschwitz trials of 1963-64.

Wolf, Friedrich. *Professor Mamlock.* (1934)*+
The Third Reich's racial laws destroy a German Jewish doctor.

Zinner, Hedda. *Ravensbrucker Ballade.* (1961)
A melodramatic play set in the female internment center.

Appendix

Great Britain

Hampton, Christopher. *The Portage to San Cristobal of A. H.* (1982)*
Adolf Hitler is captured by Israeli Nazi hunters in this stage adaptation
of George Steiner's novel.

Pip Simmons Group. *An die Musik.* (1975)
A performance piece that presents the dilemma of musicians forced to
entertain in the Nazi concentration camp.

Shaw, Robert. *The Man in the Glass Booth.* (1967)*
A fictionalized treatment of the Eichmann trial.

Taylor, C. P. *Good.* (1981)*
A "good" German professor capitulates to Nazism during the Third Reich.

Wincelberg, Shimon. *Resort 76.* (1964)*
Depiction of life in the Lodz ghetto.

Holland

de Hartog, Jan. *Skipper Next to God.* (1949)*+
A Dutch captain, with 136 Jewish refugees on his ship, attempts unsuc-
cessfully to find safe haven.

Hungary

Dery, Tibor. *The Witnesses.* (1945)*
The life of a Jewish doctor and his family in Budapest during the Nazi
occupation.

Israel

Amichai, Yehuda. *Bells and Trains.* (1966)*+
An Israeli visits his aunt in a German old-age home, all of whose inhabitants are survivors of the Nazi concentration camps.

Dagan, Gabriel. *The Reunion.* (1972)*+
Survivor-playwright Peter Stone, along with other survivors, stages a replay
of the Nazi occupation in order to reveal Third Reich inhumanity to his
uncle, who spent the war years in America.

Goldberg, Leah. *The Lady of the Castle.* (1955)*+
Two Israelis, charged with bringing back children who survived the
Holocaust, encounter an Eastern European aristocrat who continues to
keep a Jewish girl in hiding after the war has ended.

Megged, Aharon. *Hanna Szenes.* (1958)
The true story of the Jewish girl the Allies sent to Nazi-occupied Hungary
in an attempt to save the country's Jewish population.

APPENDIX

————. *The High Season.* (1967)
A retelling of the story of Job, with Job representing the Jewish survivors of the Holocaust.

Shaham, Nathan. *A New Reckoning.* (1954)
A refugee attempts to start a new life in Israel but is haunted by his having been a kapo.

Shamir, Moshe. *The Heir.* (1963)
An Israeli poses as a wealthy German Holocaust victim in order to claim the dead man's reparation payments.

Tomer, Ben-Zion. *Children of the Shadows.* (1963)* +
The effects of the Holocaust on a young survivor who tries to forget his past but is unable to do so.

Italy

Moravia, Alberto. *The God Kurt.* (1968)*
Kurt, the commandant of a concentration camp, has an imprisoned Jewish family actually act out the Oedipus myth.

Poland

Adamsk, Jerzy. *The World of Stone.* (1966)
An adaptation of the Tadeusz Borowski short story.

Bobkowski, Andrzej. *Black Sand.* (1959)*
An elderly Polish Jewish survivor murders his daughter's black lover. In the subplot, a Polish woman is married to the Latvian SS officer who saved her and her mother's life in the camp.

Brandstaetter, Roman. *The Day of Wrath.* (1965)*
An SS major, who at one time had been a seminarist, visits a schoolmate who is now responsible for a seminary in an occupied land. The SS officer discovers that a Jew is hidden in the monastery and decides to capture him.

Grotowski, Jerzy and Józef Szajna. *Akropolis.* (1962)
A metaphoric representation of the camps, loosely based on Wyspianski's classic drama, in which the inmates act out their fantasies until at the end they go to their death.

Hanuszkiewicz, Adam. *The Columbus Boys: Warsaw 44-46.* (1965)
An adaptation of Roman Bratny's 1957 novel about Polish underground fighters' lives during and immediately following the War.

Holuj, Tadeusz. *The Empty Field.* (1963)*
A survivor continues to work in a camp that has become a museum for martyrs.

Appendix

Iredýnski, Ireneusz. *The Modern Nativity Play.* (1962)*
Internees stage a Christmas play written and controlled by the commandant.

Karren, Tamara. *Who Was This Man?.* (n.d.)
The last days of Janusz Korczak as he prepares for the deportation of the orphans of the Warsaw ghetto.

Krall, Hanna. *To Steal a March on God.* (1980)*+
A present-day Marek Edelman, an actual leader of the Warsaw ghetto uprising, discusses the reality of the revolt with the 1943 Marek Edelman, with frequent interruptions by his dead comrades.

Moczarski, Kazimierz and Zygmunt Hubner. *Conversations with the Executioner.* (1977)*+
Imprisoned in the same cell at the close of the war, the non-communist Polish resistance leader, Moczarski, confronts Lieutenant General Jurgen von Stroop, the SS officer responsible for the liquidation of the Warsaw ghetto.

Nowak, Alina. *Auschwitz Oratorio.* (n.d.)
The verse drama details the horrors of the maternity barracks in Auschwitz.

Prorok, Leszek. *Freya—the Cold Goddess of Love.* (1976)*
A German doctor questions Ravensbruck survivor Agnes Sielska, a Pole who also spent two years at a Nazi controlled villa at which girls with Nordic features were used to breed "perfect" human beings.

Taborski, Boleslaw. *Guilt.* (n.d.)
Present-day encounters of Holocaust victimizers, victims, and the children of both.

Terlecki, Wladyslaw Lech. *Archeology.* (n.d.)
A radio play in which a journalist investigates a concentration camp survivor who was forced to use his training as a doctor to castrate fellow prisoners.

Wazacz, Mieczyslaw. *Prize-Winner.* (n.d.)
A female director, who has won a prize for her film on the Nazi concentration camps, explores Poland's historic relationships with Germany and Russia.

Wiernik, Bronislaw. *A Star on a String.* (n.d.)
A radio play in which a woman, who was able to survive the ghetto because her star of David was sewn on by a single string and easily removed, retells her story.

Zawieyski, Jerzy. *The Deliverance of Jacob.* (1947)*
A husband returns from a concentration camp to discover his wife with a fellow prisoner he betrayed.

APPENDIX

Switzerland

Frisch, Max. *Andorra.* (1961)*+
A supposed Jewish boy is murdered because of political pressures from a neighboring state.

————. *Now They Are Singing Again.* (1945)*
The destruction of humanism is illustrated in the story of a Nazi soldier who executes hostages.

United States

American Jewish Ensemble. *The Theatre of Peretz.* (1976)
An adaptation in which concentration camp inmates present the Peretz stories.

Bianchi, Dan. *Night and Fog.* (1978)
A stranger forces an ex-SS officer, now living secretly in the United States, to confront his past.

Cristofer, Michael. *The Black Angel.* (1982)*
A former SS officer, living in France, is confronted by his past.

Friedman, Leah K. *Before She Is Even Born.* (1982)
Raisal, who escaped pre-Nazi Europe using her sister's passport, is confronted in memory by her mother, who died before the war, and her sister and sister's daughter, who perished in the Holocaust.

Goodrich, Frances and Albert Hackett. *The Diary of Anne Frank.* (1956)*
A stage adaptation of the world famous diary.

Hecht, Ben. *We Will Never Die.* (1943)
A theatrical pageant presented at Madison Square Garden to call attention to the mass murder of Europe's Jews.

Lampell, Mildred. *The Wall.* (1961)*
An adaptation of the John Hersey novel.

Lebow, Barbara. *A Shayna Maidel.* (1984)*
Two sisters, separated when children in Poland, are reunited in New York City after World War II: one has grown up in America, the other is a Holocaust survivor.

Lieberman, Harold and Edith. *Throne of Straw.* (1973)*
An epic play about Mordechai Chaim Rumkowski, the chairman of the "Judenrat" (Jewish Council) in the Lodz ghetto.

Mann, Emily. *Annulla, An Autobiography.* (1985)*
A young American searching for her family roots in Eastern Europe spends an afternoon in 1974 with an elderly woman who recounts the true story

of how she passed for Aryan, got her husband out of Dachau and escaped to England.

Miller, Arthur. *Incident at Vichy.* (1965)*
  Set in a detention center in France, the play contrasts the fate of a group of Jews who are soon to be sent to a death camp with a "mistakenly" detained non-Jewish character.

Schechter, David. *Hannah Senesh.* (1984)*
  A one-woman drama detailing the life of the young Hungarian girl used by the Allies in an attempt to save the Jews of Hungary.

Sherman, Martin. *Bent.* (1979)*
  A depiction of the Nazi oppression of homosexuals in the concentration camps.

Tabori, George. *The Cannibals.* (1968)*
  Two survivors and sons of camp inmates relive an act of cannibalism that occurred in the camp.

Toll, Nellie and William Kushner. *Behind a Closed Window.* (1981)
  Dramatization of a diary of a nine-year-old Jewish girl in German-occupied Poland during World War II.

Alvin Goldfarb heads the theatre department at Illinois State University and is co-author of the textbook *Living Theatre.* He has written numerous articles, reviews, and notes on theatre and the Holocaust.